Allen G. Noble

WOOD, BRICK, AND STONE

The North American Settlement Landscape   Volume 2: Barns and Farm Structures

Drawings by M. Margaret Geib

The University of Massachusetts Press

Amherst, 1984

Publication of this book was assisted by the
American Council of Learned Societies
under a grant from the
Andrew W. Mellon Foundation.
Designed by Mary Mendell

Printed in the United States of America
Library of Congress Cataloging
in Publication Data
Noble, Allen George, 1930–
Wood, brick, and stone.
Includes bibliographical references and index.
Contents: v. 1. Houses—v. 2. Barns and farm
structures.
1. Vernacular architecture—North American
I. Geib, M. Margaret. II. Title.
NA703.N6 1984 728'.097 83–24110
ISBN 0–87023–410–2 (v. 1)
ISBN 0–87023–411–0 (v. 2)

Contents

Preface to Volume Two

Interest in the material culture of North America is growing steadily. In part, this situation may be a consequence of the environmental and preservation movements of the 1970s, when the consciousness of the American public over the erosion of their heritage was raised by so many diverse groups. It may also stem partly from the diversification of university study to include more non-traditional academic ventures.

Volume 2 of *Wood, Brick, and Stone* illustrates a part of the wide range of structures that warrant study by cultural geographers, folklorists, architectural historians, architects, social historians, anthropologists, and specialists in American studies. Even so, only rural farm structures are included. It remains for this inventory to be extended and completed by others.

The acknowledgments given in the first volume also pertain to this volume, with certain additions. At the University of Akron, Judy Woods has helped with the typing and Mohammed Haque with some of the research, augmenting the continuing efforts of those listed in Volume 1. Professor Howard Marshall of the University of Missouri read the entire manuscript and offered many useful suggestions for improvement.

Finally, several individuals at the University of Massachusetts Press have given advice and assistance which is greatly appreciated. Leone Stein was the first to recognize some value in the project and Richard Martin saw the book through to its successful completion. Mary Mendell has labored successfully to improve the style and appearance of both volumes. Pam Campbell has taught me much about writing. Not only has she carefully searched out and corrected my errors of both fact and expression, but also she has provided insightful criticisms.

To all of these people, as well as those mentioned in the earlier volume, I remain perpetually indebted.

PART ONE
Evolution of Barns

---

1 The North American Farm Barn: Simple Cribs and Transverse Frame

Houses are clearly among the most significant indicators on the landscape. Folk houses demonstrate a strong ethnic connection, defining areas of cultural influence. Furthermore, the design of folk housing is sometimes strongly influenced by local environmental conditions. Beginning in the nineteenth century, popular housing, which has largely supplanted folk housing, added additional cultural dimensions, often pointing to connections not immediately or obviously apparent. Thus, many of the nineteenth-century American house styles, such as Classical Revival, Gothic Revival, or Italianate, demonstrate either an academic or an indirect association with foreign influences. Because urban landscapes are crowded with a distractingly large variety of buildings, and because urban growth and renewal have often resulted in large-scale replacement of houses, it is in small towns and their surrounding rural areas that folk and popular houses are most clearly seen.

In the same rural countryside, the American farm barn is an even more important landscape element. No other rural man-made structures are more distinctive or more characteristic than the great farm barns that dot the countryside of America.[1] Despite the continuing rapid disappearance of the barn and associated buildings from the landscape, few studies have been made of these structures. A comprehensive bibliography of barns published in 1978 contained only 120 entries,[2] and a more detailed one published a year later had only 165 entries.[3]

Given the large variety of studies on house types, it seems strange that changes in the function, structure, and plan of barns and farmsteads have received little attention. This deficiency is all the more perplexing because a majority of the population throughout both the eighteenth and nineteenth centuries lived in rural areas, and, even today, farmsteads, although frequently occupied by nonagricultural families, are still a dominant feature of the rural settlement landscape.

R. W. Brunskill has noted a similar situation in England and he also has found the lack of farm-building studies perplexing:

The association of the farm-housing with roses round the door and ivy on the wall compares favorably with the manure underfoot and dust up above which are more commonly associated with the other buildings of the farmstead. Perhaps for this reason, as well as others more academic, the design and construction of farm buildings has received even less attention from scholars than the planning, choice of materials, and architectural detailing of farm-houses. And yet the sheer volume of space enclosed, quite apart from the construction problems presented by farm buildings should remind us that the expense and effort devoted to farm buildings has, for the past three centuries been greater than that devoted to farm-houses, while the architectural qualities of cathedral-like barns and elegant granaries are often superior to those of the farm-houses they served.[4]

In the few studies of barns and other farm structures, most attention has been focused simply on the identification and analysis of the basic types, with little thought given to the evolutionary processes at work. Scholars following

Fred B. Kniffen's pioneer work, "Folk Housing—Key to Diffusion," which did propose an evolutionary sequence for crib barns,[5] have concentrated on identifying types, associating them with cultural groups and particular geographic areas, and analyzing the range of variation within each basic type. Several scholars have attempted to provide classifications of barns,[6] but none has been comprehensive. Up to the present work, none has attempted to cover the entire range of major American barn types. One difficulty in establishing a complete classification system is that, because so little work has been done, not all types have even been identified. The problem is not one of securing an orderly arrangement of diverse types, but rather one of providing a system flexible enough to accommodate those types that surely will be discovered in the future. (See chapter 4 for an example of an as-yet-unidentified barn type.)

This chapter will be devoted to a discussion of crib barns, perhaps the earliest of American barn types, and the various transverse-frame barns, which have been derived from the more basic crib form (fig. 1–1). Chapter 2 traces the connection between early ethnic groups and barn types that were introduced in the colonial cultural hearths of eastern North America. Chapter 3 completes the discussion of barns with an examination of those structures that have evolved during the nineteenth and twentieth centuries, as agricultural operations changed and new building forms were required.

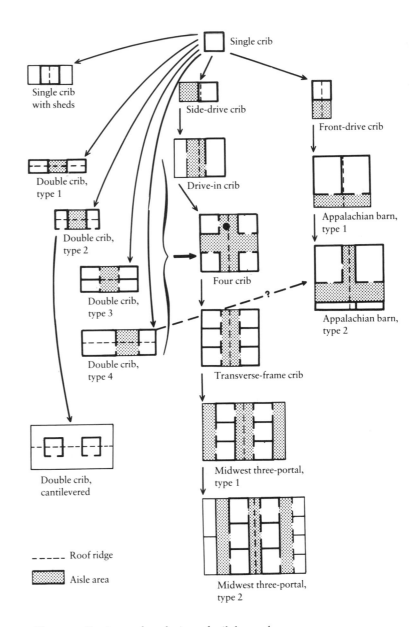

Fig. 1–1 Conjectural evolution of crib barn plans

The single-crib barn

The simplest, most elemental barns are the single-crib barns. In their crudest form, they are merely a crib,[7] or pen, constructed of rough-hewn logs and covered by a simple gable roof (fig. 1–2). The most common length of these cribs is between eight and twelve feet; they usually possess a single door located on the gable end, which is the narrower of the two dimensions of the plan.

The single-crib barn originally may have been a component of most early farmsteads. However, today it persists only in those areas in which farming never advanced much beyond a rudimentary or subsistence stage. In some instances, it was utilized as a stable or granary, but more often it was a structure for storing ears of corn, the principal field crop of Appalachia.[8] In many cribs, a small side window or door ex-

Fig. 1–2 A single-crib barn near Ghent, Kentucky, October 1979

Fig. 1–3 The single-crib barn with flanking sheds

ists to facilitate the loading of grain or corn.

The single-crib barn is most likely encountered today in the hill country of Appalachia, especially in the southern portions. Its domain stretches from Maryland and coastal Virginia westward entirely across Appalachia to the Ohio River and "throughout the Deep South."[9]

Even on the hill farms, however, the basic single-crib barn failed to satisfy all agricultural functions. At an early stage of development, lean-to shed additions flanking the crib were added (see fig. 1–1), and it is this version of the single-crib barn most commonly encountered today (fig. 1–3). The sheds, which usually are built of lighter material than the central crib and have a roof of lower pitch, are used as stabling areas, for equipment storage, or to house additional grain production.

Double-crib barns

Several lines of evolutionary development seem to have been followed from the single-crib form. One sequence, roughly similar in its form to that which produced the dog-trot house from the log pen house, resulted in the double-crib barn (fig. 1–4). In these barns, a second crib, sometimes identical to the earlier crib and sometimes of rather different dimensions, was erected so that it could share with the first crib a common roof, which extended across a central aisle or breezeway (fig. 1–5).

Henry Glassie has suggested division of the double-crib barn into subtypes based upon the form of the cribs and the position of the crib doors. In barns of the first subtype, the larger dimension of the two cribs parallels the ridge line and the crib doors open onto the aisle. The ground level "is usually used for stabling in the Upland South and corn storage in the Deep South; generally the further south this barn is found the smaller are the cribs and the more likely they are to be used for corn storage."[10]

In the second subtype, the cribs are more nearly square, but the shorter length parallels the ridge and the doors open to the barn side. To give these door openings some additional protection, a pent roof is sometimes placed on the barn, supported by a gable log extension. Glassie notes that greater variety is found within this subtype than in others and suggests a possible connection to the English barn (see chap. 2).

Fig. 1–4 A double-crib barn with an open central passageway
(Cades Cove, Tennessee, 1972)

Another connection is with the German bank barn through a Middle Atlantic variant of the double-crib barn, subtype 2. This latter structure has, in addition to the standard attributes of the subtype 2 barn, a frame shed addition to one side and forebay extensions on the opposite side. The forebay is usually divided into two sections separated by the barn's central threshing doors.[11] When used as stables, the cribs typically have two sets of entry doors, one for the animals and one that functions as a feeder entry.[12]

The third subtype double-crib barn represents a composite of the earlier subtypes. The cribs are divided by a lighter central partition and the doors open onto the central aisle.

A fourth double-crib barn subtype has been identified by H. Wayne Price from barns studied in Calhoun County, Illinois.[13] The same barn is also reported by Howard Marshall for the Little Dixie region of Missouri.[14] Subtype 4 barns have rectangular cribs of unequal size. The larger crib has its long dimension parallel to the ridge, but the smaller crib is transverse. Generally, crib doors open onto the interior aisle, although doors directly to the outside are not unknown. The larger crib, normally used for hay storage, is usually sixteen feet deep and between sixteen and twenty-one feet long. The logs of the crib may be hewn or not, and are held in place by V or saddle notches. The smaller crib, used for corn storage, is of similar construction,

but, in addition, has vertical wooden slats attached to the inside of the crib logs to prevent the corn ears from falling out. Small access doors are sufficient for corn loading, but are not large enough to admit animals or to permit easy hay loading.[15] Typical dimensions of the smaller crib are sixteen feet deep and nine to eleven feet long.

Typically, the double-crib barn is not only larger in plan than the single-crib barn, it is also a much taller structure and sometimes contains two levels, with the upper used for hay or grain storage. The desire to create a weather-tight structure to keep the hay or grain dry often resulted in the upper portion of the barn's being faced with siding as was seen in figure 1–4.

Frequently, especially when used for grain storage, the loft floor has batten strips laid down to cover the crevices between adjacent floor boards, thereby

Fig. 1–5 The Tennessee cantilevered double-crib barn

4

Fig. 1–6 The front-drive crib

making a tight floor (see fig. 6–35). For the rest of the structure, a sound roof is always more important than weather-tight siding, because most of these barns are in the southern part of the country and are built to shelter animals and farm equipment from rain rather than from cold.

The ultimate development of the double-crib barn occurred in eastern Tennessee and western North Carolina,[16] where an oversized loft area was created by cantilevering the upper portion of the barn so that the loft considerably overhangs the crib on all sides (see fig. 1–5). Since the doors to the cribs open to the barn side, it can be argued that the cantilevered double-crib barn is a derivation from the subtype 2 structure. This barn is always based on log cribs, but the upper portion is as likely to be of frame construction as of log. The loft overhang is most often encountered only on front and back, suggesting

a tie with the German construction of southeastern Pennsylvania. This is perhaps the most unusual, and certainly one of the most attractive, of American farm barns. Fortunately, one of these structures is being preserved in the Cades Cove settlement within the Great Smoky Mountains National Park. Others are less likely to survive.

Front-drive cribs and Appalachian barns

In all the variations of the basic double-crib barn, the ridge line is at right angles to the aisle, which runs through the barn from front to back. A second line of evolutionary development from the single crib involves structures in which the aisle is *perpendicular* to the line of the ridge. The main aisle runs from side to side, but just behind the front wall of

the barn (see fig. 1–1). The earliest and smallest of these structures has been termed the *front-drive* crib (fig. 1–6).[17] The building is merely a single crib with a projecting front roof supported by corner poles. About eight feet wide, the total depth of both crib and shed could be about sixteen feet in the smallest examples. The triangular loft area may be enclosed to provide hay or grain storage and is often extended forward over the open, unsided driveway which functions primarily as a wagon shelter.

Throughout the southern and central parts of the Appalachian hills, front-aisle barns are fairly common (fig. 1–7).

Fig. 1–7 An Appalachian barn near Abingdon, Virginia. The rear aisle, the clerestory roof, and the square ventilator are unusual features. (1975)

Fig. 1–8 The Appalachian barn, type 1

They seem to be elaborations and expansions of the elementary front-drive crib barn. Their plans also bear a resemblance to certain double-crib barns of south central Pennsylvania and adjacent Maryland.[18] The only discrepancy is that in these latter barns, the aisle runs along one side of the building rather than along the gable. Hence the resemblance may be incidental rather than evolutionary.

The name *Appalachian barn* appears to be suitable for all the front-aisle structures, although two subtypes can be distinguished. The two types are different in plan and external appearance, but both have rather similar overall dimensions. The Appalachian barn has not been given the careful study that its wide distribution and numbers war-

rant. Not only is it a common barn in Appalachia, it also is the most typical barn in parts of Missouri.[19]

The Appalachian barn, type 1 (fig. 1–8) consists of two (sometimes three) cribs with a cross aisle in front. The doors to each crib open onto the aisle, which functions as a vehicle or equipment shelter. Often the side of the aisle which forms the front end of the barn is left open, so that light reaches the aisle and cribs. Many variations of the basic floor plan are encountered as one moves from area to area.

The basic plan of the Appalachian barn, type 2 (fig. 1–9) incorporates a short transverse aisle lying between the two cribs and forming a T with the main front aisle. In certain instances, the cribs may be subdivided into smaller units by light-weight partitions. Crib doorways usually open onto the transverse aisle. The front gable of the barn in some cases is comprised of a narrow, interior corn crib, which lies between the gable wall and the front aisle. The exterior of the barn has a heavier, more massive appearance than type 1 barns, which is due partially to the large hay hood, a characteristic feature of these buildings.

Fig. 1–9 The Appalachian barn, type 2

Hay hoods

The hay hood is the extension at the ridge of the barn roof that provides weather protection for the loft door located high in the gable. Hay hoods appear to be much more common on barns derived from the crib form than on other types of barns. This is probably because crib barns are often loaded from outside, whereas the lofts of other barns are usually loaded from within. In part, this also may be a response to climatic conditions. Loading the loft from outside the barn is much less uncomfortable in the scorching heat of late summer. Southern barns, which fall mostly within the crib-barn family, are more apt to be loaded from outside through a loft door than are barns in the northern part of the country, where tripartite structures are covered by open interior lofts.

Originally, the ridge projection was simply a pole to which a pulley was attached to facilitate the raising of hay into the loft (fig. 1–10A). To retard the rusting of the pulley and pole, and perhaps to improve the aesthetic appearance, the roof was extended in a triangular projection called the *hanging gable* (fig. 1–10B and C). Such an extension also helped to exclude weather from the loft-door opening. Some farmers preferred a roof extension that was square and thus easier to build (fig.

1–10D). The square projection was modified by filling in the small gable triangle and providing triangular side-boards to create a box gable (fig. 1–10E).

The box-gable hay hood provided additional protection for the somewhat more sophisticated method of hay loading adopted in the nineteenth century. Large hay forks (fig. 1–11) were suspended by a pulley that moved along a track attached to the underside of the barn's ridge pole. The fork load was lifted by horse power and then manually pushed to an appropriate spot in the loft where a trip rope opened the forks.

The final elaboration in the development of hay hoods was the total enclosure of the hood, which was accomplished by extending the sides of the hood's front surface, so that the only opening was from below (fig. 1–10F

Fig. 1–10 Typical variations in hay hoods (after Francaviglia)

Fig. 1–11 A hay fork inside a box gable (Carter County, Kentucky, 1981)

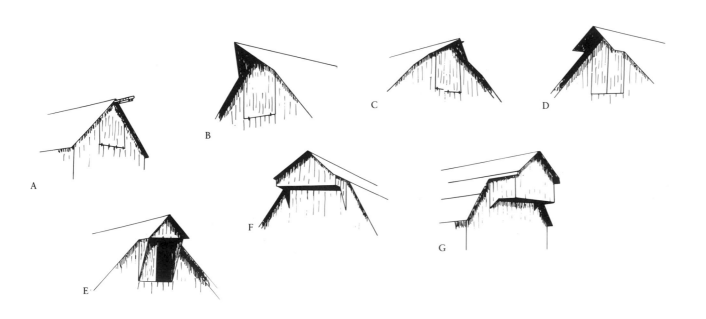

Fig. 1–12 Barn with an enclosed hay hood (Near Salem, Oregon, 1978). Photo by Brian Coffey.

and G). Richard Francaviglia has suggested that this form is restricted to the Willamette valley and is a response to the rainy climate (fig. 1–12).[20] Such a relationship appears unlikely, however, since identical hay hoods can also be found in Morrow County, Ohio (fig. 1–13), along Route 250 in West Virginia, and in the Brushy Creek valley of Carter County, Kentucky. The entire subject of hay hoods needs further study. Francaviglia's pioneering work is the only serious study of this important and diagnostic barn feature.

Side-drive and drive-in cribs

The third line of evolutionary development from the single-crib barn is most significant because it produced barns that are widely used throughout southern and central United States. In all the barns evolved in this sequence, the ridge line is *parallel* to the main aisles of the building, and the aisle (or aisles) runs from front to back (see fig. 1–1).

The side-drive crib barn should not be mistaken for a single-crib barn with one flanking shed, to which it has a superficial resemblance. The latter building has a definite break in the roof line between the shed and the crib, each of which may be of different size (see fig. 1–3). The side-drive crib (fig. 1–14) has an aisle and a crib of about equal dimensions, and each is covered by approximately one-half the roof, the slope of which is unbroken.[21] The basic struc-

ture sometimes has a later, additional shed on the side away from the aisle. As was true with the double-crib barns, the loft is often covered with more tightly constructed siding than the crib. The aisle is frequently quite open to the weather, which presents little problem in the mild winters of the southern Appalachian hills. When closed in, the aisle functions as a gear shed for storing farm tools and equipment.[22] The side-drive crib barn is a small building rather square in plan and with dimensions ranging from twelve to twenty feet, with the crib occupying roughly half the area (see fig. 1–1). The side-drive crib is widely scattered across Kentucky and may be present elsewhere in Appalachia.

Fig. 1–13 Barn with an enclosed hay hood (Morrow County, Ohio, 1977)

Fig. 1–14 The side-drive crib

Fig. 1–15 A drive-in crib near Jefferson City, Missouri. Note the side laths that permit air circulation, the roof hatches, and the driveway crib door. (1979)

The other early building in this sequence is the drive-in crib (fig. 1–15), which may be differentiated from the double-crib barn by the relationship of its aisle and ridge line, the elongated form of the two cribs, and the absence of a loft. These structures have a very wide distribution. I have observed them from Virginia to Nebraska and Kansas, and in many places between. They are among the most successful structures to survive the transition from log building to that of frame. In the cash grain-farming areas of the eastern Midwest, the roof is often broken by hatches through which the cribs are loaded. In the older examples, however, loading was done from the aisle (fig. 1–16), or through the front end of the crib.

Except for the Appalachian barn, all the barns already mentioned in this chapter are small buildings. Because of their restricted size, they perform only

Fig. 1–16 Close-up of a drive-in crib barn, near Abingdon, Virginia. Note the open siding and the hatches and doors that permit loading from the center aisle. (1974)

Fig. 1–17 A typical Appalachian farmstead, with its cluster of small farm buildings substituting for a single large barn (Near Tazewell, Virginia, 1974)

one or, at best, very few agricultural functions. In areas of high farm productivity, the small early buildings were gradually replaced by larger structures as farming operations expanded in the nineteenth century. In the poorer agricultural regions, including much of Appalachia, because of the lack of capital, the small early buildings were not replaced, or they were replaced selectively as needed. Hence the hill-country farm is characterized by clusters of small, rather simple buildings, each performing one or two functions (fig. 1–17). Furthermore, the harsher winters in northern areas also may have contributed to centralization of agricultural functions in a large barn, in which livestock acted as the heating plant.

Four-crib barns

The desirability of erecting a larger barn as agricultural operations expanded produced the four-crib barn (fig. 1–18), an attractive and very simple structure. It combines elements of the double-crib barn with some from the drive-in crib. Four separate cribs are erected, one at each corner of the barn, and a single

Fig. 1–18 The four-crib barn

Fig. 1–19 The transverse-frame barn

gable roof is put over the entire structure (see fig. 1–1). The two aisles thus formed cross in the middle of the building. The cribs are usually of nearly or exactly identical size, with dimensions varying from about eight to sixteen feet. Since the aisles are normally about eight feet wide, the dimensions of the entire barn may reach between twenty-four and forty feet. The aisles are not normally closed with any doors but remain open to weather, and are used as threshing platforms, wagon and implement shelters, and for protected access to the cribs. The cribs, used for storing corn, other grains, or hay, or as stabling areas, frequently open onto both aisles. The loft stores hay c. grain.

Apparently, no frame examples of four-crib barns can be found, which suggests that the transverse-frame barn supplanted the four crib at an early period.[23] It has been proposed that the four-crib barn originated in southeastern Tennessee,[24] although Lynwood Montell and Michael Morse place the greatest concentration in Tennessee between the Cumberland and Obey rivers.[25] This barn type is only mentioned, and generally very briefly, in a half dozen or so publications, which points up the need for much more careful study of folk, and even popular, barns before most of them disappear. The years remaining in this century will be most critical.

Transverse-frame and Midwest three-portal barns

The four-crib barn gave way quite early to a transverse-frame barn, which was made by boarding up the side aisle openings and constructing frame cribs on the sides between the corner cribs. The great question that has not been answered, indeed has seldom been asked, is why it was the side aisles and not the aisles that run from gable to gable that were boarded-in. In virtually every folk barn in other parts of the country, doors occur on the sides of the structure. Why, then, in the transverse-frame barn was the gable chosen for the door openings? A possible explanation may be found in north German barns, which do have gable doors.[26]

A few four-crib barns have been found in which intermediate, frame, side cribs have been built, but virtually from its beginning the barn was built as a finished unit, with three or four frame

Fig. 1–20 A transverse-frame barn used for drying tobacco. Note the addition of multiple flues along the ridge and the narrow ventilator panels on the barn sides.

cribs for stabling or storage on either side of the gable-to-gable aisle (see fig. 1–1). Most transverse-frame barns (fig. 1–19) tend to be longer than wide. Gable wall widths are about twenty-four to thirty feet, and side walls are slightly longer (twenty-eight to thirty-six feet). The loft or mows may be loaded from the outside, or inside directly from a vehicle standing in the aisle. Front and back doors permitted the horse- or mule-drawn wagons to pass through the structure for ease of unloading.

Fig. 1–21 A rack-side barn (Near Glasgow, Kentucky, 1981)

Fig. 1–22 A Midwest three-portal barn, type 1, in Pasquotank County, North Carolina (1978)

Fig. 1–23 A Midwest three-portal barn, type 1, in central Kansas. Photo by Robert Webb.

In Kentucky, several important variations of the basic transverse-frame barn exist. One is associated with the Bluegrass Basin and is the result of U.S. Department of Agriculture attempts to provide farmers with standardized barn plans.[27] The hallmarks of this variant are the lower roof pitch and the greater length of the barn (fig. 1–20). This barn may be used for livestock or drying tobacco.

A second variant is restricted primarily to the central Kentucky region called the Pennyroyal. Its distinctive features are inward slanting sides, which enclose interior mangers fed from the loft above (fig. 1–21). According to Karl Raitz, who has made a detailed study of these rack-side barns, they originated late in the nineteenth century and gained favor immediately after World War I as a result of a shift of agriculture on the Pennyroyal from dark tobacco cultivation to dairy and beef cattle raising. Adding hay racks permitted the stock capacity of the barn to be increased. Also, uneaten hay remained in the rack, and off the floor until it was consumed later. The rack could be emptied and cleaned

Fig. 1–24 The Midwest three-portal barn, type 1

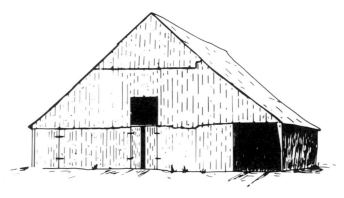

easily; indeed, many of the hay racks were hung on top hinges so that "after a few days of feeding, the unpalatable weeds and stems that remained in the rack were removed simply by unlocking the bottom of the rack, lifting it away from the outside wall, and allowing the tare to fall to the floor where it was spread about as bedding."[28] Furthermore, forking the hay from the loft was no more difficult than in barns of conventional design.

In the Midwest, and perhaps elsewhere, the transverse-frame barn appears to have been expanded into a building that typically had three aisles, the Midwest three-portal barn (see fig. 1–1). Alternately, these midwestern barns may have been introduced directly from Europe by German settlers. The form and plan of many barns in Lower Saxony, Westfalen-Lippe, and Mecklenburg are quite similar to those of the Midwest. No one has yet looked carefully at the barns of the central part of the United States. In any event, the Midwest three-portal barn became the standard farm structure throughout the south central parts of the country in the late nineteenth and early twentieth centuries (fig. 1–22 and 1–23). They are sometimes locally referred to as *feeder barns* because they are used in housing livestock. Two variations can be identified, primarily on the basis of plan. The Midwest three-portal, type 1 (fig. 1–24) is merely an expanded barn achieved by adding enclosed side aisles.

In some instances such additions are clearly an afterthought and the roof line is broken, indicating the addition of a later roof to cover the added aisle (fig. 1–25). Such an aisle is sometimes used

Fig. 1–25 A Midwest three-portal barn, type 1, in Knox County, Ohio.
The sheds are clearly later additions to the original transverse-frame barn. (1978)

to stable livestock. Early gable roofs in many cases have been replaced by gambrel roofs, but the addition of the aisle roof is still easy to identify. In the twentieth century, barns were built with original gambrel roofs spread to cover the side aisles (fig. 1–26).[29]

The Midwest three-portal barn, type 2 (fig. 1–27) represents the culmination of this line of evolutionary development. The central aisle has been reduced to a narrow walkway, but flanking cribs or stables have been added. The dimensions of this barn are between thirty-six and forty-two feet on a side, and often the gable wall is longer than the side wall. The roof line may or may not be broken, depending upon whether or not the barn was fully conceived or simply grew by accretion. In addition to providing hay storage, these barns are used to house livestock and machinery, and often grain as well. They are in many respects the rivals in size and diversity of function of the great ethnically derived barns of northeastern United States.

Fig. 1–26 A three-portal barn with a spread gambrel roof (Near Conway, Arkansas, 1974)

Fig. 1–27 A Midwest three-portal barn, type 2 (Jefferson County, Kentucky, 1979)

14

2 The North American Farm Barn: Early Ethnic Origins

Throughout the nineteenth and twentieth centuries, as changing architectural fashions became ever more important, a uniformity of housing styles, albeit of a steadily growing variety, gradually came to characterize all regions of the continent. The great differences, which had existed in the eighteenth and early nineteenth centuries and which were the result primarily of ethnic origins, largely disappeared. However, early and often ethnically associated characteristics persisted and identified the other common major structure of the countryside, the farm barn. To be sure, as time passed the original barn structure often was changed, but its modification was much slower than that of the house, for it was a much simpler structure.

In some instances, the modifications ultimately produced a complex structure (fig. 2–1) not easy to identify by type, even though the original barn might have had strong ethnic connections. It is also true that not all barns conformed to type, but this was more likely with later barns than with those erected by immigrants or their first-generation descendants.

Barns often reflect environmental conditions, especially those of the areas where the design originally evolved. Perhaps the extreme case occurs in eastern Kentucky, where rough, log cliff barns are built into the overhanging rock shelters along sandstone cliffs that border the narrow ravines and creek valleys. Such a location protects the cliff barns from the danger of flash flooding and, at the same time, offers shelter from rain and snow.[1] Certain design features may be responses to temperature, especially seasonal variations. One instance of this is the prominent hay hoods that are built on barns in Appalachia so that hay loading can be done from outside during the hot summer days. In other areas, barn design may reflect a response to the amount of rainfall, or, perhaps, to wind direction, the prevailing angle of the sun's rays, or ground slope conditions. Since barns are features associated with primary economic activities, even minor variations in environmental components can produce differences in barn types. For example, in Columbiana County, Ohio, the types in unglaciated areas are different from those of the glaciated parts of the county.[2] Further studies undoubtedly will reveal additional instances of environmental associations in other areas.

The early barns of North America were structures whose basic design was worked out in Europe. The areas to which these barns were introduced in North America often had quite different environments, and hence the barns were not always suitable to the new conditions. That modifications in design were so slow to evolve to accommodate the new environmental conditions is a tribute to the tenacity of man's cultural heritage and testimony to the inertia that usually permits changes to take place only gradually in such basic cultural phenomena. It is thus that cultural origins are preserved, so that each initial ethnic group brought at least one distinctive early barn type to its North American cultural hearth.

Fig. 2–1 Eclectic barn with numerous later additions to the basic structure (Westville, Ohio, 1976)

The English barn

The dominant early colonial people, the English, brought to the New England and Chesapeake Bay hearths the idea of a small rectangular barn (fig. 2–2). Although most widely identified as an English barn, the structure has been variously termed a New England, Connecticut, Yankee, and three-bay or two-bay barn, the last from its basic plan, which is that of a central floor area or runway with two spaces of roughly equal size on either side (fig. 2–3). Thus, they are *two-bays* if the runway is not counted and *three-bays* if it is. Above the bays is a loft for hay.

The plan of the English barn provided for hand threshing in the central space. Unthreshed grain was commonly stored in one side bay, and during the fall and winter threshed by hand using a flail on the central threshing floor. The threshed grain and straw were separately stored on the other side in the opposite bay, the grain in built-in bins. In some examples of this barn, back doors to the central section permit winnowing of the grain by creating natural drafts when both sets of doors are opened. The effect is much like that of a wind tunnel. This arrangement was fairly common in such barns in England.[3] However, many English barns built in America have only front double doors, which is probably a concession to the much colder winters of northeastern United States. Doors are always centered on the side, never on the gable (fig. 2–4).

The basic structure of the English barn may be expanded into a five- to nine-bay building by adding alternating bays and runways. In one county of upstate New York, where the English tradition of barn building predominates, Henry Glassie found over a fifth of all barns to be of this expanded type.[4]

16

Following the English tradition, New England barns are timber framed, held together by mortise-and-tenon joints. Each upright unit, consisting of posts and beams or girts, and lying across the width of the barn, is termed a *bent*. The bents are joined together by the plates and sills and the roof superstructure. By tradition, the distance between bents is sixteen feet, the space required to stable a team of draft animals.[5] Hence, each unit of internal space, called a *bay,* was sixteen feet long, or eight feet, or some other convenient variant of the basic length. Many early English barns in New England thus were twenty-four, forty, or forty-eight feet long. The heavy timber frame was covered with a roof frame consisting of a pair of rafters joined together by collar beams, and joined to the other rafters by purlins. The pitch of the roof often exceeded forty-five degrees, especially if thatch

was used as the original roofing material. Even when wooden shingles or shakes were employed (as was more common), the roof pitch remained fairly high because of design inertia.

The barn frame rested on large boulders or, in some cases, on a more elaborate stone foundation held in place with or without mortar. In New England, stone foundations penetrating below the frost line were required if the barn was to survive many winters; otherwise, the alternate freezing and thawing would cause the building to shift and, ultimately, to become unsound.

The English barn normally was sided with vertical pine boards. Because an absolutely weather-tight structure was not needed or desired, since stored hay generated heat so that spontaneous combustion was always a danger, the siding boards often had small gaps between them. If the siding had been

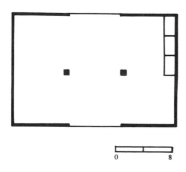

Fig. 2–2 The English barn

Fig. 2–3 Floor plan of an English barn. Lightweight interior partitions locate the position of grain bins.

Fig. 2–4 An English or three-bay barn (Trumbull County, Ohio, 1977)

placed in a horizontal position, these gaps would have permitted rainwater to collect on the upper edges, thus hastening the boards' rotting. To obviate that, the horizontal boards would have to have been overlapped or very tight fitted, requiring additional labor, resulting in unnecessary expense, and increasing the fire danger. Not only do English barns have vertical siding, so do most other early barn types.

Fenestration is mostly lacking, but small openings do appear on the gable ends, high up under the ridge, to provide ventilation for the hayloft. These openings are often cut in quite decorative shapes and are small enough so that pigeons are excluded, while martins, barn swallows, and other small birds are encouraged to nest in the loft. A small row of transom windows over the main door sometimes provides additional interior light. Illuminating the interior of the barn was always a difficult task, and often a dangerous one, given the highly combustible nature of hay, straw, and grain dust when exposed to open oil or kerosene lamps.

Fred Kniffen has remarked that the English barn moved westward to the grasslands of the central United States with remarkably little change.[6] In making his observation he implies that the English barn has been the dominant design north of Appalachia. Before exploring the subject of barn-type diffusion, however, the contributions of the other original culture source areas to barn design must be considered.

The Quebec long barn

Along the St. Lawrence and elsewhere in French Canada, another barn type, which can be called the *Quebec long barn* (fig. 2–5), was built. Gable-roofed, rectangular in shape, of timber frame construction, sided with vertical boards, and consisting of a hayloft over a single story, this barn has many similarities with the English barn.[7] It also has some important differences. Most apparent is its elongated plan (fig. 2–6), which may be derived from the continental practice of incorporating the house at the end of the barn.[8] Only a handful of such attached barns and houses have been reported from French Canada, but the elongated barn persists, incorporating within the structure several barn functions, often accommodated in separate structures in most of New England. Such a construction arrangement is economical and has the decided advantage during the bitterly cold Quebec winters of permitting farmers to do most of their work without venturing outside. The Quebec long barn is often eight or more bays wide, so that structures of forty-eight to eighty

feet are not uncommon (fig. 2–7). At the same time, these barns are rarely much deeper than the English barn.

Another distinctive feature is the dormer entrance to the barn loft. Always off-center, the dormer entrance breaks the clean roof line and provides a vertical balance to the otherwise horizontal composition of the structure. It would be difficult to imagine a more effective artistic device, despite the fact that the loft entrance was designed not with aesthetics in mind, but merely to provide a convenient entrance through which to load hay.

The Quebec long barn did not migrate out of French Canada. None is found in the Mississippi valley, in areas of later French settlement. In this latter area, a basic three-bay barn, flanked on three or even all four sides by roofed and sided aisles may be of French origin. Some additional and specific study must be made before more definitive statements can be given. In the Door peninsula of Wisconsin an elongated barn of Belgian origin (see chap. 8) is obviously related to the Quebec long barn.

Fig. 2–5 The Quebec long barn

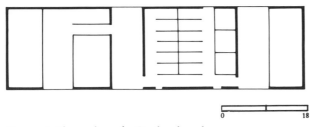

Fig. 2–6 Floor plan of a Quebec long barn

Fig. 2–7 A Quebec long barn on the Isle d'Orleans, Quebec. The ell in the foreground is a milk house built at a later date. (1976)

Closely connected to the Quebec long barn, but also having affinities to the English barn, is a structure that has been termed the Madawaska twin barn (fig. 2–8). Consisting of two gable-roofed rectangular barn buildings, often elongated, placed parallel to each other, and connected by a low intermediate passageway, the Madawaska twin barn did not appear until the very end of the nineteenth century. It is limited to the St. John valley in the extreme northern part of Maine, although isolated antecedents may be found further north in Drummond, Yamaska, and Bagot counties of Quebec.[9] The twin barn provides the same solution to the rigors of winter climate as the Quebec long barn or the New England connected barn does (see chap. 3), by eliminating the necessity for venturing outdoors. But it does so by utilizing a different and much more compact form than either of the other two types of barn.

Fig. 2–8 Sketch and floor plan of the Madawaska twin barn (from Victor A. Konrad and Michael Chaney, "Madawaska Twin Barn," *Journal of Cultural Geography* 3 [Fall/Winter 1982]: 66)

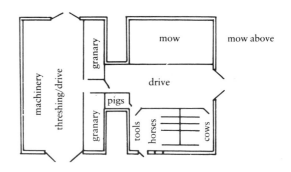

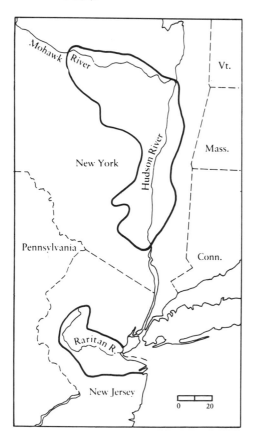

Fig. 2-10 Area in which Dutch barns have been located in mid-twentieth century. Based on studies by Fitchen (1967) and Wacker (1974).

The Dutch barn

Another compact barn of a rather different type was built by Dutch settlers in New York and New Jersey. The Dutch barn (fig. 2–9) did not spread much outside its original hearth. The area within which surviving Dutch barns have been identified includes the basins of the Mohawk, Schoharie, and Hudson rivers in New York State and the Raritan in northern New Jersey (fig. 2–10). All such areas are within or very close to the original hearth of Dutch culture. No Dutch barns have been reported from any location outside the original source area, although a later Dutch barn occurs in southwestern Michigan.

The Dutch barn differs from the English barn in several important aspects. Wagon doors are centered on the gable end of the barn rather than on the side, although in some barns there may be an additional wagon entrance on the side. At least one of the wagon doors is a Dutch door (i.e., divided so that the upper and lower portions swing independently of each other). Single, smaller doors occur near one or both of the corners of the gable end. These smaller doors give access directly to side aisles.

Dutch barns are roughly square in plan, and, when not square, are wider than they are long (fig. 2–11). The interior supports of the barn consist of rows of columns, held together by great anchorbeams spanning the central aisle (fig. 2–12). These massive anchorbeams are the most noteworthy interior feature of the Dutch barn. Their ends are shaped into rounded tenons that pass through slots cut in the vertical posts and are securely anchored by stout oak pegs.[10] The central aisle, originally utilized as a threshing floor, is always much wider than, and often twice as wide as, either of the side aisles.

Other distinctive features of the Dutch barn involve roof characteristics. The pitch of the roof is steep, so that the height of the gable at the ridge is always more than twice the height of the side walls.[11] Also, both the eave overhang

Fig. 2–11 Floor plan of a Dutch barn

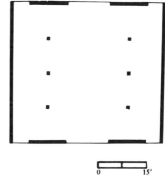

Fig. 2–9 The Dutch barn

Fig. 2–13 A Dutch barn with both gable and side doors. Note the pent roof. (Coxsackie, New York, 1979)

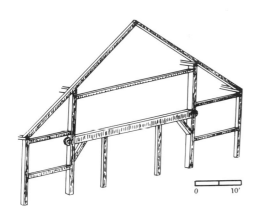

Fig. 2–12 Sketch of one bent of a Dutch barn, showing the characteristic anchorbeam (after Fitchen)

and the projection of the roof beyond the gable wall are extremely small. The eaves are much lower than in English barns (compare figs. 2–9 and 2–2). Unlike the English barn, the Dutch barn often has a small pent roof over the wagon doors (fig. 2–13).

Finally, the Dutch barn is sided with horizontal clapboards or flush boards. The explanation for this, when virtually every other early ethnic barn uses vertical siding, is probably related to the fact that barns in Holland in the seventeenth century (and to a considerable extent still today) normally were combined with the farmhouses as a single structure under a single roof. Use of horizontal boarding on houses is a well-established tradition. The separation of house and barn, which occurred in the New World, did not involve a reorientation of the siding. This situation might also explain the placement of the barn doors on the gable rather than on the side as in other early ethnic barns.

The Dutch barns performed different functions from those of the English barn. The latter structure was essentially a crop barn for grain storage and threshing, whereas the Dutch barn accommodated not only these functions, but was also a shelter for animals as well.[12] No existing Dutch barns still function as animal shelters, but the existence of some side aisles that are depressed below the level of the threshing floor proves that they once served the purpose.[13]

The only detailed studies of Dutch barns have been by Peter Wacker for barns in New Jersey, and by John Fitchen for New York Dutch barns. In addition, Theodore Prudon has examined the European connection of the Dutch barn.[14] Beyond this, nothing exists.

In assessing the aesthetic character of Dutch barns, Fitchen has drawn an attractive picture that captures much of these structures' appeal:

New York Dutch barns are of noble proportions on the exterior: broad, capacious looking, spreading expansively to either side of the central wagon doors above which the roof rises in uncomplicated symmetry. These barns are big, but not overwhelmingly so. The simplicity of their shape is frankly utili-

21

Fig. 2–14 The German bank barn

tarian, but not impersonally or austerely so. Doors—even the Dutch door of the wagon entrances—are for human use too; and both these and the martin holes above them combine usefulness and concern for good husbandry with an unself-conscious sense of good design. The shape of these barns is neither squat and sunken looking nor narrow and tall. Even when they are viewed from a distance there is a quality of integrity about them: an integrity of purpose, of materials and craftsmanship, of complete adaptation to the conditions of their being.[15]

Fitchen appears to have caught the essence of this barn. It must be admitted, however, that the Dutch barn cannot be found much outside eastern New York and northern New Jersey. It had little influence on later barn types, which were derived from the English barn and from a barn type contributed from the original German settlement area of southeastern Pennsylvania.

The German bank barn

Apparently, not until the seventeenth century was drawing to a close was the German bank barn introduced into the southeastern corner of Pennsylvania. The relatively late origin of this barn type, coming as it did at a time when agriculture had grown in scale and complexity, may account in part for the greater elaboration of the barn as compared to the earlier barns associated with English and Dutch cultural hearths. Most barns in North America were essentially crop barns, structures designed to house harvested crops and to offer shelter in which threshing could take place after the growing season. The German bank barn, like the Quebec long barn, combined these functions with that of animal shelter.

The design of the German bank barn resembles barns and other hillside structures found in southern Germany, Switzerland, and other parts of hilly and mountainous central Europe (fig. 2–14). A considerable debate exists, however, over whether the barn designs utilized in the New World were in fact evolved in this country, or whether they are transplants from Europe.[16] What seems likely is that German, Swiss, and Austrian emigrants introduced several barn types, probably all related to one another and demonstrating an evolution from simple to complex.

The most detailed study, although far from definitive, of the variants of the German bank barn has been made by Charles Dornbusch and J. K. Heyl, who have identified eleven subtypes of Pennsylvania barns.[17] Subtype B is almost identical to the English barn, consisting of three units of roughly equal size. Subtypes A and C add a partially excavated basement floor (figs. 2–15, 2–16). In both barns, the ridge line lies perpendicular to the slope of the hill. Subtypes A and B usually are built of logs and represent early designs. Glassie labels the subtype B barns as *double-crib* barns,[18] thereby suggesting a possible connection with the evolutionary sequence of crib barns already discussed in chapter 1.

Subtype C is also called a tri-level ground barn or *Grundscheier*. In southeastern Pennsylvania and central Maryland it was the most common eighteenth-century barn. Small in size (thirty-five to fifty-five feet wide by twenty to thirty-five feet deep), it usually lies athwart the slope of the land. The Grundscheier has "a threshing floor in the middle and stables on both sides: The threshing floor is invariably on the highest level; the cow stable is usually on the next lower level; the horse stable most often on the lowest level. The relative elevation of the horse and cow stable may, however, vary." The threshing platform is raised above the stables for sanitary reasons and to facilitate the loading of the mows, which surmount each of the stables. Because the draft horses were more valuable than the cows, the former were kept in individual stalls, whereas the cows were permitted to share a common stable on the opposite side of the threshing platform.[19] The Grundscheier is essentially a barn for traditional subsistence agriculture. As agriculture grew and farmers prospered in southeastern Pennsylvania more elaborate barns were needed.

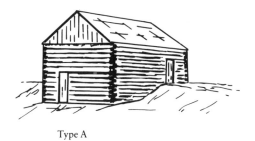

Type A

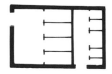

Fig. 2–15 Pennsylvania barns, types A and B. Type A is a primitive two-level barn comparable to type C. The logs are squared and carefully joined at the corners. Spaces between logs are filled with clay or lime mortar. Wood siding was later applied to give greater protection from the elements. In type B, a common roof joins two rectangular units separated by a runway. Logs are often round, variably sized, and crudely shaped. No clay or lime mortar is used, and the logs are covered with vertical wood siding. (From Charles Dornbusch and John Heyl, *Pennsylvania German Barns*)

Type B

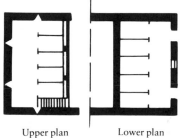

Upper plan   Lower plan

Fig. 2–16 Pennsylvania barn type C is one form of a transitional barn. It is placed with its narrow dimension in a bank or sloping grade. The wall is all stone and the wagon entrance at the back is level with the hay mow over the stable on the lower grade. The mow over the stable on the upper grade is a half level above the threshing floor. It is three bays wide and three bays long. The construction is similar to other simple barn types. The ventilators are of the slit-loop hole variety. (From Dornbusch and Heyl)

Subtype D is the first of the large structures, although it is a single-level, three-bay barn (fig. 2-17). The central threshing floor is slightly elevated to facilitate cleanliness and avoid drainage from the stables that occupy the outside bays. Such barns are normally built in stone and possess ventilator slits. These narrow openings frequently have been identified as gun or rifle ports by overly romantic writers. The best examples occur in Berks and Bucks counties in southeastern Pennsylvania. The subtype E barn is quite similar, except it is a bank barn, i.e., it is partially excavated into the slope or bank of the hillside (fig. 2-18). It is built most usually in stone and has ventilation slits and often pairs of pent roofs on the down slope side of the structure, which faces the feeding lot. Entry to the basement level, in which the animals are housed, is through a series—normally five—single doors.[20] At a higher level, the rear threshing doors open out *over* the feeding lot and cannot be reached from the ground. Such inaccessible threshing doors are characteristic of many other two-and-a-half-story barns (fig. 2-19), including those falling under the heading of *Sweitzer* barns.

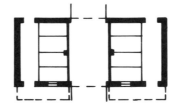

Fig. 2-17 Pennsylvania barn type D is an all-stone, ground-level barn. A slight ramp raises the runway about a foot above the stalls to the left and right, separating the horses and the cows. There are large doors that permit entrance from either side. The hay mows are on raised platforms over the stalls. (From Dornbusch and Heyl)

Fig. 2-18 Pennsylvania barn type E is an all-stone masonry, two-level barn. It is either a bank barn or a barn on level ground with a high ramp to the hay mow floor. Occasionally a wood forebay cantilevers beyond a continuous stone wall. It is three to five bays long and three to four bays wide. The animal stalls are sometimes an island surrounded by aisles with entrances from the gable wall. Most barns of this type have a shed-hood or pent roof over the doors on the stable yard front. (From Dornbusch and Heyl)

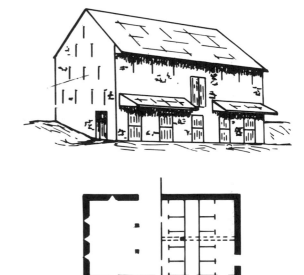

Upper plan   Lower plan

ment in summer. The lower story is constructed of stone or concrete.

The upper floor is conventionally divided into three units—either two cribs and a drive-space or three bays. Entry to the upper floor is by double wagon doors centered on the upslope side of the barn. The center area of this level was designed originally, as in the English barn, for use as a threshing floor. This use is verified by the occurrence of threshing doors in an opposing position, opening out over the feeding lot (see fig. 2–19). These doors have no entry or access function, but serve only to allow for the creation of a draft to promote the winnowing associated with grain threshing by hand. Side bays permitted storage of farm machinery and

tools as well as unthreshed grain. Often a bay was used as a hay mow.

Threshed grain usually was stored in granary bins built into the forebay of the barn. The most distinctive structural feature of the Sweitzer barn is this forebay, the second-story projection or overhang on the downslope side of the barn (fig. 2–21). The forebay, also sometimes called the *vorshuss* or the *forbau*, offers several advantages. First, because it extends out over the feed lot, it affords protection for stock in inclement weather. Second, the projection obviates the necessity of shoveling snow away from the basement doors. Third, chutes cut into its floor provide a means by which feed, straw, and hay can be dropped directly to the stock in the feed

Fig. 2–20 The Sweitzer barn

The Sweitzer barn

The term *Sweitzer* barn refers to two other German barns, which Dornbusch and Heyl classified as subtype F and G. Also called *Schweitzer* or *Swisser* barns, these structures are among the most commonly encountered barns, extending from Pennsylvania all the way to the central plains of the United States, from the Shenandoah valley of Virginia to southern Ontario. Hence, this barn will be described here more fully than other German bank barn types.

The Sweitzer barn (fig. 2–20) is basically a two-and-a-half-story building. The lower floor, devoted primarily to cattle stalls, stables, and other space for animals, is normally partially excavated. Such a situation in which the structure is built into the hillside helps conserve heat in the winter season and, conversely, provides a cooler environ-

Fig. 2–19 Close-up of threshing doors on a Sweitzer barn (Summit County, Ohio, 1978)

Fig. 2–21 A Sweitzer barn showing the unsupported forebay. Note the threshing
doors. (Summit County, Ohio, 1978)

Fig. 2–22 A Sweitzer barn showing the cantilevered forebay (Summit
County, Ohio, 1976)

Fig. 2–23 Photo showing the framing of a Sweitzer barn forebay
(Stark County, Ohio, 1979)

26

lot below. Finally, the forebay permits a larger second story than is provided by the foundation walls (fig. 2–22). The forebay is supported by cantilevered beams. Posts or columns are not normally used for support of the forebay. In some instances, the forebay is framed independently of the rest of the barn, but in other cases it is integrated. The barn may be constructed of logs, timber frame, brick, or stone, but the forebay is invariably of timber frame (fig. 2–23) covered with plank siding. In early designs, the gable roof of the barn is asymmetrical, with the forebay continuing the roof line, but in later designs a symmetrical roof line appears. In some in-

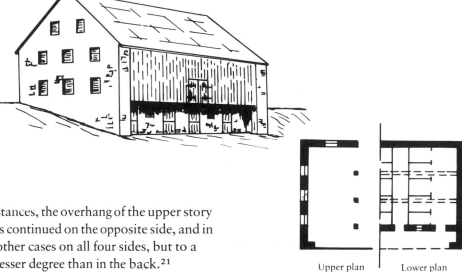

Fig. 2–24 Floor plan of a Sweitzer barn

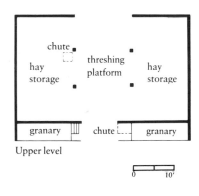

Upper level

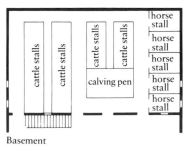

Basement

stances, the overhang of the upper story is continued on the opposite side, and in other cases on all four sides, but to a lesser degree than in the back.[21]

The Sweitzer barn is crowned by a commodious loft used for hay storage. The internal plan of the barns is simple. There are usually three units on the second floor and rows of cow stalls and stables separated by aisles on the lower level (fig. 2–24). Access to the lower level is provided by a number of Dutch doors positioned on the wall under the forebay. Barn proportions are usually three to two, i.e., three bays wide and two bays deep, although barns four to seven bays wide are not unknown. Furthermore, the width and depth of a bay may not be equal in size.

At least four variants of the basic Sweitzer barn may be identified. One is labeled subtype H by Dornbusch and Heyl (fig. 2–25). Its chief distinguishing characteristic is the fact that the stone gable walls enclose the frame forebay, giving the barn a more massive appear-

Upper plan | Lower plan

Fig. 2–25 Pennsylvania barn type H is similar to the Sweitzer barn, its major difference being that its gable wall includes a cantilevered forebay that is visible from the stable yard front. It is sometimes found on almost level ground, and when this occurs additional stable entrances are placed in the gable ends. This type is found in all areas and its form, already established in the late eighteenth century, continued in favor until the end of the nineteenth century. (From Dornbusch and Heyl)

27

Fig. 2–26 A gable-enclosed forebay barn (Near Reading, Pennsylvania, 1979)

ance than other Sweitzer barns (fig. 2–26). On the upslope side, the center section of the side wall is usually framed, and the rest is constructed of stone. These barns are found throughout Pennsylvania, central Maryland, extreme northern Virginia, extreme eastern West Virginia, and in eastern and central Ohio, with the later examples built entirely of wood.

A second variant has a much more limited disribution, being found mostly in southeastern Pennsylvania, from Chester and Delaware to Berks counties. It has been identified as subtype J, and represents a further evolution of the Sweitzer barn, especially of the subtype

H. The forebay is greatly enlarged and extended, producing an awkward looking structure (fig. 2–27). The large forebay is a forerunner of the straw shed, a nineteenth-century barn addition discussed in the following chapter. Because of its size and consequent weight, the wooden forebay is supported on large tapering stone piers.

A third variant, not identified by Dornbusch and Heyl but noted by both Glassie[22] and Joseph Glass,[23] occurs scattered over a large part of Maryland, Pennsylvania, Ohio, and areas of the Midwest. The distinctive feature of this subtype is a large wagon runway on the lower level, which occupies the space just inside one gable of the barn (fig.

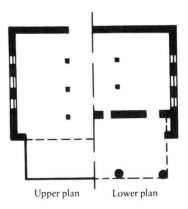

Upper plan   Lower plan

Fig. 2–27 Pennsylvania barn type J is a further development of the type H barn, a change brought about by a need for more space for hay and grain storage. A large wooden forebay is added to the original structure and is supported by stone piers or wooden columns. This type, supported on round tapered columns, is most common in Chester County. (From Dornbusch and Heyl)

28

2–28). The exterior wall of the runway includes a narrow corn crib. Most of these barns are built on level or very gently sloping land, so that a front-to-rear runway is possible, especially if the barn is catty-corner to the slope of the land. In these barns, access to the second floor is often by means of a ramp, and the forebay is broken by the runway opening.

A final variant of the Sweitzer barn is seen in Dornbusch and Heyl's subtype K (fig. 2–29). In this barn, the forebay is completely enclosed and incorporated within the barn proper. The forebay is no longer cantilevered, but is supported by a stone wall through which three arched openings provide access to the lower story. The threshing doors usually are much reduced in size. These barns are always built in stone and their distribution is quite limited and unusual. In the East this barn is restricted primarily

Fig. 2–28 Another type of German barn. The forebay, which is unsupported, extends only partially across the structure. An open wagon driveway extends from the front to back along one gable. (Near Sharpsburg, Maryland, 1979)

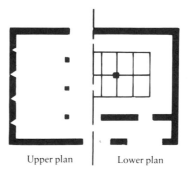

Upper plan | Lower plan

Fig. 2–29 Pennsylvania barn type K is an all-stone, two-level barn and a specialized development in areas where H type barns are frequently found. The masonry arches form a kind of loggia and shelter for the stable area, and also provide support for the extended beams, which were cantilevers in the H barn. Ventilators have occasionally been omitted. (From Dornbusch and Heyl)

29

Fig. 2–31 A Sweitzer barn built in brick with a wooden forebay (York County, Pennsylvania, 1979)

Fig. 2–30 A small Sweitzer-type barn typical of the Harpers Ferry, West Virginia, area. These barns are much smaller than Sweitzer barns elsewhere. The lower story is log and the upper is frame. It may date from the late eighteenth century. (1978)

to Montgomery and Lehigh counties in southeastern Pennsylvania, but it also occurs in central Missouri and south central Nebraska. Such a pattern is intriguing enough to warrant additional attention.

Obviously, barns considered under the heading of the Sweitzer type encompass a large number of variants. Even within the basic type itself, considerable variation exists. In some instances, this is a matter of size. For example, in central Maryland between Harpers Ferry and Antietam and stretching up into the northwest, a distinctive Sweitzer half barn of very small proportions occurs (fig. 2–30).

In south central Pennsylvania and adjacent Maryland, the variation is in type of building material. Here a number of large Sweitzer barns have been constructed in reddish-orange brick (fig. 2–31). Into the brick walls, decorative ventilators have been opened with attractive designs (fig. 2–32). In the words of J. W. Stair, "Brick-end barns are among the finest classics of rural American architecture."[24] Because of the intricate designs provided by gaps in the brickwork, "each barn stands as a unique work of art as well as of architecture." Of course, this unique brickwork provides lighting as well as ventilation.

Fig. 2–32 Close-up of decorative brick-work (Cumberland County, Pennsylvania, 1979)

Some other Sweitzer barns have other variations, such as pent roofs to shelter wagons and machinery (fig. 2–33). Such roofs are normally on the east or south sides of the barn. In certain other barns, a roof extension protrudes over the wagon doors providing some modest rain and snow protection for the door opening. Elaborate entrance structures or vestibules, such as those found on some raised barns (see next chapter) are lacking, however.

Much of the earlier discussion has focused upon the changes in the Sweitzer forebay and the downslope configuration of the barn. Modifications to the upslope facade also occur. The most

Fig. 2–33 A pent roof on a German bank barn. Such features are usually found on east or north sides of barns. (Wayne County, Ohio, 1976)

31

Fig. 2–34 A German bank barn with up-slope bays

common alteration was the addition of one or two large projecting bays, whose roof slope continued that of the main structure (fig. 2–34). Such bays are normally used for tool or equipment storage.

The basic proportion of a width one-third longer than the depth appears to be a good general index for identification of Sweitzer barns, which have antecedents in southern Germany, Switzerland, and Austria.

The Wisconsin porch barn

Another type of German bank barn appears to have come from the rolling plains of northern Germany.[25] The Wisconsin porch or Pomeranian barn (figs. 2–35 and 36) has a longer, generally lower, silhouette than the Sweitzer barn. First identified in Wisconsin, these

32

Fig. 2–35 The Wisconsin porch barn, early phase

barns are also quite numerous in eastern Ohio, and may be present elsewhere. The Wisconsin porch barn is a timber frame structure, usually between five and seven bays wide, so that several pairs of threshing doors are present. The overhang is always supported by wooden posts (fig. 2–37). A series of wooden louvers, often in a Gothic pointed-arch shape, provide ventilation instead of open ventilator slits. The early versions of the Wisconsin porch barn possess an asymmetrical roof, whereas later ones have the forebay incorporated within the symmetry of the barn's gable roof. A large dormer above the forebay is a conspicuous feature of many of these barns. Recently, Robert Ensminger has proposed that these barns are variants of the forebay barn of Pennsylvania.[26]

Double-decker barns

The final subtype identified by Dornbusch and Heyl is designated L and refers to a double-decker barn, i.e., one that has three levels plus a loft (fig. 2–38). The threshing floor is raised one floor above the hay mows on either side and is reached by a ramp.[27] The granary occupies the space immediately below the threshing floor, and it thereby benefits from the possibility of gravity filling. Often the threshing floor is entered via a covered barn bridge that protects a lower entry directly into the granary.

Double-decker barns are usually located against a steep slope, so that the ramp to the threshing floor is not too steep for easy utilization.[28] Early double-decker barns were built of stone, but by the third quarter of the nineteenth century, timber frame examples were being built throughout the German settled parts of the Midwest. However, some of the best examples of the double-decker barn are still found in the vicinity of York, Pennsylvania.

More study has been given to the German bank barn than to any other farm building. As early as 1864, Frederick Watt was proposing improvements to the German bank barn to make it even more efficient than he recognized it already to be.[29] Yet, it seems surprising that the structure has not commanded more scholarly attention, given its obvious significance, its large number of variants, and its very wide distribution. The early Grundscheier barn has been the subject of just a single article.[30] The entire literature, which is cited in this chapter, consists of just two books and not more than two dozen articles, book chapters, and other published sources, both specifically dealing with German bank barns or including material on them as incidental to other concerns.

Only Dornbusch and Heyl have attempted to identify and differentiate the subtypes of the basic building, and their classification system certainly is not exhaustive.[31] Nevertheless, it forms the basis for most later studies, several of which have provided important additional subtypes. Glass examined the

Fig. 2–37 A Wisconsin porch barn. Note the asymmetrical roof and the supported overhang. The raised roof over the threshing doors is unusual. (Wayne County, Ohio, 1975)

Pennsylvania German barn in considerable detail, but largely outside the context of the Dornbusch and Heyl classification system.[32]

Robert Bastian suggested the existence of a distinctive barn built by Pomeranian immigrants in central Wisconsin.[33] Although he tentatively called it a Wisconsin porch barn because of its supported forebay, the same type of building can be found in Ohio and Virginia,[34] and it probably exists elsewhere (see above).

Charles Calkins and Martin Perkins have called attention to a smaller stable barn that also has Pomeranian connections but that occurs mostly in the southeastern counties of Wisconsin and not in the central part of the state, where the Wisconsin porch barn occurs.[35]

The Pomeranian stable barn was built

only up to about 1875, as a companion to a small three-bay threshing barn. After this date, both of the smaller barns were supplanted by larger, two-level dairy barns. No evidence has been supplied that the two-level barns are of the type found by Bastian further north.

Although similar in many respects (e.g., in their lower profile and the presence of a forebay) to the larger Wisconsin porch barn, the Pomeranian stable barn also possesses some quite disparate features, the most important of which are the unsupported forebay and the outside stairway that provides the only access to the loft.[36] Furthermore, the Pomeranian stable barn is not built

Fig. 2–36 The Wisconsin porch barn, late phase

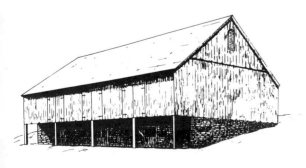

33

into a bank nor does it use the same framing system of the Wisconsin porch barn.[37]

Another study has provided some basic information on a type of German barn that seems to combine earlier eastern elements with midwestern form. This structure, like the Pomeranian stable barn, has been identified over a very limited area and is associated with a particular ethnic community. The Madison County Amish barn has several identifying characteristics: (1) a five-bay or bent form; (2) a ground level used mostly for stabling, with "each stall area functionally set apart and oriented to the long side of the barn where 'Dutch' doors provide access, fresh air, and illumination";[38] (3) an off-center wagon entry under a projecting gable structure; (4) a pent roof along the front side of the barn; (5) a right-angle straw or hay shed, which also functions as a cattle run. A comparison of this barn with the Wisconsin porch barn, which has a rather similar form, might answer some of the unresolved questions raised by Ensminger concerning the relationship of Wisconsin and Pennsylvania forebay barns.[39]

Finally, Charles van Ravenswaay has provided a tantalizing view of German barns in Missouri. Unfortunately, although the subject is worth a book it is dealt with in the space of a chapter. Consequently, his classification system is rudimentary and the discussion of several highly interesting structures is not as complete as one would desire.[40]

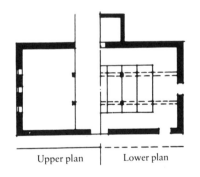

Upper plan | Lower plan

Fig. 2–38 Pennsylvania barn type L is an all-stone, three-level barn developed against a very steep natural grade. It is locally called a double-decker. The threshing floor is raised one floor above the hay mows on either side and is reached by the ramp. The granary is directly below the threshing floor and is level with the hay mow floor. These barns have a covered barn bridge that provides a secondary entrance to the granary from outside. The use of a continuous hood is common. The timber framing is similar to the more usual H type. (From Dornbusch and Heyl)

Nevertheless, a range of valuable buildings is located and described, including many that can be related to types discussed by Dornbusch and Heyl and Glassie.[41] Most important, several barn types including a rare housebarn combination are discussed. It is likely that Missouri will prove as rewarding as Pennsylvania and Wisconsin for ethnic barn studies.

Van Ravenswaay's research on Missouri is also representative of a group of studies that examines the particular characteristics or the local impact of German barns in various regions. These studies include the Sweitzer barn in southeastern Ohio,[42] the Sweitzer barn compared with the raised three-bay or basement barn in north central Indiana,[43] the double-crib barn in south central Pennsylvania,[44] the spread of German barns to the southern Appalachian region and their modifications therein,[45] a very general treatise on Sweitzer barns in Ohio,[46] and a solid general work which contains considerable information on German barns in Maryland and the Shenandoah valley of Virginia.[47] Of a slightly different character is the discussion by Terry Jordan of an unusual Texas example of a forebay bank barn.[48]

Although several authors have speculated on the origins of Pennsylvania German barns,[49] only two have provided comprehensive evidence and conclusions.[50] Both point to central Europe as the most logical place of origin.

The remaining studies fall into two overlapping categories. First are those that are secondary summarizations using materials collected and assembled from other sources. The best of these is Amos Long's definitive study of the

Pennsylvania German farmstead,[51] whose great value lies not in its treatment of the barn, but rather of all the other farmstead buildings. Less descriptive, but more pictorial, is the Pennsylvania barn chapter in *The Barn* by Eric Arthur and Dudley Witney.

Second are those studies that are partly summarizations and partly original research. These works are often of rather uneven quality, frequently romantic rather than analytical, but they do contain redeeming features. Among these is a summary article by Henry Kauffman, which makes available, although without accurate citation, a mid-nineteenth-century analysis of the Sweitzer barn, probably the earliest careful description of that structure in Pennsylvania.[52]

Bernice Ball's *Barns of Chester County, Pennsylvania* is an enthusiastic book with outstanding illustrations but rather uneven text. The most difficult book to categorize is *The Pennsylvania Barn,* edited by Alfred Shoemaker. Truly, it is *the* pioneer published effort on North American barns and it contains much valuable information. However, it suffers from the defect that mars many books of joint authorship, its material varies from scholarly chapters with carefully documented sources to chapters that are almost caricatures.

This review of the literature on the German bank barn is an example of the approaches used by various researchers to the most carefully studied of barn structures. Other barns and farm buildings have received even less attention. The whole matter of research in the field of domestic or vernacular architecture will be discussed in the final two chapters.

Other ethnic barns

Barns were also introduced in North America by other ethnic groups, but not apparently in sufficient numbers to give a distinctive character to any major region, with an exception perhaps being those introduced by the Mormons in the intermontane West (see chap. 8). The barns of later immigrant groups also have not received very much scholarly study, and additional research may reveal barn types not now recognized. Here again is another area in which much further research work is needed, and it must be done quickly, before the structures disappear or are so greatly altered as to be unrecognizable.

3   The North American Farm Barn: Changes in Time and Space

Over time, all building evolves. Innovative construction methods and materials may be adopted, functions may change, and utilization be modified. Those structures that become obsolete are often abandoned, and through disuse rapidly deteriorate (fig. 3–1) and ultimately disappear. Older construction materials are supplanted by newer and often more durable or cheaper ones. New and different structures are designed to better satisfy changing requirements. Builders borrow ideas from each other and early design weaknesses or deficiencies are gradually removed. In the process, floor plans are altered and often expanded. The form of the building changes.

However, one cardinal guiding principle that students of architecture have learned to value is the rule that "form follows function." All that this means is that the function for which a structure is intended will often determine the shape of the building itself. A good example would be a railroad roundhouse. No other shaped structure permits the switching of locomotives so quickly and efficiently with a minimum length of track.

Buildings also are affected by the materials of their construction. Houses built largely of wood evince a simple square or rectangular plan in early periods of construction. Such a form is easiest for semiskilled workers to construct. Later, a more complex building may evolve, but usually it will consist of combinations of squares or rectangles, as long as the house is constructed primarily of wood.

Farm barns are even simpler structures than houses, and also commonly have been built of wood. The previous chapter discussed the ethnic connections of early American barns. In this chapter, the major modifications that have occurred in barn building during the nineteenth and twentieth centuries are traced. In large part, changes in barn type result from modifications in the agricultural process itself. A shift from farming based upon grain crops to one emphasizing livestock encouraged a change from a single-level, three-bay barn with a central threshing platform, to a multi-level barn in which livestock were housed in the basement and the harvested crops and equipment on the upper floor. Some of these changes took place in some structures before the barn was introduced into the New World, and afterward in others. In both instances, the changing function of the barn clearly produced the new form. At a later period, the invention of the silo made the large loft used for hay storage no longer so necessary. Furthermore, the invention of hay-baling machines reduced the bulk but increased the weight of hay to be stored, making large

Fig. 3–1 Abandoned barn in disrepair (Chautauqua County, New York, 1976)

Fig. 3–2 Hay rolled for storage in the fields during the winter (Knox County, Ohio, 1978)

loft barns even more redundant. Low, one-story pole barns began to replace the earlier, bigger, bulkier barns. Still later, the process of hay making changed so much that hay after being cut and field dried was piled or rolled into gigantic mounds and left in the fields (fig. 3–2). Cattle are selectively introduced into the fields for feeding during the winter. Although the rate of spoilage is very high, the savings in labor and fuel more than compensate. The result of this system of haying and feeding ultimately will be that pole barns will be converted to structures providing only livestock shelter from winter winds and cold temperatures. Even now, pole barns completely open on one or two sides to facilitate movement of stock to water and feed are becoming fairly common in stock-raising areas.

The New England connected barn

One modification of the English barn occurred at an early period in New England. The basic detached English barn became connected to the farmhouse via a series of intervening structures (fig. 3–3). Considerable variation in the form of these buildings occurs, so a distinct type of New England connected barn cannot be said to exist, but the physical linking of house and barn in North America is restricted largely to New England. Southeastern Manitoba is the principal exception to this statement (see chap. 8). Despite variation in individual structures, a basic pattern can be discerned which "is summarized by a children's rhyme from the last century: Big house, little house, back house, barn."[1] Thus, the main house usually has an addition (which in some

instances is, in fact, the original home), and one or more intermediate structures—often built for a special purpose such as a summer kitchen, wash house, stable, or equipment storage—connect the house addition to the barn.[2]

Severe winter weather and the advantages of an enclosed passageway between house and barn often have been cited for the evolution of the New England connected barn. However, Thomas Hubka suggests that the connecting of barn and house by intermediate structures grew out of several traditions. Preserving and reusing structures was in tune with Yankee frugality and typified a conservative outlook. Moving and remodeling buildings was also a conspicuous characteristic related to

37

Fig. 3–3 The New England connected barn

the same basic traits. "Most connected farms are composed of different building types, built at different times and places, and usually remodeled or moved several times during the history of the farm."[3]

Certain standardized themes are encountered in a close examination of the New England connected barn. First, the various parts of the structure demonstrate great variety of design (figs. 3–3 and 3–4). Barns may be of the raised type or not, with side entry or gable doors, and covered with either board siding or wooden shingles. Houses are of various types, but the Cape Cod cottage predominates. Intermediate structures may be of several kinds of construction, frequently contain the oldest and newest parts of the building complex, and often exhibit the greatest degree of ongoing modification. Second, structures are typically set off from one another to produce an *en echelon* pro-

Fig. 3–4 One style of New England connected barn. One of the barn buildings has been remodeled into living quarters. (Near Camden, Maine, 1972)

38

file or plan (fig. 3–5).[4] This arrangement results from the joining of two or more separately built structures, subsequently placed to minimize wall contact and structural disruption.[5] Third, each structure of the ensemble is independent of the others. No common roofs connect buildings. Clearly, this makes the New England connected barn distinct in origin from the combined house and barn structures of Europe. Fourth, the line of the buildings usually is oriented perpendicular to the roadway. However, see figure 3–4 for one of the exceptions to this general rule. Fifth, within the line of buildings an attempt often is made to provide a farmyard opening to the south or the east (see fig. 3–3b). However, the farmyard is rarely closely or completely enclosed as one finds in the German farmsteads of Wisconsin.

Fig. 3–6 A gable-entry banked barn (Oneida County, New York, 1978)

The gable-entry banked barn

A quite different barn of English origins is found in parts of western New England, New York, and northern Pennsylvania. The gable-entry banked barn (fig. 3–6) appears to be a derivative of the type that occurs through the rough country of the English Lake District.[6] Unlike other bank barns, the gable-entry banked barn lies athwart the hill with its long axis parallel to the slope. Such a location permits upslope entry to the second story through the gable, rather than from the barn side, which is common for other barns of English origin. The basement entry is normally through the opposite gable, although small doors on one side may also be present. No study exists of this barn type in North America, but there probably have never been very many. However, its wide range is justification enough for researching its origins and associations.

The raised three-bay or basement barn

Much more commonly seen is the raised three-bay or basement barn (fig. 3–7). This structure also has been called a Central Ontario barn[7] and a Southern Ontario barn.[8] It consists essentially of an English or three-bay barn (see chap. 2) raised upon a stone, brick, or concrete foundation, thereby adding a lower story. Although an origin in central New York State or southern Ontario has been suggested, it appears more likely that this barn type also traces its origins to the English Lake Country. Unlike the gable-entry banked barn, the axis of this structure lies along the contour of the hill slope.

Basic differences in framing between the Pennsylvania German barn and the raised three-bay barn are emphasized in the lack of the forebay in the latter (fig. 3–8). Furthermore, the Pennsylvania German barn has multiple entries to the

Fig. 3–5 Floor plan of a New England connected barn

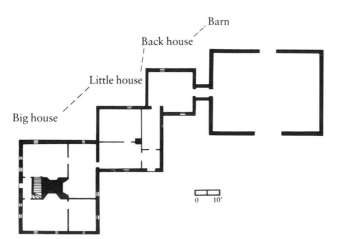

39

basement story usually only on the downslope side. The basement barn may have downslope doorways, but it also has doors centered on the gable ends of the lowest story. This placement may be a reflection of the fact that basement barns are built not only in hill country, but frequently on the more gently sloping plains of interior North America as well. Consequently, a variety of methods (fig. 3–9) is employed to provide access to the second story in the flatter areas: (1) a simple earth ramp may be constructed; (2) the ramp may be removed from the barn wall and a platform laid to bridge the gap; or (3) the bridge may be covered with an enclosed entryway. The ramp, especially if it is somewhat removed from the barn, can be excavated and used as a root or cold cellar, thereby eliminating the expense of erecting such a structure (fig. 3–10). The covered passageway, sheltered by the barn bridge, provides protected space for machinery or wagons. A distinctive, covered-entry structure is typical of raised barns throughout New York and in northwestern

Fig. 3–8 A raised or basement barn, showing the side entrance to the raised threshing floor and the gable end entrance to the basement livestock floor (Mantua, Ohio, 1973)

Fig. 3–7 The raised or basement barn

40

Pennsylvania (fig. 3–11). Stewart McHenry has found similar features in a limited area of northeastern Vermont settled by Scots immigrants.[9]

The functions of the various parts of the basement barns are essentially similar to those of the Sweitzer barn. The basement houses animals, the second level serves as a threshing floor and for crop and equipment storage, and the loft holds hay for winter animal feed. Granaries are usually built into one or both sides of the threshing floor, and threshing doors are located in the second-floor rear wall. On the average, the raised three-bay barn is considerably larger than the simple English barn

from which it is derived. Dimensions forty to fifty feet wide and sixty to one hundred feet long are quite common.[10]

The plan of the upper floor is tripartite, quite similar to that of both the Sweitzer barn and the basic English barn. The basement story contrasts sharply, in its arrangement of stalls and stanchions, with the Sweitzer barn (compare fig. 3–12 with fig. 2–24). In the former, the aisles run primarily from gable to gable, and in the latter, from side to side, with a rear aisle.

Fig. 3–9 Barn access solutions (reprinted from *Pioneer America*, July 1974). See also figure 3–7.

Fig. 3–11 A raised barn with a gable-roof entry structure (Mercer County, Pennsylvania, 1980)

Fig. 3–10 A raised barn with a ramp that has been excavated to provide a root cellar (Mahoning County, Ohio, 1978)

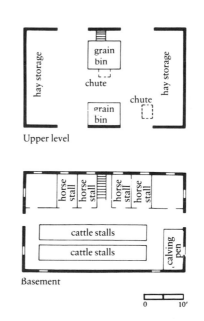

Fig. 3–12 Floor plan of a raised or basement barn

Fig. 3–13 The raised three-gable barn

Straw sheds and three-gable barns

The raised three-bay or basement barn is an attempt to combine complex and expanding agricultural functions within a single farm building by enlarging a more basic barn and raising it to introduce a basement story. As American farming became more diversified and complicated in the nineteenth century, barns were modified in other ways to make them more suitable for "scientific" farming. Throughout the nineteenth century, American farms expanded in acreage as their number declined. Thus, the barn was expected to serve a continually growing farm. Additional animals had to be sheltered and more crops processed and stored. Feed and bedding requirements also grew. Farmers began to be more concerned about proper manure application, as well as about other aspects of modern agriculture.

Mechanical threshing machines permitted the entire farm's grain crop to be processed at one time, instead of bit by bit through the long winter. As a result of all these changes, more space was needed to shelter additional animals, to store more hay for feed, and to keep both straw and manure from being exposed to rapid deterioration from the weather.

In both German bank barns and raised or basement barns, straw was normally

Fig. 3–14 Ridge level relationships in three-gable barns (from *Pioneer America*, July 1974)

disposed of at the time of threshing by throwing it out the open threshing doors into the feed lot. Here, the straw piles accumulated, but they also deteriorated rapidly. This practice is still followed on many Mennonite and Amish farms (see fig. 8–34). The advent of the mechanical threshing machine, however, made open threshing doors no longer necessary. Therefore a wing addition could be constructed at right angles to the barn to function as a straw shed, providing cover for the discarded straw. With time, the simple shed became more complex and generally larger. Its loft was expanded and used for additional hay storage; a basement was incorporated to house more livestock or to protect manure until it could be spread on the fields as fertilizer.

Eventually, the straw shed extension became as large as half the original barn (fig. 3–13). As the shed grew, the principal problem became aligning the ridgepole of the shed with the ridge of the main structure (fig. 3–14). In many sections of the Northeast, barns incorporating the straw shed and containing three gables began to be built as complete units starting in the nineteenth century.

Lumber-truss construction
and gambrel roofs

By the third quarter of the nineteenth century, forest resources had been seriously depleted in northeastern United States. The great timbers used in the frames of barns up to this time either were no longer available or had become prohibitively expensive. The invention of inexpensive nails made from wire, together with the perfection of dimension lumber cut into standardized sizes, permitted the introduction of new, lighter, but still strong, framing systems. In many respects these changes were analogous to those that had occurred earlier in house building, when sawn lumber replaced hewn timber (see vol. 1, chap. 11).

The employment of dimension lumber resulted in radical changes in barn framing in many newly constructed barns, although the old system was retained in some structures by simply nailing two

Fig. 3–16 A raised three-bay barn constructed of timber frame with a gambrel roof

by fours, two by sixes, two by eights, or two by twelves together to form the equivalent of a hewn timber. One great advantage of a lumber-truss frame (fig. 3–15) was the elimination of supporting cross members, which enabled hay forks running on interior tracks mounted just under the ridge to run the full length of the barn without hindrance. Another advantage was that lumber framing required 20 percent less wood than a timber frame of similar size.[11]

Another development of the last quarter of the nineteenth century was the popularization of the gambrel roof on barns. The lumber-truss design lent itself to the use of the gambrel roof, but such roofs were also added to barns employing the traditional timber bent construction (fig. 3–16). Their great advantage was the increase in loft capacity that such roofs provided, which therefore made barns more efficient for hay storage (fig. 3–17). Such an increase was desirable as farm sizes increased and more animals needed hay.

Fig. 3–17 Changes in barn roof design increased loft capacity, thereby making barns more efficient for hay storage.

Fig. 3–15 Changes in barn framing in the nineteenth century. Lumber truss to the left and timber frame to the right. (From Allen G. Noble and Albert J. Korsok, *Ohio: An American Heartland*)

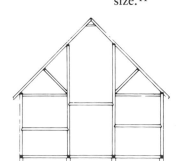

The Erie Shore barn

The first barn specifically incorporating a gambrel roof was designed for smaller, often more specialized agricultural operations, however.[12] For this reason, the Erie Shore barn (fig. 3–18) is rather small, approximately thirty by forty feet, with only one full story, plus a loft. The internal arrangement of the barn is quite unlike that of other barns (fig. 3–19). One end of the barn contains a drive floor that runs from side to side. The balance of the structure is devoted to stabling, separated from the drive floor by granaries and equipment rooms.

The Erie Shore barn appears to be a rather specialized barn, limited mostly to the Midwest. An off-center door, a feature that this barn shares with the Madison County Amish barn (see chap. 2), may be a midwestern characteristic (fig. 3–20). The origins of the Erie Shore barn remain obscure, and even its date of introduction has not been documented. Indeed, only one study of the

Fig. 3–20 An Erie Shore barn near Green Bay, Wisconsin. The exterior painting suggests the interior divisions. (1980)

Fig. 3–19 Floor plan of an Erie Shore barn

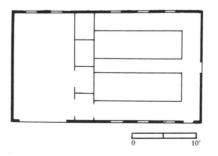

Erie Shore barn has been made.[13] The radical departure in plan and form of this barn from that of virtually all other barns requires additional careful study.

One point for future study tracing the origins of the Erie Shore barn is an examination of the barn design worked out by Professor G. T. Fairchild at the Michigan Agricultural College about 1880. Such an origin location could be reconciled with the present distribution of the Erie Shore barn (see chap. 4), and invention at an agricultural experiment station might account for the radical departure from earlier traditions in the layout and design of the structure. An illustration and brief description of Fairchild's barn is given by Byron Halstead.[14] Further study may prove that the Erie Shore barn was invented by Professor Fairchild.

Fig. 3–18 The Erie Shore barn

The Wisconsin dairy barn

The Erie Shore barn may have first appeared in the last quarter of the nineteenth century. At about the same time, the Agricultural Experiment Station at the University of Wisconsin, Madison, also was attempting to improve barn designs, especially to find one better suited to the growing dairy industry of Wisconsin. The combination of lumber-truss construction and the gambrel roof suggested an appropriate form. The Wisconsin dairy barn is normally only about thirty-six feet wide, but often a hundred feet or more in length. Because of its narrow width, the Wisconsin dairy barn provides excellent interior light, one of its most important advantages. Rows of small windows are designed to maximize light penetration (fig. 3–21).

The interior is arranged to accommodate two rows of cattle stanchions, with horse stalls at one end (fig. 3–22). The main central aisle runs from gable to gable and a short transverse aisle may connect doors midway on the sides of the structure. Because the efficiency of heating a livestock barn in winter depends upon the ratio of animals to

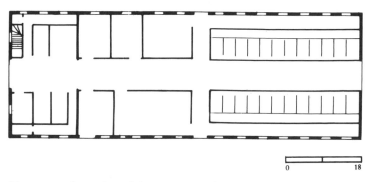

Fig. 3–22 Floor plan of the Wisconsin dairy barn

Fig. 3–23 A Wisconsin dairy barn located near Hanover, Kansas. The structure, built in 1925, measures 84 × 36 feet. Photo by Janice Seymour. (1977)

Fig. 3–21 The Wisconsin dairy barn

45

space, the Wisconsin dairy barn has an advantage, since it can be built in varying lengths to accommodate herds of various sizes. Ceiling heights are rarely higher than eight or nine feet, again to conserve the heat generated by the animals in winter. However, the summer season presents the opposite problem of how to provide sufficient ventilation for cooling. In fact, proper ventilation is a concern for the winter and the summer if the herds are to be kept in good health. Consequently, the Wisconsin dairy barn incorporates a system of ventilator chutes in its interior design. Conspicuous roof ventilators are thus usually an exterior feature of Wisconsin dairy barns. Better ventilation and better natural lighting in the Wisconsin dairy barn have both been cited as advantages resulting in better sanitation than that

Fig. 3–24 The round-roof barn

possible in the earlier banked or basement barns.[15]

The very large loft, created in part by the gambrel roof, provides maximum storage area for the hay and feed requirements of large dairy herds (fig.

3–23). In some instances, the loft is reached by a drive ramp providing for direct loft loading and offering additional machine storage space, both inside the loft and under the ramp.

The round-roof barn

The Wisconsin dairy barn was not the only new barn to make use of innovative design. The round-roof barn (fig. 3–24) carried innovation a step further, although its interior represents a compromise between the Erie Shore and the Wisconsin barn designs. Both one-story and two-story versions occur (figs. 3–24 and 3–25). Frequently, access to the second story necessitates raising a section of the curved roof.

The adoption of the gambrel roof had increased loft capacity. The round-roof barn expanded it even further (see fig. 3–17), by utilizing a nearly parabolic roof. Within the basic form some varia-

tions do occur, prompting designations such as *Gothic roof* for the more pointed roofs, or *rainbow roof* for the flatter, curving roof. Initially, the round-roof form was constructed of short pieces of lumber by the individual farmer from plans supplied by the county agricultural agent or by the state agricultural experiment station. Subsequently, the roof was formed of precut laminated rafters supplied to the farmer, already assembled, by local lumberyards. Most popular in the period just after World War I, the round-roof barn never really caught on, primarily because it was more expensive than other barn styles and could not be built by the average farmer or the local builder. One contemporary source suggested that any popularity this barn style enjoyed was due primarily to its novel appearance.[16]

Fig. 3–25 A raised round-roof barn. The loft door is raised to accommodate hay wagons. (Columbiana County, Ohio, 1975)

The pole barn

Another barn that introduced a novel form unlike that of traditional structures is the pole barn (fig. 3–26), which gained popularity only after World War II. Because of the depression of agricultural prices in the 1920s and 1930s, followed by World War II, relatively few barns were built from the late 1920s throughout the early 1940s. As barn building resumed, a few structures were built following traditional designs, others used the gambrel-roof lumber-truss system, but most barns were of a quite different type. Pole barns were only one story high because the widespread adoption of the silo had significantly reduced the need for loft storage space for hay (see chap. 5).

Fig. 3–27 A pole barn used as a cattle shelter. Note the contrast in form with the three-gable barn in the background. (Coshocton County, Ohio, 1976)

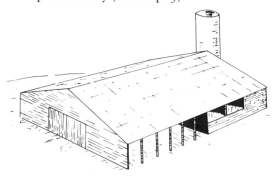

Fig. 3–26 The pole barn

The pole barn is also radically different from traditional barns in terms of its construction. Because no sills or foundation is used, the building cost is significantly less than for frame buildings. Floors are either entirely lacking or consist simply of a poured concrete slab. The framework is upright poles set directly into the ground. The siding of the barn is hung on these poles. Roof pitch is very low so that the gable is typically quite wide (fig. 3–27). Roof support is provided by steel-girder trusses, which are lightweight but possess great strength. Both the gables and the sides may be pierced by one or more door openings, or they may be completely open, as in figure 3–26.

The pole barn has been labeled a "neobarn" by Alvar Carlson[17] to differentiate it from the earlier barns with ethnic associations, but the concept of a low, wide, one-story pole building is really not that new. As early as 1881, the structure was being suggested as a suitable cattle barn for the windy central plains of America.[18] although admittedly it did not become popular until after World War II. The pole barn represents the introduction of an industrial architecture into American agriculture.

Rarely are the whims of an individual builder or the ethnic background of a resident discernible. Instead, farmers are opting for a spatial organization similar to that of a suburban manufacturing plant. Like manufacturers, they have been guided by technological factors. . . .

These features provide for the new needs of the farmers, but offer little sophistication in design or consideration for aesthetics. In fact, a national rural landscape of repetitious buildings may be coming.[19]

Pole barns can be adapted for a wide variety of agricultural purposes, although most are used as animal shelters for either beef cattle or dairy cows (fig. 3–28). One of the most commonly encountered special-use pole barns is the broiler house. Large exterior feeder cones often help identify this use of the structure.

47

Fig. 3–28 An elongated pole barn used for beef cattle (Near Conway, Arkansas, 1974)

Special purpose barns

Although the pole barn is frequently used for special purposes, most farm barns are designed for general uses. Often, however, when the structure is intended to serve a particular specialized function, its design will reflect that need. The potato barns of Aroostook County, Maine (fig. 3–29), half sunk into the insulating ground, are only one example. The design of such structures is clearly related to their function of providing long-term, cool storage space for the potato crop.

Barns primarily used as animal shelters may also show particular designs. Figure 3–30 is an animal barn located on the Columbia plateau. The barn is designed to take advantage of the swell of the ground. Loft space is limited,

compared to the area devoted to animal shelter, since outdoor feeding is possible virtually throughout the winter season. Large ventilators confirm the use of this structure for housing animals and hay.

The line separating special purpose barns from structures that are clearly secondary farm buildings is not well defined. One group shades almost imperceptibly into the other. Many farms have more than one large barn, and important farm functions are often differentiated in them. Sometimes the external shape of the barn will reflect the purpose for which it was built.

Form and function: tobacco barns as examples

Tobacco barns comprise an excellent set of examples in which function has partially determined form. The three distinct methods of drying tobacco leaves are each associated with quite

different barn forms, although some similarity of structure does exist among the three types of barns.

Fire curing of tobacco takes place in frame or log barns measuring about twenty to twenty-two feet by twenty-six to forty-eight feet.[20] These gable-entry structures are about eighteen to twenty feet high, with five or six tiers or racks of poles on which the tobacco sticks are hung (fig. 3–31). The size or capacity of the tobacco barn is determined by the number of "rooms" in the barn, a room being the space between the racks or tiers. Normally these measurements are four feet horizontally and about two feet vertically.[21] The lowest rack is fixed so that a six- to eight-foot open space at the floor of the barn is left for inspection and movement, and to accommodate the heat source.

In the fire-cured tobacco barn, the open fire is laid on the earth floor of the barn, often in shallow trenches, so that the dense smoke from the burning hardwoods, partially smothered in damp sawdust to generate smoke while retarding burning, comes into direct contact with the tobacco leaf, turning it a dark brown, and imparting a distinctive aroma and taste.[22] An attempt is always made to construct and keep the barn airtight in order to conserve smoke, making it as efficient as possible. Nevertheless, a common sight in late summer or early autumn is the wisps of smoke curling upward from the imperfectly joined eaves of the tobacco barn.[23]

The areas of fire-cured tobacco barns are very restricted. The most important is limited to the extreme western part of Kentucky and adjacent Tennessee. This area, which includes dark, air-cured tobacco as well as the fire-cured variety, is locally called "the Black Patch." A smaller, much less important area lies in central Virginia.

Even more distinctive than the fire-cured tobacco barn is the flue-cured tobacco barn (fig. 3–32). These struc-

tures consist basically of a tall squarish building, often flanked by open sheds. Measuring anywhere between sixteen and twenty feet on a side, the barn may be as much as twenty to twenty-four feet to the eaves. Barns of smaller dimensions are more nearly square, while those of larger size are more likely to be rectangular. In some areas, small square barns are sometimes enlarged by constructing an adjoining square barn, which doubles the capacity of the structure (fig. 3–33). The internal arrangement of the flue-cured barn resembles closely that of the fire-cured barn. Entrance is by small doors centered on each side of the structure.

Attached to the barn are a shed or sheds, which provide shade to workers in the late summer when the tobacco leaves are prepared for hanging in the

Fig. 3–30 A Columbia plateau animal barn

Fig. 3–31 The Kentucky fire-cured tobacco barn

Fig. 3–29 The potato barn

barn. The shed also shelters the barn's furnace and often protects the fuel supply from the weather. Finally, the shed used to offer a secure sleeping place for the attendant, who in earlier years had to keep the furnace fires going at a constant temperature throughout the night by periodically feeding the fuel.

As the most distinctive feature of the flue-cured tobacco barn, the sheds ap-

49

Fig. 3–32 A flue-cured tobacco barn

pear in almost infinite variety. One is tempted to classify these barns on the basis of the sheds. Below, a further attempt has been made to sort out the geographical pattern of flue-cured tobacco barns in eastern North Carolina, where each county seems to have a concentration of different types. "Sheds vary tremendously depending on their size and pitch and their relation to the ground and shaft. . . . They conceal as little as a portion of one side of the barn or as much as the entire central core. A shed may appear to be an element separate from the barn or it may take on proportions such that it overpowers and obscures the shaft and endows the barn with an unmistakable monumentality."[24]

A simple sloping roof attached to the barn gable and supported by simple cor-

ner posts is the plainest version of the shed. A few barns also can be found in which the single shed is attached to the side rather than to the gable of the barn.[25] Slightly more elaborate is the barn with simple sheds on each gable. A third variant is the combination of two barns connected by an elongated shed. In this instance, the shed normally connects the sides of the barns, not the gables.

At least five or six subtypes have sheds that surround the barn. In North Carolina, each of these subtypes is concentrated in a different county, but not limited to just that county. They may be differentiated on the basis of the slope of the shed roof and the height at which the shed roof is attached to the main structure.

Finally, barns can be found in which the surrounding shed possesses a roof

forming a continuous slope with that of the barn itself. In general, sheds seem to be a less prominent feature as one moves northward in North Carolina. The pitch of the shed roof seems to be less steep as well. Figure 3–34 is an attempt to graphically portray these relationships in eastern North Carolina. Needless to say, no sharp or definitive boundaries between subtypes exist, only a very general gradation. A census of both active and relict flue-cured tobacco barns should be an interesting and rewarding topic of research.

Although surrounding sheds frequently give the impression of a large structure, the enclosed space of the flue-cured tobacco barn is always small compared to barns used for other kinds of farming. The reason for such small size, and for the frequent clustering of tobacco barns, is that each barn must be

Fig. 3–33 A double tobacco barn, constructed of cement building blocks. The parapet defines the two parts. The stripping shed is on three sides. (Near Wilmington, North Carolina, 1978)

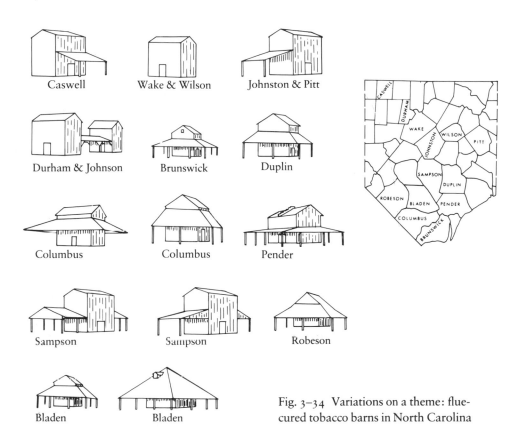

Caswell   Wake & Wilson   Johnston & Pitt

Durham & Johnson   Brunswick   Duplin

Columbus   Columbus   Pender

Sampson   Sampson   Robeson

Bladen   Bladen

Fig. 3–34 Variations on a theme: flue-cured tobacco barns in North Carolina

special barn is really needed for air-curing tobacco. Thus, in Lancaster County, Pennsylvania, the traditional German bank barn is often used (fig. 3–35), with the major modification being the addition of top-hinged ventilator panels every three feet or so along the barn sides (fig. 3–36).[27] In Pennsylvania and elsewhere, the common vertical wall ventilator panels are sometimes replaced by horizontal panels attached to outside poles, so that an entire section of panels can be raised or lowered together (fig. 3–37).

In addition to converting earlier barns to tobacco drying, barns specifically designed for this function have also been constructed. In Lancaster County, Pennsylvania, the typical tobacco shed is rectangular in plan, has a gable roof and an end entry, and is raised on a stone foundation in order to incorporate a tobacco cellar or dampening room and a stripping room (fig. 3–38). The function of the tobacco cellar is to dampen the tobacco sufficiently so that it may be stripped most easily from the stalks and then baled. Most tobacco cellars have dirt floors to help retain moisture.[28] The tobacco cellar, outfitted with poles and drying racks, takes up most of the basement.

The smaller stripping room is a narrow room along one side of the basement or else it occupies about a quarter of the basement at one gable end. The stripping room has long tables, a cement floor, several windows to provide natural light, and a stove. "The chimney

filled (or the tobacco *housed,* to put it in the local vernacular) in a single day to ensure uniform curing.[26]

Flue-curing has several important advantages over fire-curing. The fire is contained in a furnace, and hence the fire danger is significantly reduced. Less fuel is consumed by using a closed heating system. The heat is conducted through the barn in a series of flues, so that a very uniform heat is maintained. All the tobacco dries at the same rate

and quality control is easier to maintain. No smoke is permitted to come into contact with the tobacco leaves. The leaves retain the light yellow color that helps to give bright leaf tobacco its name.

Burley and other air-cured tobaccos are grown much more widely in North America than either dark tobacco or bright leaf. The barns in which air-cured tobacco is dried are widely dispersed and of great variety. Indeed, no

Fig. 3–35 Tobacco barns in Lancaster County, Pennsylvania. The German bank barn to the left has been adapted for tobacco drying by constructing vertical ventilators. The barn to the right has both wall ventilator slits and roof ventilators. (1976)

Fig. 3–36 Close-up of vertical ventilator panels (Lancaster County, Pennsylvania, 1976)

Fig. 3–37 A Pennsylvania tobacco barn with horizontal ventilators (Lancaster County, Pennsylvania, 1976)

is set in such a way as to allow it to run up just to the side of the ridge. However, some sheds have their chimneys on the outside of the shed on the gable in which the stripping room is located. When this occurs, it is usually the result of an addition rather than an original feature."[29]

Another frequent feature of many Lancaster County tobacco barns is the unusual gable ventilator. This ventilator, which is rarely found on barns west of that county, "is an extension of the cornice with the weatherboarding nailed on flush with the cornice so that it extends out about a foot or so leaving a space between where the lower siding is nailed to the nail trees."[30] In other areas, other strategies for ventilation are employed.

In southwestern Virginia standard transverse-frame barns are used for tobacco drying, the major modification to the structure being openings under the eaves and the division of the roof into three parts separated by open ventilating space (fig. 3–39). Indeed, throughout Appalachia, latticework openings under the eaves and high up on the gables are a characteristic of ordinary

Fig. 3–39 A tobacco barn in western Virginia. The roof has been divided into three parts separated by ventilator openings. (1974)

Fig. 3–38 The Lancaster County tobacco shed

barns used for tobacco drying. In Kentucky, clerestory barns occur, in which the vertical wall sections separating the sloping roofs are composed of latticework. The important consideration is always to provide the maximum facility to air circulation, in order to aid the drying or curing process. Perhaps the ultimate in this direction occurs in some of the tobacco barns of the Connecticut River valley that, although greatly elongated, have sides regularly pierced so that every third board allows outside air

to penetrate the interior (fig. 3–40). An elongated ridge ventilator is also characteristic.

Certain other common elements of air-cured tobacco barns can be identified by examining them across the extensive burley tobacco area of Kentucky. The design features of Kentucky air-cured tobacco barns appear not to be as geographically distinct as those of the flue-

53

cured tobacco barns in North Carolina. Nevertheless, the considerable range of its forms that has been depicted in figure 3–41 is presented not with the idea of pin-pointing locations, but to indicate barns with particular features that have been encountered in field observations. Most of these structures are adaptations or modifications of the basic transverse barn (see chap. 1), although they are generally taller to permit additional tiers of poles to house more tobacco. Wide panels in the upper part of the gable can be opened to increase air circulation. The very low roof pitch on some of the barns clearly indicates a late evolution of design. Although normally quite tall, the relationship between width and depth of Kentucky air-cured tobacco barns varies over a considerable range. Some barns are so narrow as to be little more than double runways, the gable just wide enough to accommodate two double wagon doors. Such tall narrow barns are especially prevalent in the Pennyroyal region of Kentucky. For other barns, dimensions of twenty-eight to thirty-two feet wide by thirty-six to forty-eight feet deep would include the most commonly found set of measurements, although virtually any barn or outbuilding of any size can be converted to tobacco curing.[31]

The most common appendage to the air-cured tobacco barn is the stripping shed, a feature that, along with ventilator panels and a protruding chimney, permits easy exterior identification of the barn, even at considerable distances.

The stripping shed can be defined as a shed, either enclosed, attached or detached with

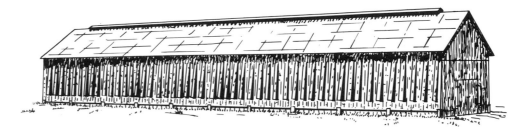

Fig. 3–40 The Connecticut valley tobacco barn

Fig. 3–41 The Kentucky burley tobacco region and the air-cured tobacco barns used therein

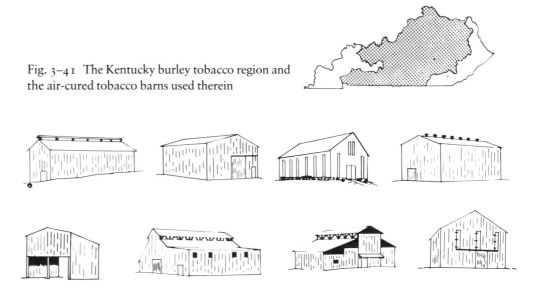

54

Fig. 3–42 The Ontario tobacco barn

respect to the tobacco barn where the tobacco is graded and sorted in preparation for the trip to the auction block. The tobacco is laboriously graded by hand and each leaf is held up to a source of indirect light for inspection by the "stripper." Because of the necessity of an indirect light source the stripping shed traditionally had been placed on the north side of the tobacco barn. With the advent of an efficient artificial light supply, especially of the fluorescent type, the siting of the stripping shed has lost its former significance.[32]

In southern Ontario, barns used for tobacco curing are of much more uniform design. In fact, they are so distinctive as to be readily recognizable (fig. 3–42). Although ventilator panels may be hinged vertical boards or wide window panels, the form of the barn is always the same, roughly cubic and capped by a simple gable roof of moderate pitch. Perhaps most notable is the occurrence of these barns in groupings or clusters of six to twelve structures, all with an iden-

tical orientation and regular spacing (fig. 3–43).

With a couple of important exceptions, tobacco barns have not been carefully studied. Fraser Hart and Eugene Mather sketched in the basic outlines in a pioneering study,[33] but few other investigators have followed up their lead. A notable exception to this lacuna is the work of Karl Raitz, who has carefully traced the diffusion of the tobacco sheds of southern and eastern Wisconsin. The barns there are usually constructed of lumber siding placed on a framework of poles set directly on the ground with little or no foundation (fig. 3–44). As in Kentucky, variations in tobacco barns exist, but the "differences in shed design from one area to another are subtle; yet when they are delineated and analyzed, they reveal that when a grower moved to a new location, he took not only the tobacco seed and the knowledge of its culture, but also took a mental floor plan of his tobacco shed, which he re-

Fig. 3–43 A typical cluster of tobacco barns. The gables are sided with asbestos shingles. The dark rectangles on the barn sides are ventilator panels. (Near Simcoe, Ontario, 1972)

constructed at the new location."[34]

In the final analysis, the plan and design of a barn may owe as much to the perceptions, limitations, and mental processes of the farmers who built them, as to the functions the structure is intended to perform.

Fig. 3–44 A Wisconsin tobacco shed

4 Diffusion of the Farm Barn in Northeastern North America

Not until recently has anyone attempted to explain the distribution pattern of barn types in any large area of North America. Even now the information on which such studies must necessarily be based is still largely incomplete. The preceding three chapters have attempted to establish a basic system of terminology for the major barn types of North America. This chapter discusses the results obtained by collecting information from, and by utilizing the expertise of, county agricultural agents who have attempted to estimate the percentages of different barn types occurring in their areas.[1] Whenever possible these data are compared with information derived from earlier studies of the different individual barn types.

A measure of the relative importance of each barn type can be gleaned from the following figures on the number of counties in northeastern North America reporting major barn types: raised three-bay or basement, 465; Wisconsin, 397; English, 383; Erie Shore, 314; pole, 300; crib, 209; German bank, 204; Midwest three-portal, 198; transverse-frame, 190; Appalachian, 168.

It is not surprising that those barns associated with dairying and general farming occur in the largest number of counties in northeastern North America. Furthermore, barns of later design generally appear more widely than earlier, ethnically-derived barns.

The patterns of barn distribution confirm certain basic facts of ethnic migration and certain earlier observations by scholars of the material settlement landscape, which will be elaborated upon below. At the same time, these distributions raise a host of questions needing more detailed investigation in future studies.

The distribution pattern of the English barn

The English barn was introduced into North America by way of English colonial settlement in southern New England. It may also have been independently introduced by other English colonists in the vicinity of Chesapeake Bay, although this has not been adequately documented. The warmer climate of the southern settlements obviated much of the need for farm barns.

The path of migration from southern New England along which the English barn was carried is not easy to trace by observing its present occurrence (fig. 4–1), but western New England and eastern New York State certainly are among its most significant areas. Fred Kniffen's observation that the English barn spread across eastern North America with little modification[2] seems to be confirmed because one of the centers of its dominance is a discontinuous triangle covering southern Indiana, lower Michigan, and northwestern Ohio. Furthermore, the form of the basic English barn was recognized by respondents throughout northeastern North America. Only the raised three-bay (basement) and the Wisconsin dairy type were reported by more sources.

The English barn was designed originally for storing and processing of grain. At first, no animals were housed in the structure, although subsequently internal rearrangements often were made to introduce animal stalls in one of the two side bays. This effectively reduced the grain storage and processing function, but only offered shelter for a quite modest number of animals. Hence, the English barn was most

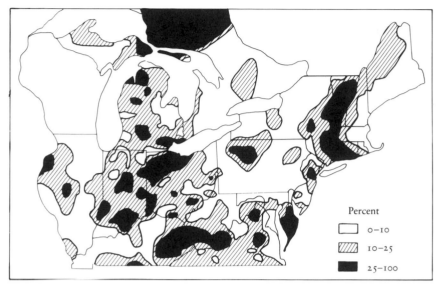

Fig. 4–1 Map showing percentage of English barns to all barns (1975)

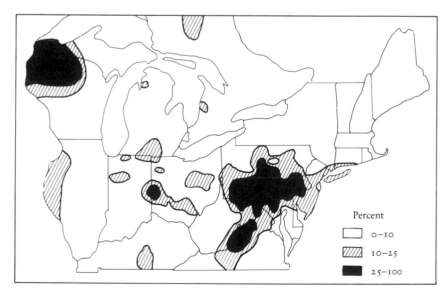

Fig. 4–2 Map showing percentage of German bank barns to all barns (1975)

suited to small-scale, subsistence farms.

These basic structural-functional relationships explain the distributional pattern of English barns in two quite disparate kinds of locations in northeastern North America. First, English barns are found in those areas that were poor agriculturally, so that newer, larger, more sophisticated barns were never needed. Farm operations always remained largely subsistent, and farms were small. For example, the Pocono Mountains and the Catskills as well as western New England are early examples of such restricted settlement areas (see fig. 4–1). A high proportion of English barns correlates with poor agricultural conditions in north central Pennsylvania, the upper peninsula of Michigan and Canadian areas north of Sault Ste. Marie, and the Appalachian hills of eastern Kentucky, West Virginia, western Maryland, and western Virginia.

A second important relationship explains the presence of the English barn in a different sort of area. The English barn is basically a single function barn, and hence it is apt to persist where agriculture is strongly oriented to crop production and where major livestock are largely absent, even in areas of high agricultural productivity. For this reason, the English barn is favored in the Delmarva peninsula, a primary vegetable growing area, and in New Jersey, where the proximity of New York City encourages truck farming and discourages the erection of elaborate farm barns in the possible path of urban expansion. English barns also occur in above-average concentrations in the Essex peninsula of southern Ontario, and in the cash-grain region centered on the Lake Maumee plain of Ohio, with extensions westward across Indiana and central Illinois and northward to encompass the lower peninsula of Michigan.

When thinking about the scattered areas of high concentrations of English barns in southern Indiana and southern Ohio where agricultural conditions are poor, one must keep that kind of occurrence separate from the high concentration of English barns in central Indiana and northwestern Ohio, where great agricultural productivity exists. The boundary of continental glaciation from southern Indiana to north central Pennsylvania provides a rough approximation of the boundary between the two quite different environments for English barns.

An additional factor favoring English barns on the plains of the old Northwest Territory is that these landforms frequently consist of the old glacial lake beds, till plains, and swell-and-swale topography that was often quite poorly drained in early periods of settlement. Such conditions would favor the construction of basementless English barns over the more sophisticated raised three-bay or basement barns that required the digging out of a considerable foundation in the face of high water tables.

The area in which the English barn is not important may be as instructive as where it does occur. The dairy areas of Wisconsin and northern Illinois, parts of Michigan, much of Ontario, and the great dairy region of New York, Pennsylvania, eastern Ohio, and the western shore of Chesapeake Bay may all be included. In these areas, the farm barn performs the dual functions of animal shelter and grain storage and processing, and hence the English barn is inadequate.

The Bluegrass Basin is another easily identified area where English barns are lacking, primarily because of the requirement for specially designed drying barns for tobacco. In western Kentucky and southern Illinois, alternative simple barns derived from the single-crib barn substitute for the basic English barn. The absence of English barns in much of Pennsylvania is probably related to the

Fig. 4–3 Ensminger's map of Pennsylvania forebay barns (*Pennsylvania Folklife*)

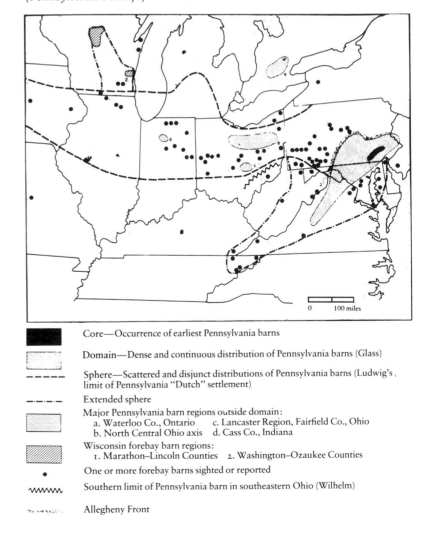

Core—Occurrence of earliest Pennsylvania barns

Domain—Dense and continuous distribution of Pennsylvania barns (Glass)

- - - - - Sphere—Scattered and disjunct distributions of Pennsylvania barns (Ludwig's limit of Pennsylvania "Dutch" settlement)

- · - · - Extended sphere

Major Pennsylvania barn regions outside domain:
a. Waterloo Co., Ontario   c. Lancaster Region, Fairfield Co., Ohio
b. North Central Ohio axis   d. Cass Co., Indiana

Wisconsin forebay barn regions:
1. Marathon–Lincoln Counties 2. Washington–Ozaukee Counties

• One or more forebay barns sighted or reported

wwww Southern limit of Pennsylvania barn in southeastern Ohio (Wilhelm)

Allegheny Front

popularity of German bank barns, an alternative structure in this area (cf. figs. 4–1 and 4–2).

The pattern of German bank barns

The designation *German bank barn* includes a group of barns introduced into the Delaware valley cultural hearth by German-speaking settlers (see chap. 2). Within this category are combined a number of different barns, but all are similar in their form, which is characterized by a two-and-a-half-story elevation and a prominent forebay, and all have an intimate connection with German settlers.

The pattern of distribution of German bank barns is much less complicated than that of the English barn. Initial diffusion occurred from the original hearth by expansion into surrounding areas of Pennsylvania, Maryland, Delaware, and the extreme western fringe of New Jersey. Two main paths of later migration also may be traced. One, along which roughly half the barns are German bank, lies within the Shenandoah valley in Virginia. A less-emphatic concentration marks the route of German movement into and through the Midwest, including the Mississippi valley. A grouping of German bank barns in Ontario southeast of Lake Huron, which is known to be significant, appears in the results obtained from county agricultural respondents to be only a small area of between 10 and 25 percent. A larger and more significant German bank barn area in Wisconsin appears north of its expected occurrence, but its importance is well portrayed.

Fig. 4–4   Type of barn common in central Iowa

The pattern of German bank barns revealed from county agricultural agent responses compares quite favorably with the map recently produced by Robert Ensminger, who relied upon a surrogate measure to provide the boundaries of the "sphere" of the Pennsylvania barn (fig. 4–3).[3] Just as one might reasonably object to the inclusion of southern Connecticut, Long Island, and much of New Jersey within the area of German bank barns (see fig. 4–2), one can also reject the inclusion of Iowa on Ensminger's map. In the former instance, these peripheral areas are included because of a combination of possible respondent error and the inadequacies of computer generalization techniques. In the other case, Ensminger's reliance on the surrogate

Fig. 4–5   Cross section of a barn from the Frisian coast of Germany (from Joseph Schepers, *Haus und Hof Westfälischer Bauern,* 5th ed. [Münster/Westfalen: Aschendorffsche Verlagsbuchhandlung, 1980])

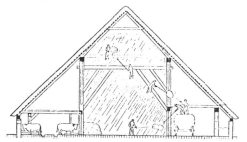

59

measure is probably at fault, because forebay barns are extremely rare in Iowa and the rest of the German-settled prairies. What does occur widely is a small, squarish (thirty-five by forty-two feet) structure with a steeply pitched roof (fig. 4–4). The plan is of a central hay mow surrounded by stabling aisles on two or three sides. This barn has not been studied in North America, but may be derived from a north German barn (fig. 4–5).[4] Throughout the vast central part of North America, no more than a half dozen or so serious studies of barns have been undertaken. Consequently, it is difficult to draw generalizations about the barns of this large area.

Returning to eastern North America, the pattern of diffusion of the German bank barn is related not only to the migration paths of German settlement, but also to the presence of competing barn types. The German bank barn is largely absent in the Middle Atlantic coast, Appalachia, much of the land bordering the Great Lakes, New York State, and New England. Along the Middle Atlantic coast transverse barns derived from the English gained an early foothold. In Appalachia, large barns were rarely built because poor agricultural conditions did not encourage expenditures on such a scale, and the milder winters permitted livestock to remain outside. In New York and New England, early barns were evolved from English and Dutch rather than German sources. The Great Lakes region falls mostly within the Dairy Belt, in which several barns compete for primacy.

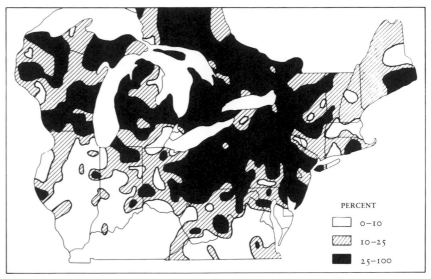

Fig. 4–6 The percentage of raised three-bay barns to all barns (1975)

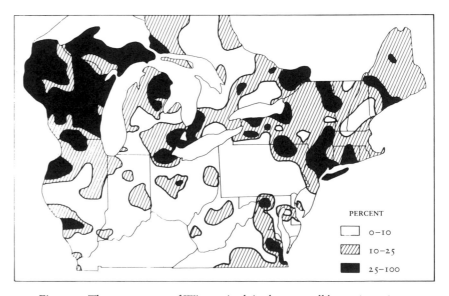

Fig. 4–7 The percentage of Wisconsin dairy barns to all barns (1975)

The pattern of raised three-bay or basement barns

The failure of the German bank barn to penetrate northward is also partially related to the use by English settlers of a somewhat similar barn. The raised three-bay or basement barn apparently first made its New World appearance in central New York, where today far more than half the barns are of this type (fig. 4–6). From here it has diffused over much of northeastern North America in a generally westward direction. Thus, it is the earliest multipurpose barn to gain widespread popularity.

Although similar in both appearance and function to the German bank barn, the raised three-bay or basement barn has been adopted over a much wider range. Probably the strong ethnic association of the German barns has worked to limit their adoption by other groups. The basement or raised three-bay barn, on the other hand, is often perceived as an "American" structure, and thus one that could legitimately be adopted by any farmers in northeastern North America in the nineteenth century.

Its southern limit coincides, in a rough fashion, with the boundary of the northeastern Dairy Belt. Within its area of diffusion, a few small scattered areas stand out as places where this barn type is not concentrated. The most important of such areas are east central Maine, southern New England, the White Mountains, the Catskills and the Poconos, the western margin of Lake Erie, the western margin of Lake Huron, and part of the Driftless area of Wisconsin.

The pattern of Wisconsin dairy barns

Another barn clearly associated with dairying is the Wisconsin dairy barn, which originated at the Wisconsin Agricultural Experiment Station at Madison about the time of World War I. Quite in contrast to most other barn types, the Wisconsin dairy barn diffused primarily eastward (fig. 4–7).

The Wisconsin dairy barn was specifically designed to provide a structure for efficient dairy farming (see chap. 3). Consequently, its distribution reflects those areas in which dairying is the most effective and prosperous type of agriculture, those areas where dairy income is highest. More county agents reported more occurrences of this barn than of any other except the raised three-bay, which may well confirm the effectiveness of this barn for dairy farming. In many counties of Wisconsin, between a half and three-quarters of all barns are of this type. Elsewhere in the Dairy Belt, in Michigan, southern Ontario, New York, and parts of New England occurrences range between 25 and 50 percent. Other important concentrations appear around St. Louis, the Quad Cities area of Illinois, Chesapeake Bay, and northern New Jersey–southern New York. In each of these areas a dairy industry is based upon the supply of fluid milk to nearby urban markets. Less easily explained is a four-county concentration of large Wisconsin dairy barns in north central West Virginia. Generally, however, the barns of Appalachia belong to the crib and crib-derived types.

The pattern of crib barns

As with the German bank barns, various types of crib barns have been included within a single heading. Single-crib, double-crib, and four-crib barns were all on the identification chart sent to respondents, and their totals have been combined in figure 4–8.

As expected, crib barns show a strong association with southern Appalachia. Particularly high percentages, i.e., above 50 percent, occur in Kentucky. Crib barns also are spread throughout the Chesapeake Bay area, suggesting that this is possibly their place of origin in North America.

Other areas of crib barns include much of Illinois, the western part of the upper peninsula of Michigan, the eastern part of the lower peninsula, and a large contiguous area extending across northern New England, northern New York State, and into Ontario. This last area and the upper peninsula of Michigan are both heavily forested and also only marginally productive for agriculture. Log crib barns, representing primitive structures built of rough materials, are to be expected in such areas, although no study has yet been given to crib barns in these places. Indeed, crib barns from these locations have not even been reported in the literature.

The presence of crib barns in the lower peninsula of Michigan and across Illinois is less logical, because both these places are of moderate to high agricultural productivity, so that one would expect more sophisticated barn types. The reported occurrence of crib barns in such locations needs much careful analysis.

The Appalachian barn

The Appalachian barn is a derivative of the basic crib barn (see chap. 1). The front gable normally does not have a main door, but there are usually a large hayloft opening and some sort of prominent hay hood. In plan, form, and appearance the Appalachian barn is quite distinctive and thus may be considered separately from the crib barns.

As would be expected, the distribution pattern of the Appalachian barn (fig. 4–9) is greater than that of the crib barn from which it is derived. At the same time, however, it was reported in only slightly more than half as many counties as crib barns. Two large but discontinuous areas can be identified. The more important one stretches from south central Pennsylvania across West Virginia to eastern Kentucky and southwestern Virginia. Five counties in West Virginia reported more than 50 percent of all barns to be of this type, a pattern suggesting a place of origin in western Maryland or south central Pennsylvania, if one assumes a general southwestward drift of settlement.

A more scattered and less dense area of Appalachian barns lies in western Kentucky, Indiana, and southern Illinois. The close association of Appalachian-

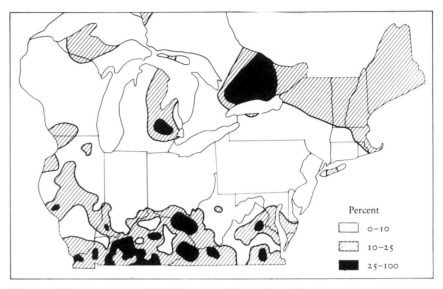

Fig. 4–8 The percentage of crib barns to all barns (1975)

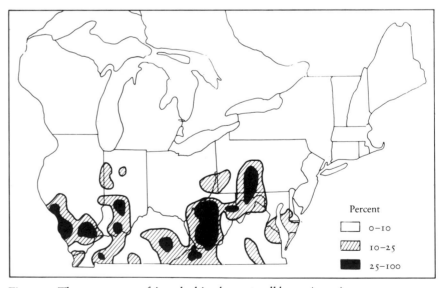

Fig. 4–9 The percentage of Appalachian barns to all barns (1975)

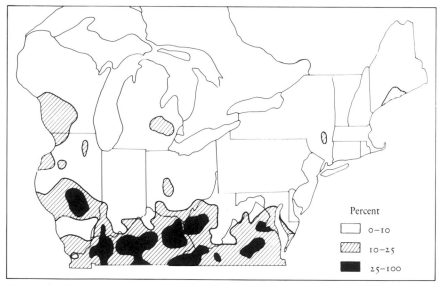

Fig. 4–10 The percentage of transverse barns to all barns (1975)

Fig. 4–11 The percentage of Midwest three-portal barns to all barns (1975)

type barns and the Appalachian physiographic region is clearly evident. However, the same barn also occurs outside of northeastern North America.[5]

The transverse barn

Another barn derived from the basic crib is that termed the *transverse barn*, which has doors on the gable and a centered main aisle from front to rear. In general, its pattern of occurrence resembles that of the Appalachian barn (fig. 4–10), with its highest concentrations in Kentucky. Elsewhere in Appalachia and southern Illinois it appears to coincide with the area of general farming. The Driftless area of Wisconsin shows up as an area of transverse barns, although this association has not previously been documented. Similarly, those areas of transverse barns in eastern Michigan and coastal Maine are places needing additional research before definitive statements can be made.

Because it derives from the crib barn, much of its range lies outside northeastern North America. Indeed, Henry Glassie has proposed that the place of origin of the transverse barn lies in eastern Tennessee.[6] The structure has also spread westward to become one of the most important barns in Missouri.[7]

The Midwest three-portal barn

The Midwest three-portal barn represents an evolution of the crib-barn sequence beyond the transverse barn. In contrast to the earlier types, the Midwest three-portal barn has a very widely diffused pattern, with occurrences spread from coastal Virginia to western Wisconsin (fig. 4–11). Western Kentucky, southern Indiana, and much of Illinois are major areas of concentration. In southwestern Michigan, the Midwest three-portal barn may have been confused by respondents with Dutch barns, which also have three doors on the gable (see below).

Two areas of Midwest three-portal barns present problems. Both eastern Ontario and southern New England–Long Island are areas where this barn type would not be expected, and yet significant concentrations are reported. All previous indications have been that the Midwest three-portal barn diffused *westward* from an Appalachian source region. It is quite possible that barns of an as-yet-unidentified and unstudied type have been included by respondents in these areas.

That the identification chart sent to agricultural agents was not exhaustive must be conceded, although all the major types were included. Detailed field study of smaller areas within northeastern North America will certainly reveal additional barn types. One such instance, which took place after this 1975 survey of county agents, can already be cited. A number of small, narrow barns

Fig. 4–12 An unidentified barn type from the area of southeast Ohio–northwest West Virginia

of quite distinctive form (fig. 4–12) are scattered over an area between Keyser, West Virginia, and Coshocton, Ohio. Not much can be said yet about this barn, but it appears to be a distinct type. Not including this barn in the identification chart casts some doubt on the validity of estimates of other barn types, at least within the West Virginia–southeastern Ohio area. Obviously, the present study of the distribution patterns of barn types represents a beginning, rather than a definitive study.

The pole barn

The latest major barn type, called the pole barn, was evolved in the eastern Midwest. The walls of the building are hung on poles that are driven into individual footings buried in the ground below the frost line. The pole barn has no folk antecedents or ethnic connections at all (see chap. 3).

The most significant area of pole barns is still the eastern Midwest, covering Illinois, Indiana, and Michigan (fig. 4–13). Elsewhere, with some significant exceptions, counties responding with high percentages of pole barns were more widely spaced, although over the entire study area only the raised three-bay or basement barn appears to be more significant.

The pole barn, being a recent innovation, appears as an important type in more prosperous agricultural areas, especially in those near urban markets where farm income is high. In such areas, in order to remain successful, farmers must adopt innovations. The pattern can be seen in south central Pennsylvania and adjacent Maryland and Delaware, in southern New England, and in the St. Lawrence valley–Lake Champlain lowland. The pole barn, which requires no foundation, seems to compete best with other barns in the colder northern areas. The crib and transverse barns appear to be more successful in the southern parts of the study area.

In certain locations, among which are those of poor agricultural productivity, the pole barn is encountered infrequently. Such areas include the Maine coast, the Catskills, the Poconos and northern New Jersey, and the pine barrens of

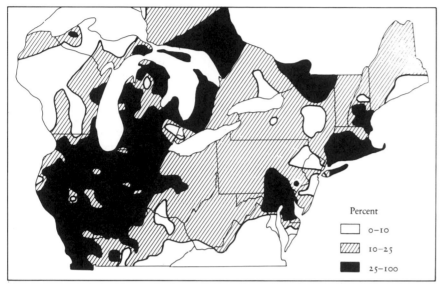

Fig. 4–13 The percentage of pole barns to all barns (1975)

Fig. 4–14 The percentage of New England connected barns to all barns (1975)

coastal New Jersey. In some other areas, such as Virginia, the tobacco-growing region of northern Kentucky and southern Ohio, and much of Wisconsin, the pole barn is apparently not utilized as fully as elsewhere. In these regions, the transverse barn and recently evolved barns such as the Wisconsin and the Erie Shore substitute for the pole barn.

Distribution of other barn types

The nine barn types that have been mentioned are the major ones of northeastern North America. However, several other barns are either important within more restricted areas or of secondary significance over much of the entire area.

The New England connected barn has not spread much outside New England (fig. 4–14). However, in coastal sections of southern Maine, New Hampshire, and northern Massachusetts, this type of barn is clearly in the majority. The New England connected barn is one of the very few barns whose distribution has been mapped by field study (fig. 4–15).[8] Thus, it offers an opportunity to compare the Symap pattern used herein with that recorded earlier by Wilbur Zelinsky from field observation.

The Symap distribution shown in figure 4–14 indicates a greater concentration of New England connected barns in southeastern Massachusetts and western Connecticut than is shown in Zelinsky's field survey. By the same token, southeastern Maine appears as a less

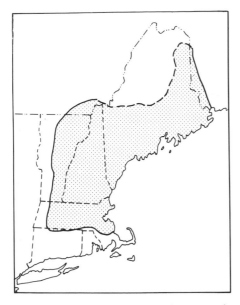

Fig. 4-15 Area of New England connected barns, according to Zelinsky

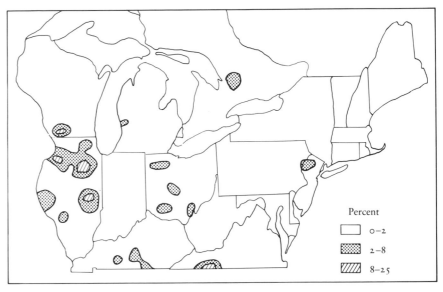

Fig. 4-16 The percentage of Dutch barns to all barns (1975)

Percent
☐ 0-2
▦ 2-8
▨ 8-25

important area. Most surprising of all is that the Mohawk valley is given as an area of New England connected barns. This identification is made on the basis of a report from a single county, and must be accepted with considerable reservation. Cursory field reconnaissance in the summer of 1983 confirms the existence of some connected barns south of the Mohawk valley in northern Schoharie County.

The Dutch barn is another structure for which field observations have been mapped (see fig. 2–10). Unlike most barns in that it is more or less square in plan, the Dutch barn has doors placed on the gable; its roof is steeply pitched with low eaves; and its siding is usually horizontal instead of vertical, as in most other barns (see chap. 2). This barn was never built in large numbers. Its colonial hearth extended along the Hudson valley of New York and the Raritan valley of New Jersey. However, the pattern shown on figure 4–16 does not identify this area well. Although northern New Jersey shows up, the Hudson and Mohawk valleys are not differentiated at all, despite the use of a magnified scale. Furthermore, the Dutch barns of southwestern Vermont reported by Stewart McHenry do not appear.[9] However, several other areas in which Dutch barns were reported by agricultural agents are clearly defined. Dutch-settled areas in the Holland Marshes north of Toronto and in southwestern Michigan around the city of Holland show up clearly. Other areas in Illinois, Ken-

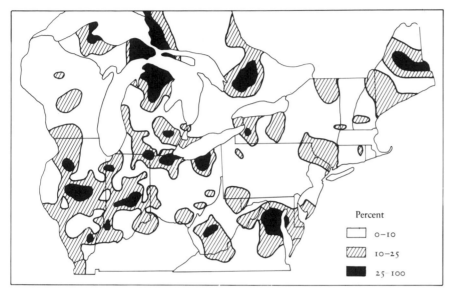

Fig. 4–17 The percentage of Erie Shore barns to all barns (1975)

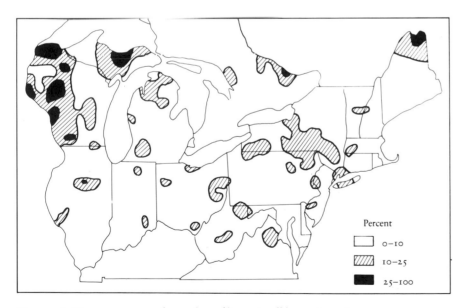

Fig. 4–18 The percentage of round-roof barns to all barns (1975)

tucky, Ohio, and Virginia represent a problem of identification because these are likely to be places in which the Dutch barn has been confused with the somewhat similar appearing Midwest three-portal barn.

In contrast to those barn types that are highly localized, both Erie Shore and round-roof barns are widely scattered. The Erie Shore barn is a multipurpose barn, with a gambrel roof and off-center side doors. The Erie Shore barn occurs in such widely dispersed places as central Maine, the Chesapeake Bay margins, and central West Virginia (fig. 4–17). Southern Ontario, where the Erie Shore barn was first described,[10] is part of a larger area of concentration which encompasses the western end of Lake Erie. Scattered across lower Michigan, Indiana, and Illinois are extensions of the original Erie Shore barn area. The Erie Shore barns reported in the upper peninsula of Michigan and the Parry Sound area of Ontario, however, may well be Finnish barns, which also have a gambrel roof and a rather similar overall form.[11] The Erie Shore barn is one of the most elusive of barn types. It apparently has no ethnic connections, although it may be confused with barns built by Finns. Its place of origin has not been identified, nor has the rationale for its development been defined. Yet, it does appear to be a distinct type, quite different in form from other barns (see chap. 3). The wide distribution of this barn may be a result of misinterpretation of the identification chart by respondents. In any event, barns of this form, whether they are truly Erie Shore barns or not, have a surprisingly wide pattern of occurrence.

The round-roof barn, perfected in the 1920s, is distinguished by its roof, which is made of preformed, laminated rafters. The new roof form permitted a larger loft space and made this barn particularly suitable for livestock areas. This barn is encountered in a number of locations mostly in northern parts of the study area (fig. 4–18), with a particularly important concentration in the upper Great Lakes region.

Barn regions of northeastern North America

American farm barns do demonstrate regional variations in their concentration. In part, such variation is related to the cultural hearths from which ethnic diffusion has taken place. Thus English barns, while widespread, have a strong concentration in western New England and eastern New York. German bank barns predominate in Pennsylvania and Dutch barns can be traced, albeit faintly, in the New Jersey Dutch hearth.

The pattern of barn types also is related to changing agricultural conditions. In some instances, simple earlier structures survive in areas of poor environmental settings, where agriculture has not prospered. The persistence of crib barns in Appalachia is an example.

In other areas, where agriculture has flourished, the original small barns have been supplanted by larger, more flexible structures. In several regions, barns specifically designed to accommodate a particular type of agriculture have become concentrated. The existence of the Wisconsin barn in dairy areas is well recognized.

Throughout northeastern North America the pattern of barn types is slowly changing. The barns of yesterday and today will gradually be remodeled or replaced by more appropriate structures, and the face of the landscape will thereby be changed.[12] These changes will come inexorably, making it always more difficult to identify the patterns of the past. Even today, we know relatively little about the past occurrence of barns or other farm structures, such as the silo, and even less concerning the rationale for their distributions.

PART TWO
Evolution of Other
Farm Structures

---

5   The Diffusion and Evolution
of the Silo

Earlier chapters in this volume have examined the kinds of American barns, as well as their distribution across the countryside. Other prominent structures also typify the rural landscape and of these the most conspicuous is the farm silo.[1] Because of their height, these rural sentinels are visible across miles of farmland. For over a hundred years silos have been an important, easily recognized feature of American farmsteads (fig. 5–1), but even farmers usually are surprised to learn that silos are a recent phenomenon, employed only after 1875 and not truly established until shortly before the turn of the century.

Preserving grain in tight containers from which air and water are excluded as much as possible is a very old and widespread practice found in many primitive agricultural societies. Normally, however, the containers are not airtight and thus the grain must be thoroughly dried before storage, in order to reduce moisture content and retard spoilage. In contrast to bins and similar devices used to store dry grains, the silo is designed to preserve *green* fodder crops, principally field corn, in a succulent condition. The stored material is termed *ensilage,* which is shortened to *silage.*

The antecedents of the ensilage process can be found in Europe, where in a number of areas the making of "brown hay," or "sour fodder," or "green sour grass" was undertaken, at least by the end of the eighteenth century. Apparently the process was not successful enough to encourage a great many farmers to adopt it on any large scale, probably because of the difficulty of excluding humid air from the stored fodder. Thus, the fodder tended to partially decompose and a large portion of it was always lost.

Diffusion of the silo

The development of the modern silo can be traced from Adolph Reihlen, a German beet-sugar grower and refiner, who appears to have been somewhat of an innovator and experimenter as well. After residing in the United States for several years, he returned to his home in Stuttgart. In addition to growing sugar beets, Reihlen introduced American varieties of large-dent corn. Much to his disappointment, such corn would not always ripen in the climate of southern Germany. By 1862, and probably earlier, Reihlen was experimenting with preserving the green corn plant in those years when the growing season was shorter than average, when the corn could not ripen. His successful experiments were reported in the German agricultural press, and, by 1870, accounts also were being published in French agricultural journals.[2] Publication of such reports in the *Journal d'Agriculture Pratique* in 1870 was the real beginning of attention to silos in France because this journal was widely read by ordinary French farmers.[3]

One of the French agriculturists who then began experiments to develop green fodder was Auguste Goffart, who is generally credited with popularizing ensilage procedures in France.[4] Returning from the Franco-Prussian conflict, Goffart found his farm operations in a state of disarray and deterioration. He was thus receptive to agricultural innovations on a large scale. Goffart's writings on silos and ensilage were collected in book form in 1877, which was the first monograph to be published on this subject, and were translated into English in 1879 as *The Ensilage of Maize and Other Green Fodder Crops.*[5]

Even before this, however, silos had come to the attention of American agriculturalists. Especially important in this process of informing American farmers of European agricultural innovation was the *American Agriculturalist.* In 1875 this journal presented a condensed version of a significant portion of several articles from the *Journal d'Agriculture Pratique,* along with illustrations of simple pit silos.[6] This report and other intelligence prompted Professor Manly Miles of the University of Illinois to conduct a series of experiments beginning in 1875 in which he preserved corn fodder in two pit silos and broom-corn heads in two others.[7] Shortly thereafter, Francis Morris in Maryland and C. W. Mills in New Jersey constructed silos. The results of Morris's experiences were published in 1877 and of Mills, in 1881.[8] Henry Alvord in 1887 noted that Morris was the first person in the United States to build silos and make ensilage for cattle food, implying that he inaugurated the practice among actual farmers.[9] A claim also has been advanced that Fred L. Hatch built the initial silo, in northern Illinois.[10]

Fig. 5–1 Grain and silage storage facilities on a dairy farm in southern Wisconsin (1976)

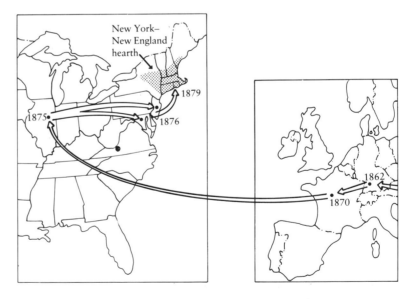

Fig. 5–2 Early diffusion of the silo (reprinted from *Landscape* 25, no. 1 [1981])

These pioneering efforts became the subject of considerable discussion in the American agricultural press. Some farmers rushed to construct silos only to find them defective. Most of these failures can be attributed to the imperfect knowledge of building techniques, which resulted in many of the early silos not being airtight. Others experimented successfully with silos, but many more were reluctant to invest time, effort, and capital in such an unproven endeavor. Many farmers, especially the more conservative, argued against adoption of silos. Aside from being "new-fangled," silos bore the brunt of other criticisms. Some were not convinced cows would eat fodder preserved in such a novel fashion. Because ensilage fermented to some extent, many dairy operators, sensitive to religious arguments against the use of alcohol, objected to feeding cows "liquor." The more conservative farmers "argued that feeding cows silage would cause them to lose their teeth, eat out their stomachs, cause trouble at calving time, and affect the quality of milk."[11] A more serious problem was that some of the creameries and dairy processors refused to accept milk from cows fed on silage.

By June 1882, the U.S. Department of Agriculture could identify only ninety-one farms in the entire country that had silos,[12] although many more undoubtedly existed. Of those identified and located, four-fifths were in the New York–New England region, which apparently led the way in the perfection of this agricultural innovation, and thus may be considered the American hearth from which subsequent dispersion took place (fig. 5-2).

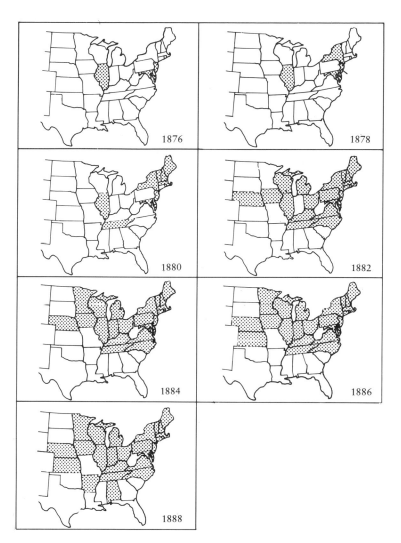

Fig. 5-3 Diffusion of the silo in the northeastern United States (reprinted from *Landscape* 25, no. 1 [1981])

Several reasons combined to account for the concentration of early silos in the New York–New England hearth. First, of course, was the size and significance of the already existing dairy industry, and its orientation to the production of fluid milk.

Second, northeastern United States, in the final quarter of the nineteenth century, was rapidly industrializing and there were consequent shifts from rural to urban settlement. Urban dwellers constituted a steadily growing market for milk, a market that existed throughout the year despite fluid milk's seasonal availability. Feeding green silage to cows throughout the winter kept them "fresh," i.e., giving milk. The same cows fed on dry grain and hay would normally go dry in November and not freshen until late April or May.

Third, the climate favored the use of the silo to preserve crops that had difficulty maturing in a short growing season with cool summer temperatures. The climate had been a major factor in determining the dominant agricultural system, a system that emphasized rapidly growing hay crops and dairy production. The silo permitted greater utilization of field corn, a more productive crop per acre than hay.

Finally, several influential "gentlemen farmers" took the lead in promoting the new device. Especially important was John Bailey, who built an experimental silo in 1879 and wrote a book, widely circulated among New England and New York farmers, on his successful experiences.[13] Bailey's book, written from a practical point of view and giving construction details, is generally credited with bringing the subject of the silo to the attention of ordinary farmers.

The acceptance of the silo and ensilage came very gradually (fig. 5–3). Fifteen years after the first experiments in this country, articles with titles such as "Has the Silo Come to Stay" were still being read widely,[14] and as late as 1910 articles still implored the conservative farmers not to continue to look upon a silo "as an extravagance to be indulged only by those able to gratify their desire for fads."[15]

Initial reluctance did eventually give way to acceptance, however, especially as the various state agricultural experiment stations began work with silos.[16] The perfection of the silo, and especially its construction in an easily built, relatively cheap version, was just one of the changes that came about in American farming as the impact of scientific and experimental agriculture fostered by the state agricultural experiment stations began to be felt.

Silos came to be enthusiastically accepted by farmers because they offered certain advantages. First, larger numbers of cattle could be kept on the farm because the food value of corn is greater than that of a combination of hay and grain. Thus, many marginal farms could be made profitable. Second, less water was needed for stock in the winter. Hence, labor requirements were greatly reduced since strenuous efforts were no longer required to break ice and thaw water. Finally, because succulent green fodder could be fed throughout the year, cows produced milk during the entire winter season. Income from dairy farming suddenly extended throughout

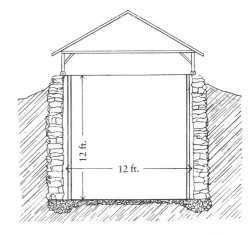

Fig. 5–4 Diagram of an early pit silo (from Bailey, *The Book of Ensilage*)

the year. Indeed, those farmers who adopted the silo first benefitted the most, because higher prices were paid for fluid milk in the winter season.

By 1895, estimates of silos in the United States put the number above 50,000,[17] and by 1903 the figure was between one-third and one-half million.[18] The silo *was* here to stay, and the period of silo building was really only beginning. One writer in 1910 estimated that at least a thousand silos would be built that year in Ohio alone.[19] By 1960 the number of silos was approaching the 1 million mark.[20]

Silos have always been emphasized in dairy regions. The early lead in silos of the New England–New York region slowly shifted to the northern Midwest as the center of dairy farming shifted there also. In 1924 Wisconsin had more silos (100,060) than any other state, followed at some distance by New York (53,300), Michigan (49,000), and Ohio (36,850).[21]

The pit silo

The earliest silos were wholly or partially excavated pits lined with stone and masonry (fig. 5–4). Normally they were located inside the cattle barn. The inconvenience of excavation inside the barn and the loss of interior usable space was counterbalanced by the ease with which ensilage could be transported from the pit to the animals housed in the barn and by the convenience of loading.

Pit silos had several other disadvantages, which were sufficient to prevent widespread adoption in their original form. Not only were they expensive to excavate, they also required considerable skill to construct in order to ensure their being watertight. Their below-ground location made pit silos bothersome to empty, and the heavy weights and covers thought to be necessary to exclude air were cumbersome to manipulate. Finally, pit silos were dangerous because of the possibility of toxic gas accumulation at the bottom.

Fig. 5–5 The rectangular wooden silo

Fig. 5–6 A rectangular wooden silo in an offset gable location, near Parkman, Ohio (1973)

Evolution of the upright silo

Despite all the drawbacks of these early silos, farmers found the value of ensilage sufficient enough so that they continued to search for a suitable silo form. It is hardly surprising that such a quest followed a path of least resistance to a simple, above-ground, rectangular form consisting of structural members of dimension lumber covered with ordinary barn siding. Vertical, above-ground silos are sometimes referred to as *tower silos*.

The rectangular wooden silo (fig. 5–5) was easy to build, almost any farmer could construct one with hired help, and the materials were inexpensive and readily secured. Most rectangular wooden silos were built outside existing barns (fig. 5–6) so that construction did not disrupt or restrict the normal farming operations inside the barn. Furthermore, the addition of the silo itself was likely to expand farm operations, creating demand for even more barn space. Thus it made sense to built an exterior silo, rather than reduce barn space just at the time it would be needed most. Several standard locations could be used.[22] A study of rectangular wooden silos in northeastern Ohio revealed a position centered on one gable of the barn to be the most frequently chosen (fig. 5–7). An offset gable position (see fig. 5–6) or a side location were the next most popular. Detached or independent locations were quite rare.

73

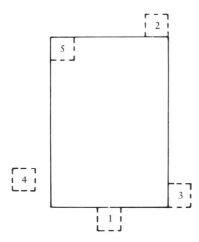

Fig. 5–7 Plan showing typical positions for rectangular wooden silos

Several construction errors were frequently committed in the building of rectangular wooden silos. First, the bracing and framing were often not strong enough to ensure long-term integrity of the structure when it was subjected to the pressure of the ensilage. Second, the foundations were often faulty so that they rotted after a time or were penetrated by rats digging under them to get to the ensilage. Finally, the lining of the silo was often defective and, hence, not airtight. As soon as air entered, spoilage began.

More serious than any of these problems was the fact that the corners of the silo provided sufficient drag to create air pockets in the silage as it was loaded

and as the load settled. Thus, pockets of mold and spoilage were interspersed in the body of the silage. The problem was especially pronounced in low silos where the weight of the silage was not great enough to exert sufficient pressure to eliminate many of the air spaces. As a consequence, considerable effort was expended in trampling down the ensilage and weights continued to be employed, but the best solution proved to be to construct taller structures. Thus, the silo began to assume the form so well known on American farms today.

A survey of county agricultural agents in northeastern United States that was conducted in 1974–75 revealed that rectangular wooden silos were still found in at least 135 counties. One especially significant concentration of such silos occurs in northeastern Ohio, where construction in a rectangular form persisted until after 1910.[23] In most parts of the country, rectangular wooden silos were seldom built after the turn of the century.

Taller silos reduced the problem of corner friction, but did not fully solve it. Only the elimination of the corners themselves would do that. By 1891 the process of feeding ensilage had proven valuable enough so that serious efforts were made to perfect the form of the silo. Many farmers must have experimented with round silos (fig. 5–8); at least one circular cement silo (at Whitewater, Wisconsin) is known from the 1880s. Large numbers of farmers modified their rectangular silos by rounding off the inside corners (fig. 5–9). Some farmers attempted to reduce corner angles by constructing octagonal silos (fig. 5–10). Finally, a practical low-cost design for a circular silo was perfected

at the Wisconsin Agricultural Experiment Station. The structure was formed of tongue-in-groove boards thoroughly soaked in water and bent into gigantic hoops (fig. 5–11). The problem for the farmers came, of course, in forming the hoops. If they were not thoroughly soaked, the boards were apt to split, and hoop ends had to be securely fastened. Furthermore, if the lumber was not thoroughly dried before use, the boards might subsequently warp, thereby rupturing the silo and negating all the farmer's labor.

Fig. 5–8 An early circular fieldstone silo with its original wood-shingle roof (Near Waukesha, Wisconsin, 1979)

74

Fig. 5–9 Close-up of the interior of a wooden rectangular silo, showing the rounded corners (Ravenna, Ohio, 1980)

Fig. 5–10 An octagonal silo with a hipped roof in northern Vermont (1977)

Fig. 5–11 Drawings of early circular wooden silos. Note the different styles of roof. (From King, *Silage and the Construction of Modern Silos*)

The advantages of the circular form were sufficient to ensure other attempts to built round silos. The most successful early effort resulted in the wooden-stave silo (fig. 5–12), whose origins have not been documented completely although the structure apparently originated about 1894.[24] It is quite possible that the concept of the stave silo was hit upon by several individuals independently and at about the same time. After all, wooden barrels were common on the farm and in the local market towns, and the concept is the same. Vertical tongue-in-groove boards are inserted into a narrow trough scratched into a round cement foundation. Alternatively, the boards were placed along the walls of a shallow pit formed in the center of the masonry foundation. The vertical boards were held together by great iron bands fastened with turnbuckles (fig. 5–13). These wooden-stave silos were not, of course, the most stable structures and many of them have disappeared, replaced by later, more efficient silos or cannibalized for their boards. Not many are still in use, but now and then one sees an abandoned one leaning gently away from the prevailing wind, a position reached through countless years of inactivity and no periodic tightening of the turnbuckles.[25]

With the introduction of circular silos, the problem of how to conveniently roof them was created. When silos were rectangular, a gable roof was most common (see fig. 5–5) and, at first, the circular silos often used such an incongruous

Fig. 5–13 Close-up of iron turnbuckles on a wooden-stave silo (Schoharie County, New York, 1979)

Fig. 5–12 Wooden-stave silos. One has a conical roof and the other, a hipped roof.

Fig. 5–14 Another method of roofing circular silos (Portage County, Ohio, 1975)

covering (fig. 5–14). After a while, roofs specifically designed for circular structures were evolved. A cone was used initially, followed by a hipped cone (see fig. 5–12), and, still later, by the low dome (figs. 5–15, 5–16) and the hemisphere (fig. 5–17).

Perhaps as important as changes in the roof form was the shift in construction material that occurred about the time of World War I. Wooden staves were replaced by stronger and more durable masonry silos. A bit later, poured-concrete silos were built, formed of separately poured, interlocking rings that were stacked one upon the other. Still later, the use of a cement stave, which was perfected about 1906, gave rise to a period of intensive research and development by cement companies who recognized the profit potential. The first cement-stave silos were erected in southwestern Michigan. Many of these original silos are still in use today and the cement-stave silo has diffused throughout the entire country. Other

Fig. 5–15 The circular masonry silo

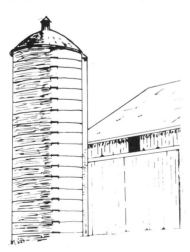

Fig. 5–16 Circular masonry silos. This type of silo and cap is typical of older silos in the eastern Midwest. (Near Madison, Wisconsin, 1977)

building materials were used, especially during the decade of the 1920s. Tile building blocks were occasionally employed (fig. 5–18), but generally they were too costly for widespread adoption. Also, the blocks were somewhat brittle and an accidental sudden impact would often cause the blocks to crack. A few silos were even built of brick, although generally this was much too expensive a construction material.

Regardless of the particular building material, all these silos had certain advantages over wooden silos. First, they could be built higher and hence had greater capacity. Second, airtight construction was more nearly achieved. Less attention had to be paid to lining materials. Third, these silos required less maintenance because their building materials were more durable.[26]

At the close of World War II, a radical-

Fig. 5–17 Circular cement-stave silos with hemisphere covers dominate this Wisconsin dairy farm. To the right are a masonry silo and a tile-block silo. A metal bunker can be seen in the center.

ly different kind of silo, called by its trade name *Harvestore*, made its initial appearance (fig. 5–19). Constructed of fiberglass bonded to sheets of metal, the Harvestore silos attained the long-sought objective of a completely airtight container. As early as 1881 the desirability of a hermetically sealed container had been recognized,[27] but it was not until 1945 that it was finally produced by engineers of the A. O. Smith Company.

The Harvestore silo had several important advantages. First, the fiberglass provided sufficient insulation so that ensilage did not freeze during the winter, and therefore continuous unloading was facilitated. Second, the unloading process was mechanically accomplished from the bottom of the silo by means of an automatically operated auger. Previously, unloading had to be done by hand, from the top of the stored material. This meant that the farmer had to climb to the top of the silo, loosen boards fixed into a vertical slot in the side of the silo, and pitch out the topmost portions of the ensilage, letting it drop to the ground, from where it then had to be hauled into the feeding areas of the barn. Obviously, considerable effort was expended in this process, which was also dangerous. In order to reduce the risks and to protect the farmer in cold or inclement weather, the ladder on the outside of the silo was usually enclosed in a long wooden box (see fig. 5–10), which also then functioned as a chute down which ensilage was pitched. Finally, because all oxygen was eliminated in the Harvestore silo, no heat was produced, decomposition was effectively eliminated, and the ensilage was preserved in optimum condition.

The Harvestore silo was perfected in Wisconsin and the first few such silos were erected in the southeastern part of that state, or just across the border in northern Illinois. The initial impetus to widespread adoption of the Harvestore silo came in 1948 when it was exhibited at the centennial Wisconsin State Fair, although manufacture of units was subsequently delayed by steel shortages in 1949 and 1950. After 1950, the conspicuous Harvestore silo with its bril-

Fig. 5–18 A tile-block silo with an original hipped wood-shingle roof topped with a decorative lightning arrestor (Near Waukesha, Wisconsin, 1979)

liant metallic blue color, sixty-one feet high and twenty feet in diameter, has increasingly come to be the mark of a commercially successful farmer (fig. 5–19). During the 1960s, the cost of a Harvestore silo ($11,302) was more than twice that of a concrete-stave silo ($5,435),[28] so that normally only the most efficient farmers operating on the largest scale could afford the investment. Both silo types were estimated to

have a life span of between thirty and forty years and the initial advantage of the Harvestore was that its use significantly reduced the labor costs involved in emptying the silo. Subsequently, bottom unloaders were perfected for other types of silos.

Because the Harvestore silo is manufactured by a single company so that its point of origin is well known, and because it is a recently evolved phenomenon, the structure is well suited to the study of diffusion patterns and processes. Sales records allow detailed analysis of the spread of this type of silo, and at least two studies already have been made for small areas.[29]

Evolution of the horizontal silo

At about the time that the Harvestore silo was first being popularized, trench and bunker silos were coming into favor, especially in the Great Plains. The shift to horizontal silos was accompanied by a shift toward the utilization of grass ensilage. Such silos were especially

adapted to the mechanical harvesting and silo filling and the self-feeding employed in grass silage operations.[30] These horizontal, rectangular silos represented, in a sense, a return to very early forms, especially the trench silo, which was an excavated structure (fig. 5–20). Bunker silos are similar in form to trench silos, but are constructed of wood or metal and are not placed below ground level. The differences between the trench silo and the early pit silo were basically those of scale and method of construction. The trench silo is often simply a long, wide cavity excavated by a bulldozer.

Fig. 5–19 Harvestore silos in front of cement-stave silos. On a farm in Winnebago County, Wisconsin. (1975)

Fig. 5–20 An empty trench silo with an earth floor and wooden sides (Near Meadville, Pennsylvania, 1977)

Fig. 5–21 A concrete trench silo showing the cover weighted with numerous rubber tires (Near Hebron, Nebraska, 1977)

The silo as a landscape feature

Despite variations in its particular form, the silo is one of the most conspicuous elements of the rural landscape of North America. During the past century, it has maintained or increased its significant position. Although the number of farmsteads has decreased steadily, the number of silos has actually increased everywhere except in New England. Where formerly a single upright silo identified each farmstead on which livestock was kept, today the silos appear in clusters or rows of three or four or more, as in figure 5–19. Furthermore, as barns have increasingly assumed lower profiles, silos have added to their height until they commonly tower over sixty feet. It seems likely that silos will remain for some time as prominent rural landscape features.

Horizontal silos of 100 to 300 ton capacity could be constructed in the mid-1950s at about one-third the cost of upright silos.[31] Although they can be made quickly, cheaply, and in varying sizes to serve large or small herds, trench silos have certain serious disadvantages. Where soils are heavy, drainage excessively slow, or the water table too high, trench silos are rarely successful. Furthermore, rates of spoilage are higher than in upright silos, unless elaborate precautions are taken to seal the silo against the entrance of air as well as of water.[32] One commonly employed method of sealing a trench silo is with large plastic sheets weighted by large numbers of used tires (fig. 5–21). Such a covering is obviously not entirely airtight. Other problems include a tendency for walls to cave in during rainy weather, the inconvenience of unloading, and the accumulation of toxic gasses below ground level.[33]

Since the 1950s trench and bunker silos have spread gradually from the Great Plains to other sections of the country, as grass silage has become more popular. Still, trench and bunker silos are rarely dominant outside the Great Plains.

Although houses, barns, and silos are normally the most conspicuous and most important buildings in the countryside, a large variety of secondary structures frequently contribute a distinctive appearance to farmsteads in different sections of the continent. Not all these features have received serious or extensive study. Nonetheless, the same things can be said about secondary structures as about the main buildings: they frequently have strong ethnic associations; sometimes their design, and often their very presence, is related to the environmental conditions in which they appear; and their form is derived in part from the functions they were designed to perform.

Because of this latter relationship, it seems logical to attempt to investigate these outbuildings within a broad framework based upon their functions. Four major categories can be suggested: (1) water-associated structures; (2) household-related outbuildings; (3) crop storage or processing facilities; (4) buildings connected with livestock. It is true that these categories are not mutually exclusive, so this classification scheme must be viewed only as a device of convenience to facilitate discussion.

Water-associated structures

As everywhere, water is a vital commodity on the North American farmstead and a number of structures were designed to serve water-related functions. During the initial phase of land occupation everywhere, settlement sites often were chosen because of their proximity to dependable springs. Not only did these springs provide drinking and domestic water, they also served to cool, and thus preserve, perishable farm products during the summertime. Hence, spring water was especially significant for those farms on which dairy products were important.

Spring houses

Spring houses were those structures erected at sources of water to ensure the protection of the spring, to keep the flowing waters from pollution, and to provide a cool, clean environment for storing dairy and other farm products. The spring house can be constructed of any material, although because stone and brick offer the best insulation properties they were most successfully employed. Furthermore, wood was susceptible to rot if continually in contact with, or in proximity to, water or the damp earth of the spring's vicinity.

The spring house generally was located at the base of the slope, where the spring issued from the ground. In order to capture the flow of water, the building often was excavated into the hillside. Sometimes this permitted the water intake to be located high enough so that one or a series of connected troughs could be employed at a raised level (fig. 6–1). In other instances, the water occupied shallow troughs or pools along the spring house floor (fig. 6–2). In all cases, the floor of the spring house was constructed of stone, brick, cement, or some other tight, impervious material.

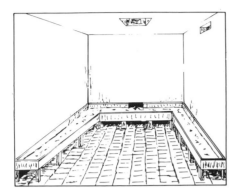

Fig. 6–1 Interior of a spring house, with raised water troughs (from Halstead)

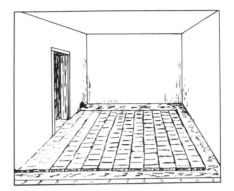

Fig. 6–2 Interior of a spring house, with floor-level water trough (from Halstead)

Fig. 6–4 The American farm windmill

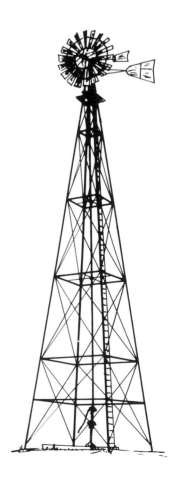

The water moves constantly through the spring house, always introducing a steady supply of cooling water. Adequate ventilation is desirable to prevent damp and mold. Louvers and a roof ventilator, therefore, are common characteristics of the spring house.[1] In other respects, these structures are difficult to differentiate from other farm outbuildings except for their distinctive location and the external water intake and outlet.

Wells and windmills

Although many farmsteads depend on water from springs, an even larger number draw upon wells for their water supply. In the simplest instances, the water is raised from a dug well covered by

a well-head structure, which may be round or square, about three feet high to prevent accidental entry, but low enough so as not to hinder water drawing, and covered usually by a gable roof raised up on wooden pillars.

In other wells, water is lifted by mechanical pumps usually placed on a simple, square wooden platform. Oftimes when the local water table is high and groundwater plentiful, these pumps are inside the farmhouse, the summer kitchen, or some other outbuilding. The labor involved in operating the pump to lift water is so considerable that the power of the wind was frequently harnessed to serve as the driving force. Windmills came, in the nineteenth century, to be among the most conspicuous of farm objects (fig. 6–3). Derived from the European wind-driven gristmills which were established along the North American colonial coast,[2] the American windmill used to lift water was invented

in the middle of the nineteenth century in Connecticut.[3]

Rapidly adapted by farmers to lift water, for livestock especially, they also were later used to generate electricity. From Connecticut, windmill manufacturers diffused primarily to the "eastern margins of the Great Plains,"[4] largely in response to the greater demand for windmills by farmers in central United States. In this area, winds were less obstructed by high vegetation and successful farming or ranching depended upon lifting significant amounts of water from the ground.

The standard farm windmill consisted of a light, but strong, steel frame of four sloping legs, braced at intervals (fig. 6–4). A steel ladder provided access to the blade and rudder mechanism which required periodic maintenance, repair, and, especially, lubrication. Unlike traditional European windmills, which had enormous paddle blades, the American windmill possessed a series of curved steel blades set in a rosette pattern. The advantage which the American windmill had over European windmills was that only the blades and rudder rotated and these were designed to automatically follow any wind shifts. Thus, the windmill worked constantly no matter what the wind's direction, and often in very light breezes, too.

California tankhouses and Louisiana Cajun cisterns

The farther west settlement proceeded, the greater was the need for windmills because water became ever more scarce. Furthermore, water had to be stored in some quantities in order to provide for irrigation of crops, as well as for watering livestock and household use. In California, this situation gave rise to a structure that has been called the *domestic tankhouse* (fig. 6–5).

In its simplest form the structure is merely a large wooden tank, elevated on an open, sturdy wooden frame to ensure gravity flow, and it is frequently boxed-in within a roofed enclosure (fig. 6–5K). Some of these can still be found in the Tulare Basin and probably elsewhere. The frame must be exceptionally strong

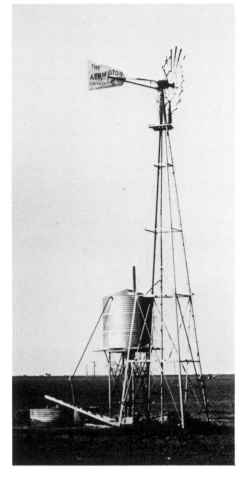

Fig. 6–3 Windmill used to raise water for livestock (Near Brownfield, Texas, 1974)

in order to support a weight of up to forty tons of water. Although already utilitarian, the lower framework can be made even more so by using it to provide an enclosure for one or more rooms under the tank (fig. 6–5J). Limited to a single room on each level, the thirty- to forty-foot tower provides two or even three levels for enclosure (fig. 6–5H).

Leon Pitman has suggested that the California domestic tankhouse may be divided into six types, differentiated on the basis of the taper, or lack thereof, of the frame, and of the relative size of the tank enclosure. The most popular type, the *straight box,* found especially in the Sacramento and San Joaquin valleys, has straight sides, and the tank enclosure is flush, both with the platform and the vertical frame members (fig. 6–5E). This type "was most likely the simplest fully enclosed tankhouse to build. Besides its simplicity, another advantage was the ease by which a windmill tower could be attached to floor joists extended from the platform and directly over a well just outside the tankhouse."[5]

Second in popularity is the *tapered-tower overhang* type (fig. 6–5, B and H). Exceptionally tall with large capacity tanks, the tapered-tower frame offers maximum strength. Despite its widespread occurrence in all parts of the state, this type is concentrated in valleys to the north of the Bay Area.[6]

The *inset-top* type (fig. 6–5F) and the *straight-box overhang* type (fig. 6–5G) are similar in form, the major difference being the relationship of the tank enclosure to the frame. Of the two, the former is quite rare, appearing only in the Fresno area of the San Joaquin valley. The latter, on the other hand, is more commonly encountered, and has a concentration in the Bay Area. The *full tapered* type (fig. 6–5A) and the *tapered-tower box* type (fig. 6–5D) also have similarities of form.

In addition to the basic types identified by Pitman, more elaborate tankhouses do exist. Some have partially open tank compartment walls (fig. 6–5I), others may adopt the Spanish mission architectural style (fig. 6–5L), but the most elaborate are those that are attached to houses as integral structures (fig. 6–5C). All in all, the California domestic tankhouse

is a conspicuous though fading element in California's countryside. It is an important phase in the history of agricultural technology, that period when wind energy was effectively applied on the farm.... Finally, the tankhouse represents a phase in domestic vernacular architecture . . . a time when the farmer could afford to demonstrate pride in the appearance of his farmstead. In style he covered up what he considered an unsightly though useful tower and structurally incorporated it as an extension of his house.[7]

Partially similar in form, but arising out of quite different environmental conditions, is the Louisiana Cajun cistern (fig. 6–6). These large water tanks usually are constructed of cypress wood, but on wealthier farms they may

Fig. 6–5 Water, water, everywhere! The domestic tankhouse and its California range. Numbers indicate valleys of concentration: 1, Sonoma; 2, Napa; 3, Sacramento; 4, Santa Clara; 5, Salinas; 6, San Joaquin; 7, Tulare Basin.

be made of brick. The tank is frequently raised on brick or masonry piers, which enables a fire to be built under the tank to provide warm water for the household. The silo-like cistern stores rainwater collected from the roof of an adjacent house. This is desirable or necessary in an environment where salt water lies close beneath the ground and prevents use of well water. Even on the upland prairies of Lousiana, where salt water penetration was not so serious a problem, the "soft" rainwater was desirable for washing.[8]

The cistern was sited almost always at the rear corner of the house. There was no need here, as there was in other parts of the country, to bury water-associated structures to prevent their freezing in winter. Indeed, the water table was so high and drainage so poor that few

Fig. 6–6 A Louisiana Cajun cistern. The cistern is in its most typical location, at the back corner of the house. Raising the cistern on cement piers permits a fire to be built under the tank. (Near Napoleonville, Louisiana, 1978)

Fig. 6–7 Cross section of a filled ice house (from Halstead)

thought of digging into the ground. As a matter of fact, even burials are made above ground in crypts or tombs in this part of the country.

It seems rather strange that the Louisiana Cajun cistern has not been given closer scrutiny or study. It is a unique landscape feature, located in an area containing perhaps the center of settlement landscape studies, Louisiana State University's department of geography and anthropology. The situation once again points up the general paucity of materials that have been assembled for study of settlement landscape features in all areas.

Household-related outbuildings

Under the rubric of household-related structures there are a number of small but quite essential farmstead buildings. Three of these, the ice house, the woodshed, and the privy, were found on every farmstead in earlier times, but although quite necessary to the proper operation of the farmstead, they perform disparate functions.[9]

Ice houses, woodsheds, and privies

Ice houses were not characterized by distinctive or peculiar architecture; they usually were rectangular and of frame structure simply because this form and method of construction were cheapest and most convenient. Occasionally the buildings were made of brick or stone, and sometimes a round form was employed. Most were free standing, and many were partially or wholly excavated pits lined with mortar or stone.

In all ice houses the critical provision was maximum insulation to guarantee preservation of the ice. Thus, thick walls of nonconducting material were desirable. Wooden frame structures typically had double plank walls filled with nogging of "bark, straw, leaves, shavings or sawdust which served as insulation and kept the ice from melting rapidly."[10] Roof ventilators drew off excess warm air, while the roof itself was often covered with hay, straw, or some other insulating material. In winter, the door of the empty ice house stood open for several days in order to freeze the ground beneath the structure before it was filled.[11]

Within the ice houses, insulation normally was provided by great quantities of hardwood sawdust. The floor consisted of bare earth to provide maximum cooling and to absorb melt water. Over this, a foot or so of sawdust was laid as a foundation for the ice blocks. The sawdust also helped absorb melt water. The ice blocks were stacked in such a fashion that each block was slightly separated from its fellows by a thin space, which was filled with more sawdust. Layers of blocks were separated by one or two inches of sawdust and the blocks were insulated from the wall by a foot of the same material. The final covering was a layer of sawdust about two feet thick (fig. 6–7).

The door to the ice house was the most critical feature because proper insulation was hardest to maintain there. One common technique was to place a series of planks edgewise, one atop the other, just inside the door frame. The pressure of the sawdust and the ice blocks held these boards in place. Long bundles of straw or some similar material were then placed between this barrier and the outside door.[12] Of course, every time ice was wanted, this material first had to be disturbed and then replaced after the ice was taken.

Mechanical refrigeration and artificial ice making, which began in the middle of the nineteenth century, sounded the death knell for natural ice cutting, although in the more traditionally ori-

ented, rural areas natural ice was harvested in ever declining amounts right up to the beginning of World War II.

A more tenacious structure is the woodshed (fig. 6–8). Originally required on virtually every farmstead, it nevertheless was almost always an unprepossessing structure, and frequently a quite nondescript one. Almost any kind of small frame building served. Its primary function, of course, was to ensure a dry supply of firewood in rainy weather. On some farms, the woodshed was an open-sided building in which lengths of wood were piled to form neat walls.

The woodshed "had a pungent, satisfying fragrance . . . from all the firewood which it housed."[13] Another pungent but much less satisfying odor attached to a third basic outbuilding, the privy (fig. 6–9). Indeed, as Henry Kauffman has observed, the location of the privy was essentially a compromise between odor and convenience (fig. 6–10).[14] In summer, aroma was a major consideration, whereas in winter, convenience be-

came more important: "The first thing which had to be done after a heavy snowfall was to quickly shovel a path to the privy."[15]

For such a necessary structure, the privy was often surprisingly poorly constructed and frequently poorly maintained. Perhaps this was due first to the primitive conditions of pioneer and frontier settlement, and later to the embarrassed attitude with which many Victorians approached this facility. One quotation from a standard architectural source will reveal the typical attitudes of the day.

There is no building which is so generally located in the wrong place, as that diminutive house to which a name is applied that expresses absolute importance of such a retreat. It is strange that a house which everyone is ashamed to be seen to enter, should be so often paraded in one of the most conspicuous positions that could be found, so that from all back windows of the dwelling house, it is the most apparent object in view. Probably there was once thought to be a necessity for this location of the building, aris-

Fig. 6–8 An open-sided woodshed (Westfield, New York, 1981)

Fig. 6–9 The privy

Fig. 6–10 A row of privies, each removed from its house by a convenient distance (Batsto Village, New Jersey, 1979)

ing from the idea that cleanliness required it to be placed at a considerable distance in the rear of the house. . . . The first improvement that was made upon the custom to which we have alluded, was to surround the front of the edifice with blinds, or with a trellis, behind which one might conceal himself before he made his entrance. The next improvement was to build a platform on which one might walk to it in muddy weather. At length it was removed to the extreme end of the shed, and the unfortunate person who was obliged to retire to it might skulk around the shed, and allow it to be conjectured that he might have gone on some less ignoble errand. How much soever it might be suspected, there was no actual proof that he entered the temple that stood there; and a modest female after having occupied it without being seen to enter it, might on coming out return to the dwellinghouse with a feeling of comparative innocence.[16]

Scatological humor, risqué jokes, and nervous laughter all were associated with the privy. It even received the nickname of "chic sale" from the foremost barnyard humorist of the day.

The structure itself was unprepossessing but distinctive enough to be readily recognizable, being much taller than wide or deep. A roof ventilator and small decorative cut-outs, especially on the otherwise solid wooden door, were the only embellishments to an otherwise strictly utilitarian building. Wooden frame construction proved to be more suitable than brick or stone because it enabled the building to be moved away from the pit when desirable, for periodic cleaning. In some cases, the pit was extended behind the privy and covered to enable cleaning without moving the building. The lower part of the back wall was sometimes hinged to aid in this process.

Cellars

In reality, the privy was as much an excavation as an erected building. Cellars, which are totally excavated facilities, were also common components of the farm. Almost as many designations of these structures arose as there were structures themselves. At various times and places they have been called *cave cellars, caves, ground cellars, root cellars, root houses, vegetable cellars, dugouts, cold cellars,* and *storm cellars.* Such facilities provided the storage area for root crops such as turnips, beets, carrots, radishes, rutabagas, parsnips, and potatoes, which were eaten by both humans and livestock. They might also be used to preserve other vegetables such as cabbage, onions, pumpkins, and squash stored in their natural state, and a wide variety of home-canned vegetables and fruit. Ground cellars were also used to store meats, cheese, butter, and other dairy products, and even home-baked goods.[17]

Few generalizations can be made about cellars. Some were large, others small, but characteristic dimensions are difficult to identify. A rectangular floor plan was usual but not required. Location against a hillside or bank reduced the labor in excavation so such a site was often used for the cellar, whose exterior consisted of little more than a door and frame.

The storage function of the cave or cellar required four conditions for maximum efficiency: darkness, cool temperatures, high relative humidity, and good air circulation.[18] Darkness caused photosynthetic growth processes to cease, aiding vegetable preservation. The cool temperatures also aided preservation, provided that the excavation could be kept above freezing in the winter. Freezing altered the composition of the vegetable material and made it inedible or at least unpalatable. Hence, the cellar had to be dug sufficiently deep to permit the ground to provide insulation, or, if partially above ground, the structure had to have suitably thick walls. The damp ground offered high relative humidity which could be kept from producing mold by inserting a ventilating pipe to circulate air and expel excess moisture (fig. 6–11).

Fig. 6–11 The open door of a storm cellar (Near Vilonia, Arkansas, 1974)

In the Midwest, the cellar performed another important function. It provided a refuge from the severe windstorms and tornados that afflict that part of the continent. Because of the flat topography, many of these storm cellars are excavated pits reached by a steep flight of steps. In these cellars, the ventilation pipe helps ensure a supply of fresh air for temporary occupants. Even though called *storm cellars* (sometimes *cyclone cellars*), they still were primarily used to store farm produce. A number of other quite specialized outbuildings also were used to process and store the products of the farm.

Dryhouses and smokehouses

Among the most interesting of the outbuildings used to process and preserve farm produce is the dryhouse (fig. 6–12). This small building used to dry out and thus preserve vegetables and fruits has been reported only from early German farmsteads in Pennsylvania.[19] It is possible that German settlers in other parts of North America also used the dryhouse, although its popularity declined rapidly after the mid-nineteenth century, a time when Germans and other cultural groups were settling these areas. The decline of the dryhouse may be linked to the popularization of the kitchen range, which provided a more convenient and efficient facility for drying.

Dryhouses apparently were always constructed of wooden frame, probably to permit facile use of multiple shallow drawers or trays. These were placed in the upper part of the building in such a fashion that they could be pulled out and filled from outside. The lower part of the building housed a stove or, more rarely, a small fireplace that provided the heat for drying.

Dryhouses were rarely more than six or eight feet on a side and smaller ones were portable. The chimney flue was detachable so it could be protected when not in use. In figure 6–12A, the opening for the flue is clearly visible. The crucial problem with the dryhouse was maintaining a small fire of constant temperature that was sufficient to aid drying, but not large enough to partially cook the fruits or vegetables or to endanger the wooden building. On many farmsteads the function of the dryhouse was performed in the farmhouse attic, in the open air under direct sunlight, or sometimes in the bakeoven.

Another structure used for a quite different type of food preservation is the smokehouse. In this building, the object is to expose meat to the action of the chemical creosote, which results from the imperfect combustion of wood.[20] The process of smoking not only preserves the meat but also improves the flavor.[21] In order to gain the maximum benefit from the smoking process, the smokehouse is kept more or less airtight and the fire is regulated so as to give off the greatest amount of smoke. Windows are normally absent and the single door, characteristically in the gable, is usually small. However, small flue openings are placed just under the eaves or high up in the gable to provide the draft required to keep the fire burning and to draw the smoke throughout the structure (fig. 6–13). Ample ventilation is also "necessary to allow the warm air to escape and to help prevent overheating the meats."[22]

Maintaining the correct size and heat of fire was most critical. The fire had to be kept in the middle of the structure away from the walls, which in the ordinary smokehouse were most often of wood. Only in later periods on wealthy farmsteads or where commercial smoking took place were very many smokehouses built of noncombustible stone or brick. In some cases, the center of the floor was excavated to create a fire pit.[23] An advanced design used two fireboxes which could be fed from outside (see fig. 6–13), but such a design was not very common.

Butchering was done usually in the late fall and during winter, which was a way of reducing herds and thereby conserving precious grain. Great care had to be taken to guard against the meat's freezing before it was cured and smoked.

It was important that the meat did not freeze while being smoked, . . . since smoke does not penetrate frozen meat. Overheating with too much fire and not enough smoke is also very damaging. Too much heat causes the meat to become soft and may cause it to fall

Fig. 6–13 Cross section of an improved design smokehouse (from Halstead)

from the hook. [It may get] so much heat that the fat melts and is forced to the outside, the meat becomes partly fried and it becomes impossible to complete the smoking process . . . it cracks in most instances and becomes moldy, resulting in rancidness and spoilage.[24]

An additional advantage of maintaining a slow fire is that it keeps the ashes from rising up with the smoke so that they adhere to the meat.[25] Green wood was often used because it produced more smoke than drier wood, but the most effective method of creating smoke and slowing the fire was to exclude as much outside air as was possible. Although hickory was the preferred wood, oak, maple, cherry, apple, and sassafras also were burned,[26] and chestnut wood, which split easily and burned rapidly, or dried corn cobs provided the material to start the fire.[27]

Fig. 6–12 Pennsylvania German dryhouses

Side opening

Front opening

89

Instead of using a separate smoke-house, certain farmers in Pennsylvania merely removed bricks from their houses' chimney flues, which permitted smoke to enter a small partitioned area of the house attic or loft at the bottom near the floor and to escape at the top near the roof.[28] This could only be done in those few dwellings where the loft or attic was not used for living, working, or grain storage space.

Although surviving smokehouses in eastern United States appear to be concentrated in tidewater Virginia and eastern Pennsylvania,[29] only one primary study exists of this feature in the latter area, and none in the former.[30] Across the Delaware River in New Jersey, Peter Wacker, working from historical records and a very few surviving structures, suggests that two distinct colonial smokehouse types can be identified—a west New Jersey type and a Dutch type. The former were of stone or brick (although frame examples were probably originally more numerous), possessed small gable-end doors, measured anywhere from seven to eleven feet on a side with either square or rectangular floor plans, and normally were used for commercial as well as domestic smoking. The Dutch smokehouses were of frame construction, smaller in size, with a square floor plan, and had large chimneys built into the rear gable wall.[31]

The descriptions of Pennsylvania German smokehouses provided by Amos Long vary somewhat from those of the Dutch. In Pennsylvania, the average size is between six and eight feet on a side, with a height of between eight and twelve feet. The ground plan may be either square or rectangular. Many times they were built of frame construction, often with wide siding and battens to cover the joints between wall boards.[32] Stone and brick smokehouses, as well as a combination of these materials with upper frame parts, are widely scattered throughout the Pennsylvania German culture area.

Smokehouses also are widely spread across the Upland South culture area, although in scattered locations.[33] Those reported from Texas are quite similar to those from eastern Tennessee. Both square and rectangular floor plans exist.

Rectangular smokehouses, derived from eastern Pennsylvania German sources, are most common. Typical dimensions range from twelve by fourteen feet in Tennessee, to slightly smaller in Texas.[34] They may be built of lumber or logs, with those of log usually earlier. A cantilevered roof extension provides shelter to the single gable door, and also supports a stout horizontal pole from which newly slaughtered hogs are hung for butchering.

In addition to butchering and smoking, the smokehouse is also the location for meat curing. In Texas sugar curing is most usual, whereas in Tennessee salt curing is more often found. Consequently, the smokehouse contains one or more sawn lumber curing boxes or hollowed-out log troughs, in which the meat is immersed for varying periods to absorb the sugar or salt.

The square smokehouse is much less common, but because it originates from English tidewater sources, it is apt to be encountered almost anywhere in the Upland South culture area.[35] In contrast to the rectangular smokehouse, which usually measures eight feet or less to the eaves, the square smokehouse, of two stories, rises sixteen feet or more to the eaves and may be capped with a pyramidal roof further accentuating its height. The square smokehouse is more likely to be built in lumber frame, stone, or brick than in log.

Almost any construction material can be employed for a successful smokehouse. The most unusual one is a charming, and perhaps unique, smokehouse built of stovewood (fig. 6–14). It stands in a dilapidated condition and in grave danger of collapse on the Dom farmstead in Door County, Wisconsin.

Fig. 6–14 A stovewood smokehouse (Door County, Wisconsin, 1980)

Stovewood as a building material.
This use as a wall material of lengths of wood suitable for burning in a stove or fireplace is quite restricted. In North America, multiple examples have been reported only from Wisconsin, the upper peninsula of Michigan, Quebec, eastern Ontario, southeastern Manitoba, Minnesota, and the Georgian Bay area.[36] The stovewood is stacked up much as firewood would be, except that it is held in place by mortar, and sometimes by a timber frame (fig. 6–15). This

use has provided its other common names: *cordwood* and *stackwood* architecture. Obviously, such construction involves an enormous amount of labor, much more than conventional log building, although it can be performed by a single individual. Stovewood construction is only feasible in those areas where there are abundant forests of fairly small trees. The cedar stands of the northern swamp and bog forests provide such an environment.

The length of the logs and, hence, usually the thickness of the wall depend upon the size of the building, but a maximum length of twelve to eighteen inches is general. In small buildings,

lengths as short as five inches with three-inch diameters have been used. For the most part, logs are laid in the round minus the bark, but those of large diameter may be split in half or thirds. Occasionally, a farmer will go to the great labor of squaring the logs.[37] Removing the bark is necessary to eliminate insect pests, to retard decay, and to guard against the loosening of the bark as drying takes place. Such drying will ultimately endanger the integrity of the wall. Corners present a particular construction problem, solved usually by employing squared log sections, much as stone quoins are used in masonry walls.[38]

For a long time, the origins of stovewood architecture in North America remained obscured. Recently, however, William Tishler has presented convincing evidence that this method of building is derived from Scandinavian sources. He cites both Swedish and Norwegian antecedents.[39] In the Door peninsula of Wisconsin, where the greatest concentration of stovewood construction seems to occur, there are several communities of Norwegian settlers. Additional research will probably reveal a connection, but a similar association in eastern Canada would seem to be more difficult to establish.

The Door peninsula in northern Wisconsin is not only known for stovewood buildings; it also is the locale of one of North America's most important concentrations of outdoor bakeovens.

Fig. 6–15 Close-up of the wall of the smokehouse shown in fig. 6–14

Bakeovens

During the early days of settlement in North America, bread was baked in one of three ways: in front of an open fire; in a Dutch oven as "johnny cake"; or in a bakeoven.[40] In areas of English and Dutch colonial influence, when separate ovens were used, bakeovens were generally built into the kitchen hearth inside the house (see vol. 1, fig. 3–12 or 4–12 for examples shown in plan). The French, Spanish, German, and other settlers, however, employed separate bakeoven structures (fig. 6–16).

A bakeoven separate from the fireplace had several advantages.[41] First, and most important, it reduced the danger of fire, thereby offering a measure of protection to the house. Second, the mess and considerable heat associated with baking were removed from the kitchen, an especially important consideration during the summer. Finally, a separate bakeoven permitted an increase in the size of the baking area, so that more could be baked at a time, reducing the number of occasions each week during which the oven had to be used. At the same time, separate bakeovens suffered from at least two significant disadvantages.[42] They were more inconvenient than ovens located within the kitchen and they were most troublesome in inclement or cold weather.

Each ethnic group or culture had a somewhat different form of bakeoven. Before contact with the Spanish, the Pueblo Indians of the Southwest used a primitive stove called a *guyave* or *piki*.[43]

Fig. 6–16 Types of bakeovens in North America and the areas of their use

1 Canadian French   2 Wisconsin Belgian

3 Pennsylvania German

4 Louisiana French   5 Spanish-Mexican
Pueblo Indian

Consisting of three rectangular stone slabs held together by mud (fig. 6–17), it rested against the wall of the adobe, either just in front of, or actually inside, the open fireplace. The major defect of this stove was the lack of any vent.

The Spanish-Mexicans introduced a quite different oven, the *horno* (fig. 6–18).[44] Made of adobe, or more likely of stones bound and covered in adobe mortar, heaped up into a parabolic or beehive shape, the horno is a separate structure, always found outside the adobe house. It may be used either for baking bread or equally well for finishing Pueblo pottery vessels.

Because their interior capacity is small, hornos often occur in multiple groupings, which "at a distance resemble nothing so much as anthills."[45] Rarely is the outside diameter larger than four feet and the height is slightly smaller, but the whole is raised on a one-foot-high plinth of adobe or stone.

Bakeovens of French derivation were built both in Louisiana and in the St. Lawrence valley. The form of the oven in both areas varies somewhat. It may be barrel-shaped or domed and the ground plan oval, pear-shaped, or rectangular. In Louisiana, ovens are formed of clay mixed with Spanish moss over a wooden form that is subsequently burned out, thereby hardening the oven's interior.[46] In Quebec, the oven is more apt to be made of brick or stone, although clay ovens are by no means uncommon. In both areas, ovens constructed of clay usually are covered by a wooden shed or gable roof raised up on wooden posts to provide protection to the easily weathered clay structure (see fig. 6–16[1]).

In Louisiana, the French bakeoven spread over a wide area, but its French association accounts for only part of the particular pattern of its distribution, because it is not known in the western part of French Louisiana (fig. 6–19). Its absence from this area, which was also settled by the French, has been attributed to the difficulty of growing wheat there and the consequent shift of that French population toward the growth and consumption of maize, a grain that is not so suited to baking in a closed oven.[47] Although some ovens are built directly

Fig. 6–18 A horno oven (Taos Pueblo, 1967)

Fig. 6–17 A Pueblo piki oven (from Mindeleff)

Fig. 6–19 The extent of French culture and French bakeovens in Louisiana (after Kniffen)

upon the ground, most are raised on a sturdy wooden platform roughly two to three feet high. The plank floor is covered with several inches of compact clay before the oven structure itself is built.

The bakeovens of Quebec (fig. 6–20) are close in form to those of Louisiana, although an oven inside the house, usually in the basement and projecting through an exterior wall, is also quite prevalent.[48] Perhaps it is the colder climate or the greater tendency to build houses in stone that favors placing the oven within the house itself. Separate bakeovens of clay or brick are raised on wooden platforms as in Louisiana. Much rarer is the massive bakeoven built of stone with a large chimney at the front. In these ovens the vault is usu-

ally constructed of brick and covered with a wooden hipped or gable roof resting on the top of the stone walls that surround the vault.[49] An insulating space thus is created that helps to retain the oven's heat. As was the case with all ovens, the facility was located so that prevailing winds would blow the smoke and sparks away from the house and other buildings.[50]

Related to the French-derived ovens are those of the Belgian community of the Door peninsula of Wisconsin. Free-standing ovens were built and used in the community, but the majority are extensions of individual summer kitchens (fig. 6–21). In Belgium, the warmer winter climate and the compact settlement pattern, as well as the fire danger, encouraged the use of communal ovens, but in Wisconsin the much colder continental climate and the pattern of individual, dispersed farmsteads removed two of the three reasons for the communal European feature.[51] Incorporat-

ing it into the summer kitchen reduced the hazard of an oven in the farmhouse itself.

The Belgian bakeoven always occupies the rear gable of the summer kitchen, and the access to the oven is through the summer kitchen interior (fig. 6–22). Both brick and stone were commonly used in the construction of the bakeoven, set on a platform of bluish-gray dolomite, six to seven feet square and about four feet high. Sometimes the oval baking chamber was built of, or at least was faced with, local dolomite, but more often the chamber and the chimney in the summer kitchen gable wall were of brick. The oval interior was about two feet high, four feet wide, and almost six feet deep. "Since baking was accomplished by radiated heat, the dimensions of the oven were critical. If the oven was too small the bread burned, and if it was too large, baking would be slow and uneven" and often incomplete.[52]

Fig. 6–20 French bakeovens of Quebec (from Michel Lessard and Huguette Marquis, *Encyclopédie de la maison québécoise* [Montreal: Les Editions de l'Homme, 1972], p. 621

Fig. 6–21 The bakeoven extends from the gable of this Belgian summer house built of dolomite (Door County, Wisconsin, 1980)

Fig. 6–22 Close-up of the brick firebox of the Belgian bakeoven shown in fig. 6–21. Note the dolomite sill and the bricked-up ash pit opening.

In many respects German practices vis-à-vis the bakeoven are close to those of the French and Belgians. Frequently the oven is an appendage of the summer kitchen, especially when the latter is of brick. In other instances, the bakeoven is built into the fireplace of the main house, but extended beyond the wall of the house and covered with a wooden roof to protect the masonry.[53] Most often, however, the German settlers made use of an oven standing in a separate structure (fig. 6–23). Generally these structures are larger than their French or Belgian counterparts, measuring roughly eight by twelve feet.[54] This includes a projecting roof overhang of some three feet. Normally, only the triangular projecting gable is enclosed, but in many instances the overhang is provided with side walls, and sometimes even with an end wall and door, so that an anteroom is created (fig. 6–24). Here firewood can be stored under shelter and often a series of shelves provides a place to put bread and pastry for cooling. The tile or wooden shingle roof is supported on corner posts that elevate it some three or four feet above the baking chamber.[55] Interior dimensions are normally 4½ feet wide, 5½ feet long, and thirty inches high,[56] very close to the sizes that Calkins and Laatsch found in Belgian ovens.

Two subtypes of Pennsylvania German bakeovens are identified by a different location of the chimney (see fig. 6–16[3]). In the most common type, a brick chimney is positioned at the end opposite the oven door, which in its turn opens into the antechamber formed by the projecting roof. Viewed from the side in outline, the structure bears a vague resemblance to a railway steam locomotive, with chimney (smokestack), baking chamber (boiler), and anteroom (cab) in that order.[57] Heat loss from the oven was regulated by covering the chimney or other flue, often with a metal pie plate.

95

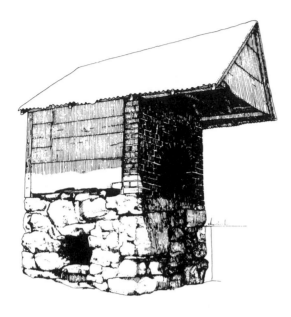

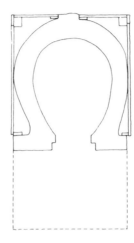

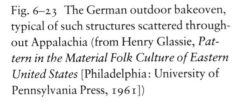

Fig. 6–23 The German outdoor bakeoven, typical of such structures scattered throughout Appalachia (from Henry Glassie, *Pattern in the Material Folk Culture of Eastern United States* [Philadelphia: University of Pennsylvania Press, 1961])

The second type of Pennsylvania German bakeoven had the chimney attached to the front of the baking chamber. In this instance, the roof enclosed the chimney, but normally a space for ventilating and lighting the anteroom was left between the chimney stack and roof projection. A front location for the chimney had at least two advantages. In winter additional warmth was given to the exposed anteroom. Additionally,

the oven flue was accessible to the baker, and it was not necessary to go outside to the rear to regulate the draft, an important consideration in the winter and during rainy periods. The flue, however, was not necessarily a direct connection between the front of the baking chamber and the chimney. For an as-yet-unexplained reason, some German bakeovens, called *squirrel-tail ovens*, possessed flues that left the baking chamber at its rear and led back across the top of the oven to enter the chimney located at the front. The flue resembled nothing more than the curled tail of a squirrel, hence its popular name. Such ovens were especially numerous in Bucks County, Pennsylvania.[58]

In nearby Berks County, an examination of both types of outdoor ovens has revealed that the earliest structures were usually built of fieldstone, whereas the

latest were most likely to be constructed of brick. Most were combinations of the two materials with the foundation and walls of stone and the baking chamber and chimney of brick.[59]

Amos Long has provided an excellent description of typical construction techniques:

The outdoor ovens were generally constructed by erecting two walls of stone or brick laid in clay or mortar to a height of two or two and one-half feet. The area between the bases enclosed by the bottom of the hearth served as the ashpit. . . . Long flat stones or planks were placed horizontally across the two walls. Over these, other flat stones were laid in clay which was often gotten from the beds of nearby streams. A layer of clay several inches thick was plastered over the stones to form the bottom of the hearth. . . . After the clay or mortar which helped form the bottom of the hearth had dried, the side walls were built up about four inches or two layers of brick. Sand, soft earth, small wood chips or bark were then placed on top and pressed down upon the

Fig. 6–24 A Pennsylvania German outdoor bakeoven

hearth in an oval shaped pile. . . . About a four inch layer of clay mixed with straw . . . was placed over the top of the pile to form the arch of the oven. . . . The brick dome was then plastered over with mortar. . . . When the oven was completed, it stood idle for several days and if the wood particles formed the arch, they were set on fire. . . . The fire not only removed the wood debris but also baked and hardened the clay. This formed the inner chamber of the oven. When earth or sand was used to form the arch, it was also removed after a like period. . . .[60]

The Pennsylvania German bakeovens have gone the way of many folk culture features. First, commercial bakeries and, later, electric and gas ranges caused the demise of the wood-burning rural oven. By 1972 not a single bakeoven that could still be located in southeastern Pennsylvania was being used.[61] Just as significant but not so thorough is the decline and the changing function of another important farm outbuilding, the summer kitchen.

Summer houses or summer kitchens

The bakeoven solved the problem of removing from the dwelling the great heat required to bake foods. The summer house or summer kitchen (fig. 6–25) carried the idea even further. Not only was heat generation eliminated from the farm dwelling, a series of other problems was solved as well. The mess associatd with the greatly augmented scale of summer cooking, when additional hired hands and helpers had to be fed, was removed from the dwelling. Flies, mice, and other pests attracted by the food were confined to the summer house. Fire danger was also confined. Finally, the summer house could be used as a place to serve meals and to bed additional help, preserving the privacy of the main house for the family.

There appear to be two origins for the summer house or summer kitchen on American farmsteads. One lies in the conversion of an earlier, cruder dwelling to summer-kitchen use when a

Fig. 6–26 A vertical plank-sided, frame summer kitchen, located close behind the farmhouse (Medina County, Ohio, 1981)

larger, more elaborate farmhouse was built.[62] Although some were attached to the later house as back wings, most were detached structures so that they offered the greatest advantages of fire protection and nuisance reduction. For maximum convenience, however, they were rarely more than a few steps from the kitchen entrance of the main house (fig. 6–26).

The more important origin of the summer house lies in continental European folk traditions. Construction of detached summer houses or kitchens in North America is reported among Pennsylvania Germans, Hungarians, French-Canadians, Belgians, Russian-Germans, and Finns.[63] Apparently, the

Fig. 6–25 The summer house or summer kitchen

97

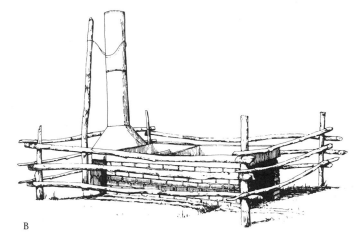

A   B

Fig. 6–27 Sorghum crushing mill and outdoor evaporator used throughout the
Ozarks and southern Appalachia (from
Henry Glassie, *Pattern in the Material Folk
Culture of Eastern United States* [Philadel-
phia: University of Pennsylvania Press,
1961])

summer kitchen was not a strong tradition among English settlers, although
separate year-round kitchens were an
integral part of the larger southern colonial farmsteads.

The separate summer house or summer kitchen (see fig. 6–25) is a rather
simple structure, frequently just a single
rectangular room about sixteen by
twenty feet. Somewhat larger summer
houses often had two first-floor rooms
for food preparation and serving and
a larger, undivided loft for storage or
extra sleeping space.

Because the summer kitchen was designated for food preparation, a large
fireplace and chimney usually occupied

one gable wall in the earlier ones. Later
these features were often replaced by a
stovepipe, as the cast-iron range replaced the hearth. High atop the ridge,
sometimes in the exact center, was an
open cupola for the dinner bell, which
was used to summon the farmhands to
meals. In some instances, the bell stood
atop its own pole in the yard, close to
the summer kitchen door.

The summer house proved to be useful
well into the twentieth century on many
farms. Eventually, however, "the introduction of pressure water systems,
modern sinks, refrigeration, gas and
electric ranges plus many other modern
devices in the home provide[d] the necessary facilities for cooking to be done
with ease and convenience in the modern kitchen."[64] Like so many other folk
features of the countryside, the summer
house went into a rapid decline, having
outlived its usefulness.

Crop-oriented structures

A third group of secondary farm structures consists of those that are closely

connected to the harvesting, processing,
or storage of the nonanimal products of
the farm. Corn cribs and granaries are
nearly universal. Structures to stack and
store hay are more restricted and to a
considerable extent controlled by climatic conditions. Very specialized
buildings to process unusual crops such
as sorghum, maple syrup, or hops occur
on a very limited basis. Despite their restricted geographical distribution, these
latter structures are most distinctive and
quite recognizable, although not well
studied by scholars of the settlement
landscape.

Maple sugar houses and sorghum mills

Sugar and syrup traditionally have been
made from three sources in three different geographical regions of North
America. In southern United States, especially in the Mississippi delta and in
southern Florida, sugar from cane was
produced on large properties using
quasi-industrial methods from the very
beginning, as a consequence of the plan-
tation system of agriculture. Hence, the

small-scale, folk contributions to the process were diluted, mostly beyond recognition, almost at once. With sorghum and maple sugar and syrup making, the folk connection has persisted, probably because the labor involved was so large compared to the output that commercial production did not succeed in many instances.

On the plains of Texas and Oklahoma and in the Maumee valley of Ohio and Indiana, and at various locations between these widely separated extremes, sorghum farmers have harvested large enough acreages to support local industrial mills. Elsewhere, in Appalachia and the Ozarks especially, sorghum syrup is still produced in small amounts by individual farmers following traditional methods. All that is required is a simple crushing apparatus and an evaporator. Rarely are either of these housed in a protective building when the scale of the operation is small; rather the operations are carried on in the open air.

The sorghum mill (fig. 6–27A) consists of a set of wooden or metal rollers supported on wooden stumps or a timber framework, roughly three or four feet high. The sorghum cane is fed into the rollers and the expelled juice is caught in pans placed under the platform. The rollers are turned by gears attached to a vertical shaft, which in turn is connected to a long horizontal sweep or boom. This boom, often counterbalanced to reduce its weight, is powered by a horse or mule walking in endless circles. As Clarence Keathley notes: "The sweep had to be just the right size to fit on the 'sweep cap,' the right length and the right crook or shape. The end to which the horse was hitched had to be considerably lower than the top of the

mill. . . . A small pole, called a 'lead pole,' was hitched to the bridle of the horse or mule to keep him in the circle around the mill. A well-trained horse or mule did not have to be driven."[65]

The evaporator (fig. 6–27B) is set up a short distance from the crushing apparatus, and consists of three principal parts: a deep brick or stone fireplace, roughly four feet wide and twelve feet long, a metal chimney about eight feet tall, and a very slightly tilted evaporating pan which rests on the fireplace. The syrup is slowly led, back and forth, from one side to the other, in narrow transverse channels beginning at one end of the pan and continuing to the opposite end, where it is ultimately drained into jugs or bottles.

The traditional production of maple syrup and sugar follows the same process of evaporation that is employed in sorghum making. The juice, however, is obtained much differently, by boring holes into the maple trees, placing a tube called a *spile* in the hole, and allowing sap to drip into covered pails or buckets hung from the spile. The season for tapping is short, limited to a few days in February, March, or April during which daytime temperatures are above freezing and nighttime temperatures below.

The sap is collected and brought to the sugar house (fig. 6–28), which is usually located in the *sugar bush*, the term applied to a grove of sugar maple trees. The sugar house and the surrounding sugar bush in some places is referred to as a *camp*.[66] The sugar house is a distinctive folk structure, yet no studies have been made of it.

The smaller houses measure about ten by eighteen feet and contain only a sin-

gle room, large enough to house the firebox, also called the *arch*, a chimney pipe, the long shallow metal evaporator pan, and various jugs, bottles, and other miscellaneous equipment. Larger sugar houses, with dimensions of sixteen by thirty-six feet, normally have two rooms, permitting separation of syrup boiling and sugar making operations.

In the earliest period, sap was reduced to syrup in a large kettle suspended over an open fire. The improved shallow-pan evaporator was designed in the second quarter of the nineteenth century. Accompanying the development of the evaporator was the evolution of the fireplace or arch: "The arch was further refined so that the fire was confined at one end and the heat was drawn beneath the pans by filling in the opposite end, from a midway point to within a few inches from the pan. A chimney or stack was added to the back, as well as doors to the front, providing more control of the fire."[67]

Firewood is sometimes kept inside the sugar house, or in an open-sided lean-to addition to one of the gables (fig. 6–29).[68] Just as often, it is neatly

Fig. 6–28 The sugar house

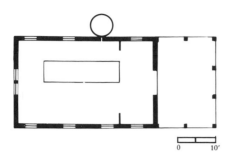

Fig. 6–29 Floor plan of a sugar house showing the attached woodshed, the rectangular evaporator, and the outside storage tank

stacked a few steps outside. Great quantities, of course, are needed to reduce the sap to syrup, a process that also generates considerable humidity. To permit this moisture to escape, the typical sugar house has an elevated ridge ventilator, with open louvers or with openings that can be closed by hinged doors.[69] These ventilators are one of the most distinctive architectural features of the buildings (see fig. 6–28).[70] Ideally, the sugar house is located at the foot of a bank or small slope, which permits gravity feeding of the sap into the evaporator (fig. 6–30). Unfortunately, as maple syrup and sugar production declines, sugar houses are disappearing from the cultural landscape, or they are being structurally modified to serve other functions. Because these buildings are as yet largely undocumented, attention must be given to recording them before they disappear entirely, especially in those areas subject to urban encroachment. The need is especially criti-

cal because sugar houses normally occur in isolated locations, away from other farm buildings. Figure 6–31, which shows the extent of maple syrup production at the turn of the century, indicates where relict sugar houses are likely to be encountered and thus where study of them should be concentrated.

Hop houses

Another specialized agricultural building in danger of extinction, at least in eastern United States, is the hop house (fig. 6–32). In western United States, the early folk structures are also being replaced by industrial buildings performing the same functions, but on a larger scale.

Hops have been grown in the United States for a very long time. The traditional date of introduction is 1629, although colonial production remained

Fig. 6–30 A schematic diagram of a sugar house: (a) evaporator; (b) floor excavated one foot below grade for ease in firing the evaporator boiler; (c) open wood storage; (d) work bench; (e) sap storage tank; (f) sled collecting tank. (K. E. Barraclough, *Maple Syrup and Sugar Production in New Hampshire* [Durham: New Hampshire Agricultural and Home Economics Extension Service 1952])

quite limited.[71] Hence, relics of the early New England and other early eastern hop growing regions are quite rare.

At the beginning of the nineteenth century, James Cooledge introduced hop cultivation into central New York and built the first hop kiln there, which survived at least up to the time of the Second World War.[72] Perhaps because of extensive German settlement and the establishment of a large number of local breweries, Wisconsin farmers also developed methods of hop cultivation,[73] although significant production was limited to the very middle of the nineteenth century. Sometime after midcentury, hop production was introduced into the West Coast valleys, which became the center of the industry by the mid-twentieth century. By 1889 the United States ranked third in world

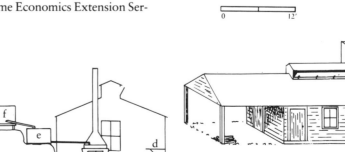

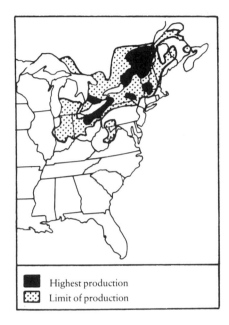

Fig. 6–31 Maple syrup and sugar production, about 1900

hop acreage, slightly behind Great Britain. Germany, at the same time, had more than double these amounts.[74]

The earliest facilities in New York for processing hops consisted of two parts. The kiln or drying house was a circular stone structure with a high, tapering upper portion, a type introduced directly from southeastern England.[75] Stone walls created an airtight space to retain heat from the open fire kindled on the earth floor, and the round form offered the least resistance to circulating air. The top of the kiln tapered to a small vent from which both smoke and moisture were exhausted. The vent was protected by a distinctive cowl, affixed so

that it rotated according to changing wind direction. (see fig. 6–32).

The second part of the structure was the hop shed or barn in which the dried hops were cooled, sorted, and packaged for shipment. The hop shed was an ordinary, framed, one-story, rectangular building with a gable roof. Both facilities normally adjoined one another, and together the complex was called a *hop house* or *hop barn*.

Fig. 6–32 Hop houses in the United States

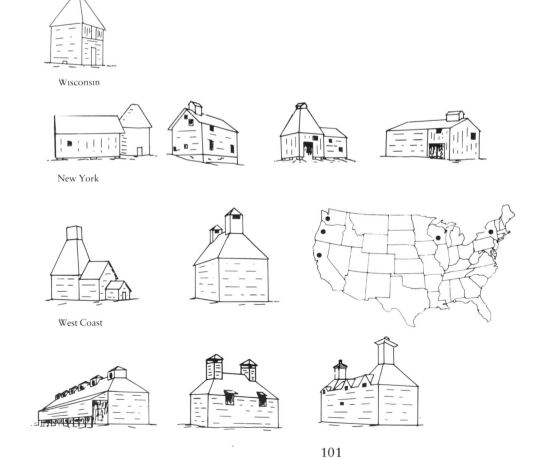

By the mid-nineteenth century, the hop house of New York and Wisconsin had evolved into a more complex structure (fig. 6–33). Each of the earlier parts had been divided, the form of the structure had also changed, and new methods of drying and processing had been introduced. The simple kiln, with its open fire and loft containing the drying hops, was replaced by a two-chamber square kiln, measuring eighteen by eighteen feet.[76] The ground level was the stove room housing a large iron stove connected to a square or rectangular system of large stovepipes for space

101

heating (fig. 6–34). The upper chamber, now termed the *drying room,* typically had an open-slatted wooden floor to permit the heated air to come in contact with the hemp or jute on which the hops were placed.[77] An open platform, outside the drying room, offered a place to feed hops into the drying room. Wood for fueling the stove was stacked up in the shelter beneath this platform. Small quantities of sulphur were expelled from pans placed in the stove room during firing and, as a result, the hops took on a golden hue.

The hop shed was divided into a cooling area on the upper level, called the *storing room,* and a *press room* on the ground level, where the hops were pressed into bales or boxes for shipment.[78] The floor of the storing room often was two or three feet below the slatted floor of the drying room in order to facilitate the emptying of the latter. During cooling of the hops in the storing room, some moisture returned to the plant, enabling it to be handled more easily in subsequent operations. When cooled, the hops were fed into a chute which conveyed them to the press or baling operation in the room below.

With these elaborations also came modifications in the form of the kiln. Square or rectangular frame kilns replaced circular, stone ones since the former were easier and, hence, cheaper to build by individual farmers. The inside walls were plastered to keep kilns airtight. Small openings that could be closed by wooden sliding doors were made on each side close to the ground to

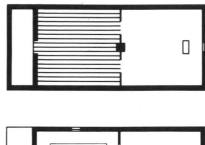

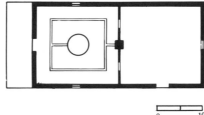

Fig. 6–33 Floor plan of a typical Wisconsin hop house (after Rudd and Rudd). Upper level: loading platform on left; slatted drying floor of the kiln; and the cooling room with the rectangular chute opening in the floor. Lower level: wood storage area on left; kiln furnace with heating pipes in center; and baling room on right.

permit entrance of air for the stove and to supply cold air to keep up a draft to the cupola, which replaced the cowled vent of the earlier kilns.

Since both the kiln and the shed were now constructed of frame materials, it was easy to incorporate them into a single building in which the functions were clearly differentiated only by the interior arrangement of the structure. The risk of fire was also increased, however, and for this reason on some farms the kilns and the hop sheds remained physically separated.

On the West Coast, in the late nineteenth and early twentieth century, as hop growing became well established, the size of the hop houses increased and a distinct form evolved as well. Stoves

were replaced by furnaces fired by coal or natural gas. The kiln assumed a squarish, hipped-roof form topped by a prominent hooded shaft, as is shown in figure 6–34.[79] Because of the scale of production, kilns were paired with the hop shed between; later, long banks of multiple kilns were built. Finally, fans were introduced either at the base of the stove room or in the cupola openings to force air through the drying area.[80]

Hardly an architectural feature, but nevertheless a most noticeable aspect of the landscape, were the numerous hop yards in which the hop plants were cultivated. Originally the hop yards consisted of a regularly spaced series of tall, thin poles upon which the vine was trained to grow. By 1954 only one grower in the entire United States was thought to be using the pole method of hop growing.[81] The alternative method of growing hop plants was to use a trellis system consisting of a series of poles interconnected by horizontal wires, ten to fifteen feet off the ground. In both methods, harvesting was frequently done by farm help wearing stilts before the invention of mechanical pickers.

Granaries

Much less picturesque are the methods of growing grains and the buildings in which those grains are stored. Grain was so vital to the survival of early settlers that it often was stored in the lofts of their houses. There it received maximum protection. Neither hostile Indians nor rapacious neighbors were likely to raid it without alarming the farmer. Furthermore, the house loft was apt to be drier and more vermin proof than other farm buildings, but there were some disadvantages to such storage. Rats and mice were likely to be attracted to houses where grains were stored and the risk of fire from spontaneous combustion was increased considerably, especially if the grain had not been thoroughly dried before storage. Buckwheat was particularly susceptible to spontaneous combustion in damp weather or if not properly dried.[82] For

Fig. 6–34 Cutaway view of a hop kiln showing the arrangement of furnace and heating pipe (from Lawrence)

these reasons, and also to obviate the considerable labor required to move grains into house lofts, many farmers followed the long-established tradition of building grain bins into barns.

Since the earliest barns (English barns, for example) were usually threshing barns, considerable labor was saved by dumping the threshed grain directly into storage bins in the barn. Because much of the grain would be used for animal feed, labor was further saved by keeping the grain in the barn near the feeding lot, or near the animals, if they were housed in the barn.[83] Many German bank and raised or basement barns have grain storage bins on the threshing level which can be emptied by chutes leading down to the lower level housing the animals. In crib and transverse-frame barns, the loft frequently was used for grain storage. Battens were laid down covering the spaces between floor boards to make the loft as tight as possible (fig. 6–35).

The practice of employing separate buildings as granaries appears to have been in response to the expanding agri-

cultural production of American farms, although separate granaries had long been used in the farming villages of Europe. The emphasis on a separate granary on each farm did not last long, however. The development of rail transportation, the perfection of mechanical threshing machines, and the constant demand for grain in the growing urban centers of North America all worked to

Fig. 6–35 Interior of transverse-frame barn loft showing floor battens to make the loft grain-tight (Greenup County, Kentucky, 1981)

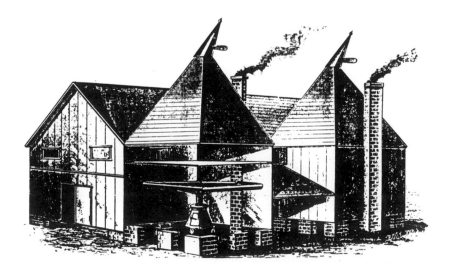

ensure that most grain was moved from the farm as soon as it was harvested. Hence, granaries are not commonly found on the large cash-grain farms of the West. More likely encountered is the small relict granary on middle-sized farms in eastern and central North America (fig. 6–36). Here there are often strong ethnic associations. German, Scandinavian, and eastern European farms seem to have granaries most often, although no scholarly studies have yet been undertaken to reveal the ethnic associations of farm granaries.

Most granaries, regardless of ethnic connection, are rectangular (fig. 6–37) and characterized by a lack of windows, doors, or other openings, primarily to keep the structure as animal proof as possible. Use of vertical battens to seal spaces between siding boards is encountered in Norwegian granaries (fig. 6–38), but overlapping horizontal clapboards is usual in German and eastern European granaries (fig. 6–39). Perhaps the most distinctive feature of the granary, one by which it can usually be recognized, is its elevation on several short piers of wood, stone, or cement block. The purpose is to raise the structure above the damp ground and to assist in making it animal-proof. Sometimes circular metal disks are added to the top of the piers just under the sills of the building to further discourage rats, mice, and other pests. The interior of the granary was usually divided into a series of bins or compartments for ease of grain handling and to permit storage of more than one grain. By the latter

Fig. 6–36 Typical granary (Lorain County, Ohio, 1980)

Fig. 6–37 A granary of German origin (Washington County, Missouri, 1979)

Fig. 6–38 A granary of Norwegian origin (Old World Wisconsin Outdoor Museum, 1977)

half of the nineteenth century, on some farms especially in the Midwest, the functions of the granary were combined with those of the corncrib in a single structure.[84]

Corncribs

The term *crib* has at least two important and quite distinct definitions. In one sense it means a square or rectangular pen formed of horizontal interlocking logs. These are the cribs referred to in discussing crib barns (see chap. 1). The other usage is related to the first and re-

104

Fig. 6–39 A series of small granaries on a farm of eastern European origin (Near Regina, Saskatchewan, 1977)

Fig. 6–40 The corncrib

fers to a log building used to store ears of corn. From this definition, a *corncrib* (fig. 6–40) has come to mean any structure used to store corn, whether log or not. Thus, timber frame, lumber, masonry, metal, and steel-wire corncribs can be identified.

The origin of the corncrib as a separate building has not been clearly established, although Halloch Raup has suggested that it is derived from crude American Indian structures.[85] In the colonial period, corn production was not large, and the corn could be quickly harvested and stored in a corner of the barn. However, as farm sizes grew the farmer began to resort to the shocking of corn (the gathering of cut corn stalks in vertical stacks) in the field where it

could be left throughout the winter if necessary. The farmer would simply husk what was needed for animal feed.[86] Amos Long states that Pennsylvania farmers did not generally begin to shock corn, however, until about 1800.[87] Nicholas Hardeman suggests that the practice of shocking began a generation or so earlier in Virginia.[88]

An emphasis on the raising of ever more livestock resulted in greater and greater acreage devoted to corn. The need for ear corn as animal feed increased so much that shocking was clearly an inadequate method of supplying the demand. Thus, in the nineteenth century, corn was husked in the field as soon as it was harvested. When the crop was large or the weather inclement, the

unhusked corn was taken into the barn, where it was stripped in a more leisurely fashion, often in husking bees, great social occasions which rotated from farm to farm. The ears of corn were then loaded into free-standing corncribs (fig. 6–41). Because they are newly harvested, the ears of corn contain considerable moisture, up to 25 percent or higher.[89] One of the functions of the corncrib is to permit the slow, steady drying of the corn, in order to reduce losses from mold and mildew. To accomplish this, the crib must possess certain basic design features, which can be

Fig. 6–41 A corncrib of unusual design (Medina County, Ohio, 1980)

development, in order to provide the maximum weather protection and, at the same time, to assist in gravity unloading, the sides were constructed to slant outward toward the top, giving the crib a coffinlike gable profile (see fig. 6–40) and, incidentally, making it a somewhat unstable structure. A hundred years ago, this type of corncrib was referred to as a *Connecticut corn house* and identified as the common type of corn storage facility "throughout the East."[92]

Because of the size and shape of ears of corn, loading and unloading always presents difficulties. Often a series of small doors or openings for unloading may be located near the base of one wall.[93] In any event, the largest opening is usually a man-size door in the gable wall. Inside the crib and behind this door is an arrangement of boards, one atop the other, blocking off the crib but permitting the opening and closing of the door. The boards are held in vertical grooves and are removed as needed to permit unloading of the corn.[94]

A final diagnostic element of the early

Fig. 6–42 Maximum optimal width of corncribs in the Midwest (from Kelley)

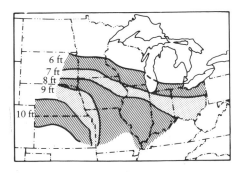

used to identify the structure. First, the walls must contain a high proportion of open area, usually attained by use of widely spaced, narrow slats. Second, the structure must be narrow in order to ensure adequate circulation of air, or it must be artificially dried. "The narrower the crib, the freer the movement of wind through the corn, and the greater the likelihood of successful natural drying. The proper width of an ordinary crib in a particular locality depends on the date at which corn normally matures and on the prevailing weather conditions during the first 8 months of storage. Among the

weather factors that should be considered are humidity, temperature, and amount of sunshine and wind."[90]

Figure 6–42, based on USDA recommendations, gives the maximum widths for rectangular corncribs for the Midwest. Circular corncrib diameters can be up to one and a half times these widths. Generally speaking, however, homemade corncribs were narrower than these dimensions, especially in eastern United States where farms were smaller and corn production lower.[91]

The earliest corncribs utilized unhewn or split logs of small diameter, usually laid up with saddle notching. The bottommost logs were placed on log or stone piers. Although many often were left open, the best cribs had wood-shingle, gable roofs. At a second stage of corncrib design was the use of an overhanging skirt, sometimes of lumber (see fig. 6–41), sometimes of metal, about a foot or two above the ground. This, of course, was a device to reduce as far as possible the depredations of rats, mice, and other small animals. In the earliest cribs, large flat stones and, later on, round pieces of tin were placed on the tops of the posts but under the crib floor, to accomplish the same purpose.

A second type of corncrib assumed a quite different form (fig. 6–43). An elongated rectangle, this crib was crowned by a shed roof and the sides were vertical rather than slanting. Initially these sides were composed of open wooden slats, but later, wire mesh was often substituted. In order to promote drying, these elongated cribs frequently are oriented in a north-south direction to catch maximum prevailing winds and drying sunlight.[95]

The rectangular, shed-roof corncrib is filled through a series of hatches in the roof. Initially, the crib height was restricted, so that loading directly from the bed of a wagon was possible. Later on, with the development of the loading elevator, crib walls became much higher.

In the latter part of the nineteenth century and in the twentieth century, as both farm sizes and corn production increased, ever more corn storage was required. One solution was to use multiple cribs, but a more efficient and cheaper one was to employ cribs of larger design. Two shed-roof cribs placed opposite one another, with a driveway between (fig. 6–44), was one such design, constructed in sufficient numbers to be a recognizable barn type (see chap. 1).

The drive-in crib may have originated in the Middle Atlantic states.[96] It occurs frequently in the Shenandoah valley and occasionally throughout Appalachia, but it is in the Midwest (and especially the Corn Belt) that this crib is most commonly encountered. The driveway would be used to store machinery and the loft space over the driveway served as a granary for small grains. Hatches in the roof replaced wall openings as elevators were introduced to load the corn. Still later, a cupola was added to permit permanent installation of inside conveyor elevators to lift both corn and small grains. The cupola allowed the placing of "the elevator head high enough so that the grain can be spouted to any part of the building with less trouble and expense than cross conveyors required."[97] The cupola also provided ventilation for the grain stored in the building.

The perfection of the loading elevator permitted the erection of ever taller cribs, which were economical because they required no larger foundation or roof structure than smaller ones. The invention and widespread adoption of the corn picker produced some difficulties in using tall cribs, however.

Fig. 6–44 The evolution of the drive-in crib barn from two corncribs can be seen from this dilapidated structure in Polk County, Iowa (1980)

Fig. 6–43 Photo of a shed-roof corncrib (Wayne County, Ohio, 1977)

When corn was picked by hand and scooped by hand, the crib was filled slowly and the corn well distributed along its entire length. Some drying took place as the crib was filled. . . . The picker plus the elevator meant rapid filling, more husks, silks, and shelled corn, and a tendency to concentrate them in one place under the elevator spout. High cribs required interior braces. Rapid filling piled the corn well above the braces before it had a chance to settle. When it did settle, as it must when it dries, the braces were broken out by the settling corn. Corn packs more densely in the bottom of high cribs, hence the farmer is faced with a ventilation problem and a loss of corn which he did not have before.[98]

Iowa masonry corncribs. To help solve these structural problems, gigan-

Fig. 6–46 Corncrib and farmhouse (Polk County, Iowa, 1980)

Fig. 6–45 A double masonry corncrib (Polk County, Iowa, 1980)

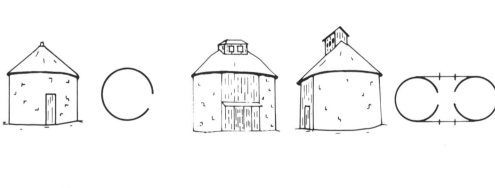

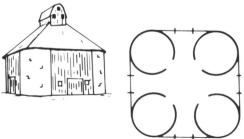

Fig. 6–47 Evolution of masonry corncribs in Iowa

tic masonry or clay tile cribs commonly were built in Iowa, and in some other parts of the Corn Belt, from the 1920s to the 1950s (fig. 6–45). The largest of these cribs are truly enormous, as large as a large house and fully as high (fig. 6–46). Constructed of masonry blocks pierced with rows of narrow slits, these cribs have evolved from simple circular cribs to complex four-chamber structures with overhead bins for shelled corn or small grains and a large cupola to assist loading and ventilation (fig. 6–47). These cribs, in addition to housing great amounts of corn, have the additional advantages of "economy in construction, fire resistance, rat resistance, and permanence, but many provide inadequate natural ventilation."[99]

When corncribs are given the scholarly attention they deserve as architectural forms and as significant elements of the American farm, other types probably will be identified. At the same time, some efforts must be made now to preserve examples of early forms. The ethnic connections of corncribs have not been clearly established, although Scandinavian and German cribs can be identified. It is not unreasonable to expect that other ethnic groups evolved different types.

Hay barracks

Although ethnic relationships are not yet clear for corncribs, the hay barrack is a structure having strong ethnic associations, especially with the Dutch (fig. 6–48).[100] Just as the granary is a specialized structure for storing small grains and the crib for storing corn, so the barracks is for preserving hay and straw.

The structure is simplicity itself, comprised of just four corner posts and a pyramidal or gable roof, with the gable ends enclosed. The building usually had no foundation other than a series of poles laid on the ground to keep the hay or straw from contact with the damp earth. What made the structure unusual was that the roof rested on four movable wooden or metal pegs placed in a series of holes in the four posts. By using a ratcheting jack, the entire roof could be raised or lowered by moving each roof corner, one peg at a time. "The first corner is the most difficult to raise because of the weight of the roof. The last corner is easiest to raise since the upward warping or spring of the roof frame decreases the weight on the unraised corner."[101] Raising or lowering the roof ensured maximum protection for the stored hay or straw (sometimes even grain was stored). Dimensions of the barrack varied normally between twelve and sixteen feet, and occasionally these structures were as large as twenty feet.[102]

Some early barracks were constructed with a raised floor to permit the shelter of one or two cows under the barrack.[103] Generally speaking, the hay barrack was so simple that it could not be converted to other functions and, hence, tended to disappear from the landscape as agricultural conditions changed. Apparently, only a handful of barracks have survived into the middle of the twentieth century (fig. 6–49). The range over which the hay barrack has been reported suggests a connection to northern German immigrants, and even to Ukranians, as well as to the Dutch with whom it has its strongest associations.[104] Among Pennsylvania Germans

Fig. 6–48 The hay barrack (from McTernan)

the hay barracks is known as the *shotscheier* and seems to have been a fairly common feature of their farmsteads.[105] Indeed, a special kind of thatched roof, used only on shotscheier, has been identified, suggesting that these structures were originally all thatch-roofed, as many still are in the Netherlands today.[106]

The hay barracks was known and utilized in other parts of Europe besides the north German plain and Rhine delta. In the Ukraine, for example, it was called an *oborohy*.[107] Furthermore, Peter Wacker has postulated that the simplicity and cheapness of the barrack encouraged its adoption in pioneering areas without strong ethnic associations. These two considerations may explain the unusual pattern of reported occurrence of scattered hay barracks in eastern Massachusetts and Virginia, Maryland and Ohio, in two separate areas of eastern Iowa, in northern Illinois, in western New York, in Rhode

Island, on Prince Edward Island, in southeastern Manitoba, and on Irish farms in eastern Newfoundland.[108] It is likely that other, as-yet-unreported occurrences will be documented in the future. Here again is a material landscape feature that warrants closer scrutiny. Such study might well begin with an examination of the large number of nineteenth-century illustrated county atlases which contain hundreds of drawings of farmsteads.[109]

In western America, where there is greater emphasis on animal raising because of the drier climate, an open-sided hay barn is frequently used to store the larger amounts of hay raised there. Although superficially resembling the hay barrack in that it has open sides, it differs by having a fixed roof, a rectangular plan, and often one closed side facing the prevailing wind direction.

Fig. 6–49 Reported locations and types of hay barracks

Hay derricks

In these western areas, hay (principally alfalfa) was often stored from the beginning of settlement in piles or stacks out in the open with no protection at all. In order to create these stacks, devices were necessary to pile up the hay to reduce spoilage from exposure to the weather.

The first mechanical device to improve on hay stacked by the pitch fork was patented in 1866 by an Iowan, and it was only when pioneer settlement advanced into the drier West that hay stackers and derricks became important features of the cultural landscape.[110]

The hay derrick (fig. 6–50) is a device associated with the Mormons. Indeed, Rick Francaviglia has used it as an index to identify the extent of Mormon settlement.[111]

The evolution of the Mormon hay derrick has been fairly clearly established (fig. 6–51). The earliest version is little more than a vertical pole held up by guy wires (type 1). Hay was raised by ropes

Fig. 6–50 Mormon hay derrick, type 13 (Near Provo, Utah, 1974)

and pulleys with horse power. Somewhat of an improvement was the addition of a horizontal cross-bar (type 2). The great disadvantage of these early derricks was that the hay could only be stacked in one spot at the base of the pole. Providing braces at the bottom of the pole added stability and rigidity (type 3). Modifying the cross-arm to make it movable over a limited radius made possible a larger stack of hay (type 4).

Another series of hay derricks used two vertical poles. The more primitive derrick consisted of two vertical poles with a horizontal cross-arm connecting them (type 5). Somewhat more rigid was a two-pole derrick (type 6), in which the slanting poles were connected at the top as well as by a horizontal cross-arm.

The next advance in design involved a change in the way the cross-arm was attached to the main boom. In earlier

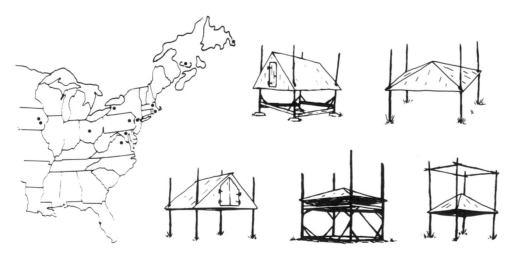

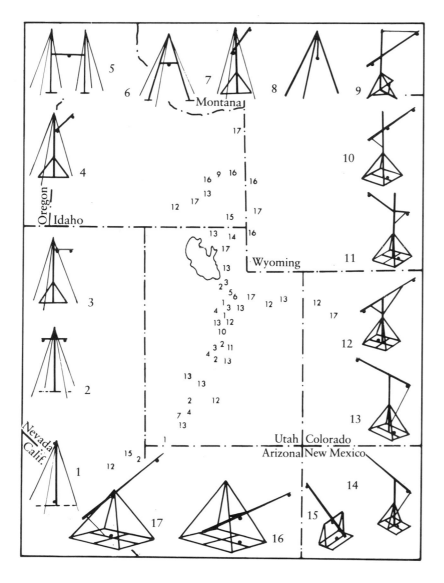

Fig. 6–51 Evolution and diffusion of the Mormon hay derrick. The small numbers represent locations where the various types have been reported.

types the horizontal member was attached by nails, pegs, or an iron collar to the vertical shaft. By substituting an iron chain, the cross-arm was given much greater freedom of movement (type 7). Austin and James Fife suggest that this slight modification opened the way to further elaborations and improvements of the derrick.[112]

A three-pointed support without guy wires (type 8) represents a transitional stage, in which the design of the derrick is shifted from that of a permanently located feature to one that is mobile, enabling it to be moved over short distances. In the mid-nineteenth century, pioneer farms were small and the number of livestock not great. Hence alfalfa production was limited and the entire hay crop could be stored within the barnyard (fig. 6–52). A simple, permanently located derrick was all that was needed. As farms and number of livestock grew, production of alfalfa also expanded, which necessitated stacking hay in the fields for the winter feeding of range cattle. "Under these conditions there was an urgent need for derricks that could be moved with relative ease so that several stacks might be built with the same derrick."[113] The normal method of securing mobility was to create a skid base that could be weighted with boulders or otherwise anchored to the ground at a series of temporary locations. The first bases were triangular, as in figure 6–51, type 9, but these were succeeded by pyramidal bases (type 10).

The next improvement was the introduction of a rotating mast (type 11) to

111

Fig. 6–52 Hay derrick located in barnyard of a Mormon farm (Millard County, Utah, 1967)

Fig. 6–53 Mormon hay derrick, type 12, near Nephi, Utah (1974). The base has been braced with additional supports to better hold the mast which rotates.

replace the earlier fixed ones. Also, in later types the boom is longer and its fulcrum is such that it becomes partially counterbalanced (type 12). The boom is located at the top of the mast (type 13), which is often shortened from earlier types. The base may be symmetrical or it may be constructed to counterbalance the thrust of the hay being lifted (type 14).

A type that lies somewhat out of the direct line of evolutionary development utilizes a counterbalanced base, but the on the horizontal cross-arm and the framing is unlike that of other derricks (type 15). The final elaborations use a large base, four slanting frame poles, and a long, counterbalanced boom. The wide base is such that the derrick can be easily dragged from field to field without danger of upsetting. The boom may be attached to a horizontal cross-bar (type 16), or it may be suspended by a short chain just below the apex of the pyramid formed by the four slanting poles (type 17).[114]

Rick Francaviglia has shown that adoption and use of the hay derrick by Mormon farmers was so strong and tenacious that it was identified by non-Mormons in the West as a Mormon cultural feature.[115] The pattern of distribution of relict hay derricks tends to confirm the Mormon connection since the simplest (i.e., most primitive) forms lie near the heart of the Utah oasis, whereas increasingly complex, and hence later, forms (fig. 6–53) are found at greater distances from the oasis center. The maximum range of the Mormon hay derrick is given in figure 6–54.

One reason for the growing complexity and bulkiness of the hay derrick frame is related to the shift from stacking loose hay to stacking compact bales, which weighed much more per volume. Thus a stronger, pyramidal, braced, four-pole frame became the standard design for the late derricks (fig. 6–55).

Hay stackers

Other folk devices, which functioned quite differently from the Mormon derrick, also have been used to stack hay throughout western North America. These hay stackers may be grouped into five major types, each of different design.

The ram stacker consists of two separate parts—a fan-shaped slide made of long, straight poles of small dimension held aloft at an angle of forty-five degrees by a framework of other poles (fig. 6–56), and a racklike structure in which

Fig. 6–54 Extent of the Mormon hay derrick

Fig. 6–55 Mormon hay derrick, type 16 (Near Vernal, Utah, 1974)

Fig. 6–56 The slide of a ram stacker. Note the gentler slope at the base to facilitate the movement of the ram up the slide. (Near Bridgeland, Utah, 1974)

the hay is held. This is attached to a very long, stout log plunger or ram (fig. 6–57), which is pushed by a team of horses up the slide until the rack tips its load of hay onto the stack.

Closely related to the ram stacker is another device also using a sloping ramp, the beaverslide hay stacker. Although its name is widely thought to be derived from some fanciful reference to beavers and the "slide they might use down a steep bank," the name is actually a shortened form of "Beaverhead County Slide Stacker" which refers to its place of origin in the Big Hole valley of western Montana.[116] The beaverslide stacker consists of a slide made of long, straight poles or narrow boards placed within a framework of heavier poles and supports to maintain a forty-five degree angle, and a two-sided hay basket which is pulled by a cable-and-pulley arrangement up the slide (fig. 6–58).

Unlike other types of hay stackers, the beaverslide has been given some study as a settlement landscape feature. Its point of origin is known, the various modifications have been traced, and the pattern of its diffusion has been studied (fig. 6–59). The advantages of the bea-

Fig. 6–57 The ram portion of the ram hay stacker

verslide stacker include its low costs, simplicity of design and repair, ease of use, ability to build large stacks rapidly, and suitability for wet and rugged territory.[117] Its principal disadvantage is its susceptibility to damage with heavy usage.

A third type of hay stacker is called the *overshot*. It functions much like a catapult. The large hay basket is mounted on two long poles, the ends of which are attached to and pivot on the base frame. The base consists of a rectangular arrangement of skids on which a pyramidal superstructure is mounted (fig. 6–60). By a series of cables and pulleys, the hay basket is raised in an arc, up and over the base and framework. The overshot stacker enjoyed wide popularity in western United States and Canada, probably because it could be used to build stacks of different sizes.[118]

The swinging stacker, a fourth type, bears a superficial resemblance to the Mormon derrick. Its base consists of a pyramidal frame of skids and poles. To the top of this a long counterbalanced pole is affixed. At the long end of the pole is the hay basket, and at the shorter end is a wooden box or frame constructed to hold boulders and to act as a counterweight to the loaded hay basket. The hay load is swung sideways and elevated, with the great advantage being that the hay can be deposited in almost any part of the stack.[119] Another advantage is that the swinging stacker can work more rapidly than other types of stackers.

Finally, at a somewhat late date, a de-

Fig. 6–58 A beaverslide hay stacker. The vertical frame at the left is a backboard which helps to form the stack. (Near Steamboat Springs, Colorado, 1974)

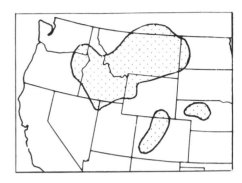

Fig. 6–59 Extent of the beaverslide hay stacker

Fig. 6–60 An overshot hay stacker next to a modern hay rake (Near Woodruff, Utah, 1977)

vice called a *combination stacker* or *jay-hawker* was evolved.[120] It combined the functions of the sweep rake and the stacker in a single unit and resembled a very crude version of the modern front-end dirt mover. The hay basket was placed in front, and the base and pyramidal frame were mounted on wheels. The stacker operated "by being driven over the ground. An elevating mechanism is engaged when the stacker is about 80 to 100 feet from the stack, and the rake with its load is then lifted, as the stacker advances, until it is high enough for the load to be deposited upon the stack." The combination stacker offered several advantages over earlier types: it was highly mobile, no time was lost in moving or setting up, hay could be delivered to any part of the stack and from any direction, which was important if the wind shifted during the stacking operation. The significant disadvantages were a rather low daily capacity and higher initial cost than other stacker types.[121]

The use of hay stackers gradually has declined since World War II. On the more prosperous farms and ranches, mobile hay balers have come to replace the hay stackers, since these greatly reduced the manpower required to harvest hay. As a consequence, hay stackers are increasingly relegated to the smaller, poorer ranches and farms in more remote locations. As with other structures and devices elsewhere, the commercially produced is steadily crowding out the traditionally crafted item. In at least one location, however, the introduction of the hay baler established an important connection with folk building.

114

Baled hay as a construction material.
The Sand Hills of Nebraska were opened to homesteading in 1904. The bleak, grass-covered sand dunes offered even less in the way of building materials than had the open prairies a generation or two earlier. Wood was virtually unknown within this vast area, and even today no railroads and very few roads penetrate the region, so that lumber shipments were not feasible. Several factors mitigated against the use of sod construction, which had been a common response of the pioneer settlers on the prairies (see vol. 1, chap. 8). First, the sod construction skills had not been used much since the 1890s and to some extent had been lost. Second, the oxen, ideal for pulling the sod-cutting plows, had been replaced largely by horses or mules. Most important of all, the sandy soils made exceptionally poor sods.[122] The only material available in abundance in this vast sandy landscape was the wild grass hay which supported the cattle herds, and which made a sparse settlement possible here. To this material the homesteaders turned to produce a method of house building not found elsewhere (fig. 6–61). Stationary hay balers and presses could produce hay bales one to two feet in cross section and of varying length. Between three and four feet was the standard, but half-length bales were also used, since the bales were stacked much as bricks or sods were. In some instances a mortar was used to bind the bales, but sometimes the bales were merely wedged tightly together and held in place by long wooden dowels inserted vertically through the baled-hay wall. Wooden door and window frames were also held

by shorter wooden dowels driven into the packed hay. The wall's exterior surface was finished by applying a coat of stucco, cement, or plaster, often placed over a netting of chicken wire.

Foundations were of concrete, floors of concrete or wood, and roofs of light lumber framing covered with various commercially made roofing materials. A large number of baled-hay houses were covered with a hipped roof, which had the advantages over other roof forms of minimizing horizontal stress on the side walls and of permitting all

Fig. 6–61 Extent of baled-hay construction. The dotted lines enclose the Sand Hills of Nebraska. (From Welsch)

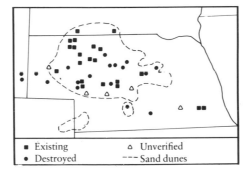

■ Existing △ Unverified
● Destroyed --- Sand dunes

four walls to be built to the same height. However, some of these houses (fig. 6–62) closely approximate the German-Russian house (see vol. 1, chap. 10). Outside the Sand Hills' environment, baled-hay construction did not prove to be a viable building technique.

Fig. 6–62 House constructed of baled-hay walls covered with stucco, built 1925 in Arthur, Nebraska (1983)

Buildings connected with livestock

A final group of rural secondary structures has a close connection with the various animals found on the typical farm. Some of these are the shelters that house the animals, others are for processing animal products, and, finally, there are those structures—the walls, hedges, and fences—that confine and separate farm animals. Often these structures have a form closely related to their function, although many are not sufficiently distinctive to warrant much discussion here.

The milk house

One facility often recognized by its location is the milk house (fig. 6–63). Originally milk was cooled in the spring house (see above), but as dairy farm operations grew, both commercial standards and government regulations forced an improvement in milk cooling methods.

Milk as drawn from the cow has a temperature of approximately ninety degrees Fahrenheit and becomes damaged after a few hours, if not properly cooled, because of bacterial action. Since bacteria require a temperature of fifty-five degrees or warmer to grow rapidly, milk and cream should be held at fifty degrees or lower. . . . The sooner milk is cooled after having been drawn from the cow, the longer it will keep, consequently quick and adequate cooling is always essential.[123]

Usually rectangular and gable-roofed, the milk house is an unmistakable trademark of the dairy farm, located as close as possible to the barn itself—so close that it is often an appendage of the barn. The milk house generally is small, just large enough to provide a cooling container, washing facilities, and storage space for the milk cans. Although most of the early milk houses were constructed of wood, concrete and tile blocks are more suitable because of the constant moisture in the building. As time passed, the milk house was subjected to ever greater restrictions as governmental regulations were strengthened and tightened. The evolution of other secondary structures was not given the same attention.

Chicken coops, sheep folds, and pig pens

The larger farm animals normally are housed in the main barns. Occasionally, a special barn is given over to some of these animals, especially on very large farms. Smaller farm animals, in contrast, are usually kept in separate structures. Generally, these are smaller, undistinguished rectangular buildings with shed or gable roofs. On secondary farm buildings, the shed roof has the advantages of simplicity of design, ease of construction, and economy. A further advantage is that all the water falling on the roof is thrown to the downslope side of the building and the structure can be located so that this is toward the outside of the farm building complex. The gable roof has the important advantages of shedding rainwater and snow more rapidly, and of permitting use of a loft, which provides additional storage space

with little additional wall construction, and an insulating area important in maintaining building temperature in winter.

In the earliest period, chickens were permitted to wander at will. They roosted in trees and barn lofts and made their nests in the hay mows. Gradually farmers began to give more attention to poultry as income from them and their eggs increased. Shelter particularly improved, especially to provide winter protection. Sometimes an old shed was converted to house chickens, or a rough frame structure was built. Many of these early, rough structures were poorly lit and ventilated. By the end of the nineteenth century, farmers, realizing that additional windows improved the chicken house by admitting beneficial sunlight, built two-and three-story (or even higher) chicken houses with multiple small windows, particularly along south facing walls. "The next step in poultry-house construction was a radical one, the change being made from the closed warm house to the open or curtain-front type, in which the temperature was kept as low as that out of doors, and in which an abundance of fresh air was provided."[124]

The exterior of the poultry house could take many forms. The interior could also exhibit a variety of arrangements, although certain features were necessary. In one area, a series of horizontal roosts had to be provided, and in another, nesting boxes for each hen. In still a third place, provision had to be made for a dust bath, while the feeding and watering arrangements occupied the remaining space.

One of the more distinctive features which marked the poultry house was the chicken walk, a device permitting chickens to enter the roosts directly. "It consisted of a wide board with thin strips or laths nailed across at intervals of six to eight inches to prevent slippage as the chicken proceeded upward."[125] Other buildings providing shelter to small farm animals have no such distinctive or easily recognizable exterior features.

The most important function of the swine house, or pig pen, is to give protection against the cold. Almost any one-story building will do, if an enclosed feeding yard is also provided. Typically, the pig pen was located as far away from the farmhouse as possible because of flies and odor.[126] The size of the structure depends upon the number of animals to be housed. Interior arrangements generally are simple, with an access aisle along one long side of the building to allow for easy feeding. The balance of the structure is made up of individual pens each accommodating one or two animals. In some instances, an ell is provided for slaughtering operations.

Another animal requiring some care, and hence usually sheltered in a separate building, is the sheep. "During the winter season, the keeping of sheep requires much care and skill, and, with a large flock, but little success can be had without a good sheep barn."[127]

Providing shelter from extreme exposure conserved both body weight and feed, but if closely confined in quarters that were too warm, sheep suffered ill effects.[128] Therefore, the sheep fold had to be a substantial structure, yet partially open to an exercise and feeding yard. Most important of all, the sheep fold had to be commodious.

Unlike pig pens, the sheep barn very often consisted of two stories, with the ground floor housing the animals, while the upper floor provided storage space for straw used for bedding the sheep and hay for feed. Such structures were rather late developments; earlier shelter was provided by simple windbreaks and temporary enclosures.

One of the most important aspects of the sheep fold was the kind of fencing that defined the exercise yard. It had to be strong and tight. Usually it was made of sawn boards. Elsewhere on the farm, fencing was among the most conspicuous elements of the rural landscape. The next chapter discusses fences, walls, and hedges in the various sections of North America.

Fig. 6–63   A milk house built of cement blocks and nestled into the angle between the barn and the drive ramp (Holmes County, Ohio, 1978)

No rural cultural element is so widely distributed as the farm fence, yet fencing was not always a common feature of early settlements in North America. Only gradually, as the population grew, did the need for fencing become imperative. Initially, farmers who raised field crops or grew vegetables were expected to fence in their fields or plots, in order to keep grazing animals out (fig. 7–1). Not until the middle of the nineteenth century did the situation change so that fencing to keep animals in became their owners' responsibility. As agriculture became more intensive and more mixed in mid-nineteenth century, laws became ever more restrictive and specific about the necessity of erecting and maintaining fences. The office of fence viewer steadily gained importance in this period. These officials were charged with the responsibility of ensuring that local fences were adequate, and they had the power to levy fines for lack of compliance.

In addition to growing population densities and increased urbanization, the spread of railway rights-of-way across the country was a powerful factor in extending farm and range fences. Cow catchers on the front of locomotives were not nearly as effective as cattle-tight fences. "The fence is a significant index of settlement stage and character, as well as often being a clue to the physical environment. Few landscape elements combine so finely the characteristics of the resource base, the cultural matrix and its historical antecedents."[1]

The fence is also an expression of the personality of the individual farmer. "Fences and walls spoke of the farmer's domain on earth, his individuality within the community."[2] They express concepts of private ownership and individual stewardship.[3] In this connection, they are clearly symbols of the material success of each farmer. Indeed, in some places such as the Kentucky Bluegrass Basin or the northern Virginia piedmont, a whitewashed, board fence has come to signify the gentleman stock breeder or farmer.[4]

Brush and stump fences

The most primitive fence of North America, although not necessarily the earliest, is one that may be called either a *brush fence* or a *deadwood fence*. It consists merely of piles of the dead branches and trunks of trees removed during the process of land clearing. In the early stages of settlement, the brush fence offers a means of disposing of unwanted materials, and at the same time converting them into a serviceable facility. Unfortunately, its disadvantages outweigh any advantages. The brush fence harbors all manner of rodents and other agricultural pests and it can be a serious fire hazard.[5] Even more important is the great amount of land taken up by this type of fence, effectively reducing the area under cultivation.

Closely related to brush or deadwood fences is the stump fence, composed of uprooted tree stumps "generally upended with the rosette of interlacing roots facing the outside of the property."[6] Halloch Raup has suggested that stump fences were particularly numerous in the Allegheny plateau of Pennsylvania and New York,[7] but they certainly occurred in virtually all forested, pioneering areas.

7   Fences, Walls, and Hedges

Stone fences and stone walls

Another type of fence closely associated with land clearing is comprised of sub-angular glacial field boulders (fig. 7–2). Restricted primarily to areas of glacial deposition such as New England, New York, Ontario, Michigan, Wisconsin, and Minnesota, the stone fence, or stone-pile fence, as it is sometimes called, has not proven to be a very effective barrier. Another defect is the considerable width required in order to achieve an adequate height to restrict animals. Consequently, the stone fence is more of a boundary marker than a barrier.

The stone fence should not be confused with the stone wall. The latter may be laid up in mortar or not, takes up much less room, and can be an effective barrier. The stone wall consists of more or less flat stones, which are usually limestone or sandstone fragments (fig. 7–3). Only on lands underlain by limestone is soil normally fertile enough to warrant expending the labor involved in constructing a stone wall and maintaining it in good order. Furthermore, limestone easily fractures along relatively straight planes. Thus, rocks of generally uniform size and flat sides are widely available in these areas. The Bluegrass Basin of Kentucky is one of the better known areas of limestone wall fencing.[8]

One exception to the general rule that stone walls are restricted to limestone areas may be found in northeastern Pennsylvania, where a thin layer of glacial deposition covers the sandstone bedrock and provides the required soil fertility to support the efforts needed to build stone walls. Here, New England traditions have been employed to construct sturdy sandstone slab walls. The wall itself is built up of two straight faces with the irregular space between

Fig. 7–2 Stone-pile fences typical of glaciated areas (northern Oneida County, New York, 1975)

filled with rock fragments and rubble. In order to exclude as much water as possible, the wall is capped with large, flat, overhanging stones.[9]

With all stone walls, the great advantage of durability is balanced by the enormous labor involved in construction, and by the relative immobility of the structure. Other fences can be disassembled and shifted if field boundaries change; the stone wall is not easily moved. However, the stone wall does not have to a be permanent feature. In the 1920s and 1930s as local roads throughout the country began to be paved, the demand for crushed stone for road surfacing material led many landowners everywhere to sacrifice their stone walls. Later on, a similar pressure from stone masons constructing fire-

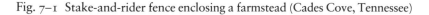

Fig. 7–1 Stake-and-rider fence enclosing a farmstead (Cades Cove, Tennessee)

Fig. 7–4 The chock-and-log fence

Fig. 7–3 A stone wall composed of lime-stone fragments laid up with no mortar (Door County, Wisconsin, 1980)

places and chimneys in new rural and suburban houses led to the further de-pletion of stone walls in northeastern Pennsylvania,[10] and probably in other areas as well.

The log-and-chock fence

In earliest times, because of the abun-dant forest cover in eastern North America, wood was the cheapest and easiest material to use for fencing. Hence, most fences before the middle of the nineteenth century were made en-tirely of wood, and at least partly of wood, even afterwards.

One of the simplest solutions to fenc-ing pioneer fields was to use the trees that covered the potential fields. Thus not only was the fence built, but the land was cleared of its forest cover as well. In order to reduce labor as much as possible, the trees were used as logs with as little modification or trimming as convenient. Stability was provided by cutting some logs into two to three foot chocks which were inserted, more or less at right angles, between the logs (fig. 7–4). Sometimes incipient saddle notches were quickly cut to add addi-tional stability. Chock-and-log fences may have been built in many originally forested regions, and were common enough in the colonial period in the Hudson valley to draw the notice of famed Swedish traveler, Pehr Kalm.[11] Today, perhaps a few of these fences re-main, but they are always in inaccessi-ble areas.[12] The basic problem of the chock-and-log fence was recognized as early as the eighteenth century: "Many fences of the same size and value could be made from the timber used in one log fence provided the timber were split. . . ."[13] Splitting the logs produced the rail fence.

120

The rail fence

The fence that has come to be most closely identified with eastern pioneering areas is the rail fence (fig. 7–5), also sometimes called a *worm, snake,* or *zig-zag fence*. These latter names refer to the crooked pattern that the fence makes, the result of a necessity to alternate directions in order to maintain stability. The angle at which rails crossed was about 120 degrees, thus requiring much more material than if the fence ran in a straight line. In glaciated areas, the angle formed by two sections of the rail fence could be used as a place to pitch stones or boulders turned up in each spring's plowing, but the space was otherwise often wasted.[14]

Because of its crooked pattern, enormous amounts of land had to be given over to the rail fence. To enclose one

Fig. 7–6 Rail fence, with upright supports providing additional stability (Near Sharpsburg, Maryland, 1979)

Fig. 7–5 A rail fence in the Great Smoky Mountains National Park (1975)

square mile with rail fencing requires the use of almost five acres of land. "If all fences in America were of this type, an area slightly larger than the entire state of Indiana would be involved."[15] Regardless of whether these estimates are totally accurate, the point is clear that rail fences consume great amounts of land and must be counted as wasteful.

The rails of the rail fence can be small saplings or they can be split lengthwise from any straight tree trunk. To reduce deterioration, the lowest rails often are supported on field boulders. These "rest" stones sometimes remain in place long after the wooden parts of the fence have disappeared, and Amos Long re-

ports they are occasionally used by surveyors in Pennsylvania to locate lost boundaries.[16] The weight of the rails alone supports the true rail fence. Care is usually taken to place the largest rails on the bottom to ensure stability, but the stack is seldom absolutely stable.

An improvement to the basic rail fence is the addition of vertical supports at each rail crossing (fig. 7–6). This solves, for the most part, the problem of keeping the rails in place even in the face of windstorms and milling stock. In later versions, the tops of the vertical supports are held together by wire loops.

The origins of the rail fence are obscure; it dates from the earliest colonial times but apparently has no clear European antecedents.[17] Its beginnings are an intriguing question that needs further research. One of the other names for the rail fence is the *Virginia fence*, which may suggest an origin.[18] because the rail fence was quite common in the Middle Atlantic states during and after the colonial period. In 1871, about 80 percent of all fences in Virginia were of the rail type. No other fence type had so wide a distribution throughout the entire country in the nineteenth century before the introduction of wire fencing. It was so common as to be regarded by the U. S. Commissioner of Agriculture as "the national fence."[19] Today, however, the rail fence remains only in the most backward parts of North America, especially in remote areas of the southern Appalachians,[20] and on the fringes of the Laurentian Shield.

The stake-and-rider, Irish, and sawyer fences

The rail fence supported by uprights requires digging post holes, so its construction involves both time and expense. Much simpler to erect is the stake-and-rider fence (fig. 7–7), in which support is provided by a pair of crossed stakes requiring no post-hole digging, although they are often hammered a few inches into the ground. A sturdy rail, the *rider*, is laid on top of the fence in the crotches of the stakes. The lower part of the fence is made exactly like the rail fence. The stake-and-rider fence is easy and cheap to erect, and it solves the problem of stability by providing a top rail difficult to dislodge. In some instances a rock is placed in the crotch atop the rider to help anchor it.

Somewhat similar in appearance to the stake-and-rider is a structure called the *Irish fence* (fig. 7–8). It consists of a series of long poles or logs, one end of which is supported in the crotch of crossed stakes, wired or nailed together. The opposite end passes beneath two adjacent stake crosses and rests upon the ground.[21] Such a fence has the virtue of simplicity of design, ease of construction, and economy of both materials and space. The principal drawback is the need to rigidly fasten the crossed stakes in some more or less permanent fashion.

Another term applied to this fencing type is the *Shanghai fence*.[22] The origin of both names is obscure, warranting additional research. In fact, the entire subject of fence nomenclature is worthy of additional study. Such work might illuminate the ethnic connections of these commonplace yet vital rural features. Wilbur Zelinsky, for example, has noted at least twenty-five synonyms for the rail fence recorded in New England.[23]

Very close in form to the Irish fence is one called the *sawyer fence*. In place of logs or poles, the main components are slabs of wood left over from sawmill operations, and this accounts for the name. The geographical location of this fence is in the immediate vicinity of sawmills. Because the slabs were shorter than the poles or logs of the Irish fence, the angle at which they were set was much greater.[24] Sawyer fences were never very popular or widely used, probably because of their construction. Inexplicably, the Irish fence also never became very widely utilized. Perhaps it needed too much timber, even though it was more economical in that regard than the rail fence.

The post-and-rail fence

In any event, neither the Irish nor sawyer fences became as popular as the post-and-rail fence (fig. 7–9). The use of the post-and-rail fence can be traced across northeastern North America. Statistics from the *Report of the Commissioner of Agriculture for the Year 1871* show a concentration in the lower peninsula of Michigan, in New Jersey,

Fig. 7–7 The stake-and-rider fence

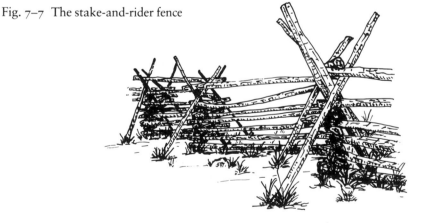

Fig. 7–8 The Irish fence

northern Pennsylvania, much of New York, and northern New England (fig. 7–10).[25] Wilbur Zelinsky has also noted the continuation of the post-and-rail fence in the St. Lawrence valley of Canada.[26] Throughout these areas today, only widely scattered relicts of the post-and-rail fence remain, although occasionally a farmer, both in these areas and elsewhere (see fig. 7–9), will take the trouble to erect this type of fence. In such cases, it is usually enhanced by a strand of barbed wire along the top rail.

Economical of timber, the post-and-rail fence consists of two or, less often, three split rails mortised into upright posts. Other advantages include its lower space requirements and hence its greater facility for weed control.[27] Balancing these advantages are the much greater amounts of time and labor required in construction. Mortises have to be cut into the posts by drilling double holes with a hand auger. Also, the ends of the rails normally have to be slightly tapered to fit into the post mortises. Most important of all, holes have to be laboriously dug for every post. Furthermore, in early years before chemical treatment, posts had to be replaced and new holes dug every few years.

Fig. 7–9 A post-and-rail fence (Near Salem, Ohio, 1981)

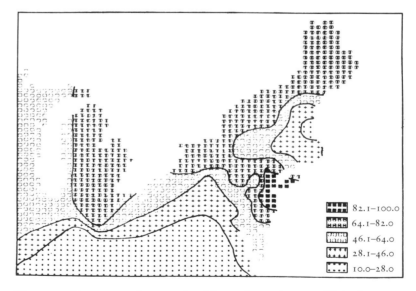

82.1–100.0
64.1–82.0
46.1–64.0
28.1–46.0
10.0–28.0

Fig. 7–10 Percentage of post-and-rail fences in northeastern United States, 1871. The original data from the *Annual Report of the Commissioner of Agriculture* has been processed by computer to generate this map. Such techniques will be used increasingly in the analysis of material cultural settlement features in the future.

Fence posts

Regardless of the type of fence, certain factors have to be taken into consideration in estimating the potential life of wooden fence posts.[28] Not only are certain woods, such as locust, cedar, and Osage orange, more durable, the conditions under which they are prepared are important. The amount of seasoning the post receives before being set in the ground, as well as soil and drainage, and the local climatic conditions to which it is subjected, bear on its life. The size of the post, as well as the season when it is cut, affects its rate of deterioration. Larger posts and those cut in spring before the sap begins to flow are more durable than smaller posts and those cut while the sap is still running.[29] Balancing this, however, is the knowledge that posts cut in the spring after the sap begins to flow can be stripped of their bark much more easily. Furthermore, in pioneer times the bark could be sold to local tanneries for tannic acid needed to cure leather and thereby provide a supplemental source of income.[30]

In the slate belt of eastern Pennsylvania, farmers attempted to solve the problem of fence-post deterioration by using discarded slabs of slate left over from the quarrying of roof slate.[31] Pieces of slate "about six or seven feet long, two or three inches thick, and fifteen or so inches wide, were morticed to take rails," but although they were more durable than wooden posts, they still succumbed to frost damage and weathering after a time.[32] In the slate region of Vermont, a somewhat different approach was used in the nineteenth century. Here the slabs were set into the earth close together, almost touching one another, and the wooden rails were dispensed with altogether.[33]

The Smoky Hills region of north central Kansas is a third area of stone fence posts. In this instance, however, the stone is a limestone, "light buff in color with rusty brown streaks."[34] Soft and easily shaped when quarried from near-surface deposits, the stone hardens on continued exposure to air. Although quarrying of these posts largely stopped after the turn of the century, thousands of these durable sentinels still dot the region.

The board fence

Post-and-rail fences were constructed of timber posts and split rails. After the advent of dimension lumber in the nineteenth century and the perfection of nail mills to produce nails in large quantities, the board fence (fig. 7–11) gained widespread popularity. Sometimes the posts were square lumber pieces, although timber posts continued to be used. The horizontal members usually consisted of four boards nailed to the posts. The boards often were nailed in such a fashion that little space was left between the bottom two. This considerably lessened the danger of injuries to the legs of large stock.[35] Often a slanting, side brace was added to provide additional strength, and sometimes a crowning piece was nailed from the flat top of one post to another, providing a kind of narrow roof for the fence and offering some weather protection.

Of sawn lumber, the board fence looked raw and unattractive unless it was stained, whitewashed, or painted. Because of the labor this entailed, the board fence has never been built extensively. It does function to restrain animals better than many other types of fencing, and consequently has been associated with livestock raising regions.[36] Indeed, it has developed as a sort of prestige item in many areas where affluent owners raise stock, especially valuable ranch stock or thoroughbred horses. The Bluegrass Basin in Kentucky, the piedmont of Maryland and northern Virginia, and smaller, more scattered stock-raising areas in the West and Midwest have particularly high concentrations of board fences. In virtually all agricultural areas, board

Fig. 7–11 The board fence

fences are used to enclose feed lots.

Combinations of several fence types are a characteristic of farmyards, although they are perhaps not quite so common as in the late nineteenth century. Views taken from county atlases frequently show three or four types of fencing in close proximity to the farmstead (fig. 7–12). Fields often were fenced with rail, stake-and-rider, or post-and-rail fences, whereas barnyards were bounded by board fences, and the farmhouse might be set off by a wooden picket fence, or even one of iron pickets.

Fencing in the dry western areas of North America

As settlement progressed westward in the nineteenth century, the countryside that was being occupied was drier and drier land. The abundant forests of the East were left behind, and wood, the most common fencing material, disappeared. As was true with housing materials, the settlers began to employ local substitutes. In the desert of the extreme southwest, plants such as the long, thin ocotillo were used to form a palisade.[37] Also in these areas, *jacal* construction (see vol. 1, chap. 8) was often employed for corrals and stock enclosures (fig. 7–13).

On the less dry but treeless interior plains, instances of sod fencing have been reported, but this material was never widely popular. For one thing, enormous labor was required to construct a sod fence.

Two parallel furrows were ploughed so that the sod turned over and lay side by side. Sods

Fig. 7–12 Sketch of the J. S. King farmstead, Clayton County, Iowa, from A. T. Andreas, *Illustrated Atlas of the State of Iowa* (Chicago: Andreas Atlas Co., 1875). In addition to rail and board fences, the sketch shows a wooden picket fence in front of the house, a very typical arrangement. Nineteenth-century county atlases often contain similar illustrations and are one of the best sources for information on cultural landscape features.

Fig. 7–13 A *jacal* fence. The light horizontal poles are held between split upright posts, fastened together with wire. (Fredericksburg, Texas, 1982)

from adjacent furrows were carried by hand to this base and laid in position on top, taking care to break the joints and to taper the wall gradually towards the top. These fences or walls were generally built three and a half feet high. . . . Usually a deep furrow was run along each side of the fence after it was built turning the soil so that it lay along the base.[38]

The sod fence could be a formidable structure. Mary Rice describes it as typically eight and a half feet across at its base and some two feet wide at the top. It stood four feet high with two-and-a-half foot ditches flanking it on either side.[39]

Obviously, sod would not solve the fencing problems of the vast plains. As early as the 1840s it was being abandoned in favor of other fencing,[40] although such earth barriers continued to be erected in Nebraska right up to the end of the nineteenth century.[41] As long as farms were widely scattered and herds could range freely, the fencing problem was not acute. But as settlement intensified, two factors were at work to make it so. First, farms steadily became smaller, and thus the amount of fencing required per acre increased. Second, as settlement proceeded westward, the productivity of the land decreased just as fencing costs were increasing.[42] The types of fencing employed in the East (rail, stake-and-rider, post-and-rail, and board) continued to be used at first in the Midwest, but they soon proved much too costly.

A further complicating factor was the expansion of the railroads, whose rights-of-way came to crisscross the prairies, and in the process became an attraction for thousands of range animals who collected there at various times of the year "in search of greener grass, shelter from winds, and higher dryer ground." The railroads, thus, became the agency for fencing much of the prairie, since it was easier to require railway companies to enclose their tracks or otherwise be liable for injuries to livestock than it was to require the thousands of settlers along the rights-of-way to fence in their livestock.[43] Consequently, board fences of lumber shipped to their point of use by the railroad itself became commonplace just before the Civil War.[44] This type of fence did not solve the problem, however. It was costly, easily damaged by recurrent prairie fires, vulnerable to strong prairie winds, and, in winter, often caused snow to accumulate in banks on the tracks.[45]

On the drier margins of the prairies generally, and to a limited extent elsewhere in the Midwest, the conflict between stock grazing and crop raising was solved by the institution of the herd law, which required the confining of livestock or their herding by attendants at all times. The herders were responsible not only for the animals, but for any damage they might do to standing crops. In 1875 in Kansas, for example, the herd law was generally in effect west of the ninety-seventh meridian and in localized areas even to the east of it.[46] The herd law was most effective in areas where crop production was limited. As settlements by small-scale farmers became more common, other solutions had to be sought.

The Osage orange and other hedges

The European practice of planting hedgerows was, of course, known to early North American settlers, but had never caught on, probably because of the abundance of wood in the eastern parts of the continent. Early French traders noted the use of Osage orange wood by Indians in the lower Midwest for making hunting bows and named the wood *bois d'arc*.[47] By the 1840s, seed was being sent from Texas and nearby areas to Illinois for experimentation and trials.[48] Central Illinois became the center from which propagation of hedges proceeded, although seed continued to be supplied from the Texas area. The normal process was for the seed to be shipped to companies in Illinois, whose salesmen distributed the seed throughout the Midwest (fig. 7–14).

By 1869 Osage orange hedges were firmly established as a fencing type in the central Midwest. They were particularly conspicuous in southeastern Nebraska in the 1860s,[49] and by 1871 had become the leading fence type in Kansas.[50] In that year the three states with the largest totals of Osage orange hedges were Illinois, Iowa, and Kansas. The use of hedges continued to increase in some parts of the area until almost the turn of the century, and throughout the region hedges were important landscape features until World War I.

The range of the Osage orange hedge was limited by several different factors. To the south, the wooded Salem Plateau of Missouri provided material for wooden fences, as was also the case for areas to the east. On the west, rainfall was too unreliable and generally insuf-

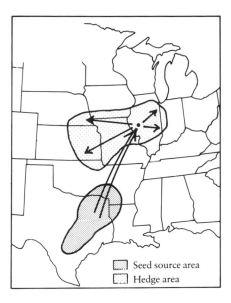

Fig. 7–14 The diffusion of Osage orange hedges in the nineteenth century (after Humphrey and Winberry)

ficient to permit the growth of the hedge. The northern boundary was determined by the severe winter temperatures. In these northern regions, the willow usually replaced the Osage orange, although not to the same extent.[51]

The expansion of Osage orange hedges was abruptly terminated by the Civil War, when the supply of seeds was cut off.[52] Willow was introduced as a substitute, but the results were mixed. Other plants often used for hedging included English hawthorne, privet, cockspur, buckthorn, crabapple, honey locust, buffalo berry, yucca, and Cherokee rose.[53]

The hedge was more than a simple bar-

rier. It offered shelter from cold winds to both stock and the farmstead itself. At the same time, it could screen out the barnyard or any other undesirable feature. Hedges were ornamental and had no dangerous aspects like ditches, barbs, or pointed pickets. Other positive characteristics of hedges were their low maintenance costs and beauty, the shelter they provided for beneficial birds, and the "hygrometic advantage" of breaking the force of the wind and thereby reducing the rate of evaporation.[54]

By way of contrast, certain quite important disadvantages of hedges were at work to prevent their widespread adoption. One of the more serious problems associated with them was that as they grew, they blocked out the sunlight necessary for crops in adjacent fields. The difficulty was most acute on the north sides of east–west trending hedges.[55]

Other shortcomings were their susceptibility to frost, the care that had to be exercised in planting, the necessity to cut the hedges back regularly in order to promote dense growth, the fact that they harbored vermin and that they had to be protected with a fence for the three to five years they took to develop.[56] Some attention, too, had to be paid to two techniques for ensuring dense growth. *Layering* was the term applied to the bending of "branches sideways and interweaving them till the entire hedge [looked] like a huge green rope." *Plashing* referred to "cutting part of the branches and entwining them with those remaining upright to close any gaps."[57] A final and most significant disadvantage of the hedge was that once planted and grown, it could not be shifted.[58]

Barbed-wire fences

Barbed-wire fencing (fig. 7–15), which largely replaced hedges, did not have the same problem of permanency. It could be rolled up and reerected with relative ease in a new location.

Barbed wire was not the first kind of wire fence. During most of the first half of the nineteenth century, farmers had been experimenting with smooth, iron-wire fences. These did not prove successful for several reasons. The iron wire snapped in cold weather, sagged in hot weather, rusted rapidly, and broke when livestock strained against it.[59] The introduction of galvanized wire solved some of these problems and the invention of barbed wire solved others. "The twist and the barb are the two major important features of barbed wire." Twisting the two strands of wire solved the expansion and contraction problem associated with straight-wire fencing. The twisted barbed wire, which is in fact a sort of spring, will "expand and contract without becoming loose and without breaking."[60]

Barbed wire was not adopted widely immediately. Early opposition, apart from the feeling that one or two thin strands were too flimsy to contain stock, centered on the rather opposite ideas that barbed wire was too cruel and inhumane, that stock would be cut, and that screw-worm infection would likely develop in the resultant wounds.[61] In some states the use of barbed wire was declared illegal for several years after its introduction.[62] As a result of these neg-

127

Fig. 7–15 Silhouette of a barbed-wire fence with rough-cut posts (Oneida County, New York, 1958)

ative reactions, the impact of barbed wire in the eastern Midwest, where it was introduced in the late 1870s, was slow to be realized.[63] Further west and a few years later, barbed-wire fences had come into their own and their impact was immense.

"Probably no other single invention of the nineteenth century had such a profound effect on the lives of people on the land as did barbed wire."[64] It enabled the vast interior plains of North America to be effectively occupied and uti-

lized (fig. 7–16). At the same time, the expanding cattle industry, the initial base of western settlement, was transformed from a primitive frontier activity into a modern industry. Small-scale operations were forced out, and cattle raising moved further westward where there was good grass, but where water was so scarce that tanks and wells had to be constructed. The quality of stock improved, both because water was dependable as a result of these facilities, and because the cost of the facilities meant that attention had to be paid to maintaining only the better animals. Finally, fencing allowed animals to be segregated so that indiscriminate breeding was prevented and herd quality was thus improved.[65]

The early center of barbed-wire modification and production was in north central Illinois, particularly around De Kalb.[66] Of 394 early patents issued for

barbed-wire fencing, 176 were issued to Illinois inventors.[67] No other area had such a significant concentration. Ultimately, barbed wire came to be employed throughout the entire continent as an effective enclosure, but it was on the drier margins of the plains that it was used almost exclusively. Its advantages included its strength, durability, cheapness, ease of erection, the fact that it occupied very little space, did not shade standing crops, and did not harbor noxious weeds, insects, rodents, or other pests.[68] Counterbalancing these favorable features were several significant disadvantages. First, stock often were wounded by barbs, particularly in the early days, and screw-worm infection frequently resulted. Second, animals were often killed in sizable numbers if lightning struck the wires, because cattle tended to collect along fence lines during thunderstorms. Finally, barbed-wire fences prevented cattle from moving in heavy snowstorms or blizzards, often trapping them so that they froze to death.

Actually, this latter disaster represented only the most extreme situation. Very often barbed-wire fences, called *drift fences,* were erected to keep range cattle under control. Previously this had been done by line riders, who "followed imaginary lines established by 'range rights'—the unwritten code of the cattle frontier."[69] In some instances, cattle were reported to have "drifted" as much as 200 miles in just a few days, driven before a raging snowstorm.[70] The problem of cattle drifting was not significant until the ranges became overstocked. Then, drifters threatened to destroy the home ranges further southward. By 1881 the first drift fence had

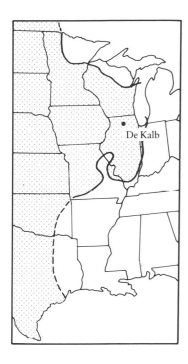

Fig. 7–16 Map of the area in which barbed-wire fencing predominated over other types of fences, 1916 (from Humphrey)

been erected and others followed quickly, always running east and west to block the southward movement of range cattle.

In Texas by 1883, not only had drift fences become common, so had all other kinds of barbed-wire fences. Unfortunately, 1883 saw one of the worst droughts ever. Many water holes had been fenced in, and the quest for water became part of a larger social protest which found its expression in fence cutting.[71]

The conflict over fencing was by no means confined to Texas. It brought clashes in nearly every part of the western range country. It was the renewal of an ancient struggle between the nomadic herdsman and the settled stockman. The rapid spread of barbed wire merely brought the conflict to a head. In Texas the clash sharpened by the fact that the public land was owned not by the [federal] government, as elsewhere in the West, but by the state. When drought pushed the landless cowman to the brink of financial ruin, violence was inevitable.[72]

Fence cutting was done not just to provide access to water holes for range cat-

Fig. 7–17 The Russell fence

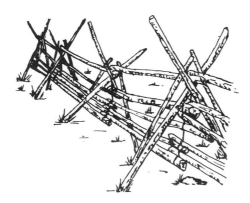

tle; it was also a response to (1) the emotional desire for free grass and open range; (2) fencing that often closed roads and obstructed travel; (3) the potential unemployment of cowboys thrown out of work as line riders; (4) the use of fencing by absentee owners or by those who did not own or lease ranges, but nevertheless used them; (5) hatred of the big pasture system that symbolized big capital and of corporations; (6) the appeal of the Greenback movement. In this latter instance, fence destruction was seen as a further phase of the struggle between labor and capital.[73]

Fence types in the montane and desert West

Even before barbed wire had tamed the prairies, the fringes of settlement were encroaching upon the mountains to the west. Here, fortunately, some supplies of timber were available, although amounts were always limited. Furthermore, many of the trees available were small and the wood twisted. Another problem in these environments was that soils were often very thin, with bedrock at or near the surface, making post-hole digging difficult or impossible. Two fences, evolved in the western mountains, solved both these problems.

The Russell fence (fig. 7–17) is clearly a variant of the stake and rider, but it does employ some distinct features, proven by the fact that it was awarded a patent.[74] The stake or post part of the fence may vary; sometimes four stakes

129

are used, two crossing at a high angle and lying in a plane perpendicular to the rails, with two others of somewhat longer length oblique to the line of the fence and resting at a lower angle. The crossing of all four stakes is secured by two or three turns of strong wire. Thus, a stable, four-point base is provided for each section of fence. In other instances, a vertical pole is substituted for the second pair of stakes, thus giving a three-point base, which is still quite stable because the vertical post is set into the ground. Another distinctive feature of the Russell fence is that all the rails, except the topmost, which lies in the crossing of the stakes, are held in place by wire loops suspended either from the crossing or from higher suspended rails.

The Russell fence appears to be limited mostly to the mountainous areas of western Canada and to the northern parts of the same ranges in the United States. Apparently, no detailed or careful study has been given to it. Since it had a single point of introduction, once its inventor has been identified, its pattern of diffusion could be a most rewarding study, illustrating how landscape features diffuse in space.

The other important fence type in the western mountains is the jack fence (fig. 7–18). This fence receives its name from the jack, which consists of two sloping posts, nailed together at or near the top, with butts resting on the ground. A third piece of timber joins the other two near the bases, thus creating a rigid triangular form. In certain cases, notches may be cut into the timbers to provide a stronger structure. These jacks, when

joined together with rails, eliminated the necessity for digging post holes. Subtypes of jack fences have been recognized on the basis of the symmetry or asymmetry of the jacks, and on the position of the rails (fig. 7–19).[75]

The jacks are normally set between twelve and sixteen feet apart and connected by rails held in place by spikes or wire loops. The posts are sometimes slightly notched to secure the rails better, and occasionally the posts are even mortised to hold the rails.

In form, the jack fence resembles the Virginia rail fence, from which it may have derived, although its exact origins remain obscure. The genetic relationship of the Russell, jack, and rail fences is an intriguing area of speculation.

The great advantage of the jack fence is that it requires no post-hole digging. A further advantage is that, because two pairs of jacks connected by rails can be a complete unit, the fence can be built of a series of individual units, which can be

shifted easily. At the same time, the units are not easily tipped over and, when wired to adjacent units, are virtually immobile.

The jack fence seems to have a wider distribution than the Russell fence, perhaps because the portability of its units encourages its use as a temporary cattle barrier. The great disadvantage of the jack fence is that it is not very economical to construct. It requires considerable timber as well as a large quantity of nails, and this has certainly worked to restrict its range.

An important variant of the jack fence is the western snow fence (fig. 7–20), which is constructed of jacks of dimension lumber, with sawn boards instead of rails. Two subtypes are in use. In the first, the jacks are connected by a series of wide horizontal boards. The second subtype employs shorter, vertical boards nailed to two or three horizontal beams.

A final western type, the Mormon fence (fig. 7–21), has such strong ethnic associations that it has even been used, along with other features, as an index of

Fig. 7–18 The jack fence

Fig. 7–19 Types of jacks (after Fife)

130

Mormon settlement (fig. 7–22).[76]

The Mormon fence is a product of the circumstances in which many Mormons found themselves during the nineteenth and early twentieth centuries. Cut off from the rest of the continent, confined to small properties in widely scattered towns, often quite poor, the Mormons built with whatever they had available.

The Mormon fence uses any bits of timber and scrap lumber indiscriminantly. Perhaps because of the need to use short lengths of lumber and timber, the form of the fence is that of pickets attached to upper and lower horizontal rails, in turn nailed to widely spaced posts. The emphasis is on variety.

Besides starting out relatively crooked because cedar or juniper are frequently used woods, they are patched with the most ill-fitting, rustic-looking boards, and the fence becomes an unpainted potpourri of different types and shapes of wood. There appears to be little concern for, or awareness of, beauty when fences are considered. In one fence one may count as many as five different picket styles, from simple two-by-fours to an ornate Victorian picket once used around the house itself. An old wagon wheel or hay rake may be seen forming part of a fence.[77]

Mormon fences are never painted, whitewashed, or stained. In time, they weather to a dull gray-white color, but they never lose their rough, chaotic, frontier character.

Woven-wire or net-wire fences

Quite in contrast to the rough-and-ready Mormon fences are the regular and smooth surfaces of the woven-wire or net-wire fences (fig. 7–23). Just as the introduction and popularization of barbed wire revolutionized the cattle industry, the woven-wire fence had a profound impact, at a later period of time, on sheep raising. Many of the consequences were quite similar.

Apparently, woven-wire fences were introduced in the early 1880s.[78] Sheep raisers quickly recognized that woven wire, unlike barbed wire, provided a wolf- and coyote-proof fence. Although they were very expensive, they were effective and the increases in productivity in sheep rearing that they ensured more than paid for their cost.[79] Other consequences included the reconciliation of cattle and sheep raising on the same pastures, the elimination of wolves and coyotes as predators, the control of diseases, improvements in the quantity and quality of wool produced, upgrading ranges and improving the ranches by keeping cattle out of cultivated fields and gardens, as well as lawns, farmyards, and even flower beds, introduction of range management and conservation practices, and the replacement of the sheepherder with the sedentary sheep rancher.[80]

Net-wire fences were also effective in combating the serious rabbit invasion of cultivated plots in Texas.[81] Hence, the services of the fence rigger began to be in great demand, since the woven-wire fence required considerable skill to erect. By the close of the first decade of the twentieth century, a common pattern had begun to emerge in Texas. "The woven wire, with a six-inch mesh and 42 to 52 inches in height, was stretched on cedar posts. Barbed wire was placed along the ground, sometimes on both sides of the posts, to prevent wolves from scratching under the fence or three barbed wires were mostly placed about the woven wire. Frequently, the barbed wire on top served as the ranch telephone line."[82]

Fig. 7–20 The western snow fence. Fence boards may be vertical or horizontal.

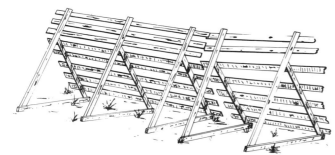

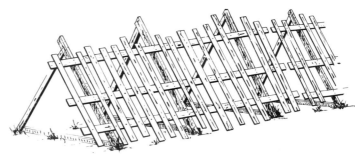

131

Fig. 7–21 A Mormon fence in the left rear ground, around a hay derrick and hay loft. A woven-wire fence is in the foreground. (Near Vernal, Utah)

H. N. Humphrey, in a 1916 study of the Midwest, reported that two distinct areas of woven-wire fencing could be discerned. Ohio, Indiana, southern Michigan, and extreme eastern Illinois were areas of wide woven wire, defined as a net-wire fence over forty-two inches high. Narrow woven wire, which was less than forty-two inches high but was supplemented by strands of barbed wire to bring it up to normal height, predominated in southern Wisconsin, southeastern South Dakota, Iowa, Illinois, and northern Missouri. Humphrey offered as an explanation for this variation that farmers in the eastern area had considerable amounts of wooden fencing when woven wire was first introduced, but farms in the western area were only partially fenced. "On account of the high price of the first

Fig. 7–22 Extent of the Mormon fence (after Francaviglia)

woven wire, it was made narrow and of lighter wires to keep down the cost."[83] The woven wire was supplemented with strands of barbed wire. Later on, when the wooden fences of the eastern area needed replacement, costs of the woven-wire fencing were much lower, and thus a higher fence was employed.

In addition to sheep farmers, the other agency effective in the introduction of woven-wire fences was the railroads. Many railroads had been unhappy with the use of barbed wire, uneasy over potential injury that such a fence could inflict. Consequently, as the cost of woven wire began to come down, it was widely employed by railroads, whose rights-of-way were mostly fenced by woven wire by the turn of the century.[84]

Electric fences

All wire fences are excellent conductors of electricity. As a matter of fact, one of the arguments against all kinds of wire fences is that they are potential lightning hazards and must be grounded frequently in order to counteract this danger.[85] But electricity also can be beneficial. In fact, a single strand of wire charged with electricity can function just as effectively as a multistrand barbed-wire fence in restraining large stock.

The electric fence may have originated on the Texas prairies in the closing years of the nineteenth century, but it was not widely adopted until the early 1930s. The great advantage of the electric fence is its very low materials and maintenance cost. Harry Symons estimates a savings of up to 70 percent over conventional fences.[86] Only one six-volt bat-

Fig. 7–23 A woven-wire or net-wire fence (Portage County, Ohio, 1982)

Fig. 7–24 Braced corner of a rubber-strip fence (Ottawa County, Michigan, 1982)

Rubber-strip fences

As the twentieth century progressed, galvanized steel wire became a steadily more expensive fencing material, one of the most important reasons why the single-strand electric fence gained popularity. This situation also caused a search for cheaper, alternative fencing materials. One of the newest of these, whose ultimate success is still uncertain, is made from rubber tires, cut and vulcanized into long thin strips (fig. 7–24). One of the major advantages of this fence is that, not only is the material cheap, but by using it in this manner, a major disposal of a worrisome surplus commodity is achieved. Other advantages are that the rubber strips are flexible and easily handled, that they do not rust or weather rapidly, that they can be easily stretched taut, and that they are more highly visible than wire.

tery and its associated apparatus is required to charge a fence five or six miles long.

If such a fence is to function properly, certain precautions and procedures must be taken, however. First, stock have to be taught to associate the highly visible white porcelain insulators with the unpleasant shock produced by contact with the electric wire.[87] Second, if weeds grow tall enough to touch the wire, the charge can be grounded and the effectiveness of the fence lost. Thus, the fence line has to be periodically mowed and checked for snags and other items.[88] Third, static arrestors have to be employed if the fence interferes with local radio or television reception. Fourth, poorly drained wetlands must

be avoided because they are potentially dangerous areas of grounding.

In the final analysis, it must be kept in mind that the electric fence will not contain an enraged animal or stampeding herds. Under normal conditions, however, the electric fence is economical, easily relocated, and quite effective in restricting cattle and other large animals.

Fences in the American landscape

The fence is probably the most common element in the American rural landscape, and yet it may be quite inconspicuous. The shift in major fence material reflects, in a way, the changes in rural technology—uprooted stumps, logs, split timber, sawn lumber, iron wire, galvanized steel wire, and electricity. Even used-tire fences reflect these changes in technology. The fence often may be an inconspicuous feature of the landscape, but it is hardly an insignificant one.

133

PART THREE
The Settlement Landscape:
Review and Prospect

8   The Settlement
Landscape

The individual structures, and even the clusters or groupings of structures, that have been erected across the face of North America arc thc components that make up the various cultural landscapes of the continent and give it its personality. Although most North Americans are now urbanites with an economy that is complex and industry based, the character of the continent is still expressed by the appearance of its small town and rural landscapes. These landscapes are complicated mixtures of ethnic heritage, regional economic development, and local social organization, placed within a series of varied environmental settings. Even the most casual observer traveling across the countryside notes such landscape changes. In the intermontane West, the Mormon cultural landscape has been perceived and carefully studied by a number of scholars.[1] Elsewhere the cultural landscapes usually are less isolated and easily identified, and so they normally have received less attention. Nonetheless, they do exist and gradually they are coming to be documented.

For many students of vernacular architecture or material culture, the analysis of individual structures, or of groupings of structures, or even of all structures of a particular type, is merely the initial step toward a more comprehensive investigation—that of the entire cultural landscape. Over much of the continent the normal settlement process has combined with growing population densities to produce a series of American settlement landscapes that are the result of the intermixing of diverse cultural elements. In truth, this mixing has not been without its limitations and restrictions. Cultural spheres and, to a lesser degree,

cultural domains have overlapped and coalesced (see vol. 1, chap. 1). Regional cultural personalities have evolved. New England, the South, Appalachia, the Midwest, and the Pacific Northwest are all widely recognized regional landscapes, although their exact character, as well as their geographical extent, are the subjects of continuing lively debate, which is certainly beyond the scope of this study.

More to the point is an examination of the techniques that scholars have used to try to determine the cultural landscapes based upon material culture, specifically vernacular architecture. Some of these cultural landscapes also will be examined in greater or lesser detail later in this chapter.

Review of methods of studying cultural landscapes

Among the most active researchers attempting to unravel the mysteries of the cultural landscape have been scholars from several disciplines: cultural geographers, folklorists, architectural historians, social historians, anthropologists, and archaeologists. Their investigations have been directed on several levels of inquiry, which are summarized graphically in fig. 8–1.

The directions of research have tended to vary not only with the orientation and bias of the particular discipline, but also according to the objectives of each research project. Some investigations concentrate on local areas, or have the even more restricted focus of a single structure or group of structures; others are much more wide ranging.

Studies of individual
elements or groupings

In the final analysis, however, the validity of all cultural landscape studies rests upon the accuracy with which individual structures have been perceived. Thus, virtually all cultural landscape research gives some attention to individual elements, even when it primarily synthesizes existing studies done by others or when it attempts to sketch in the cultural landscape of vast areas. At the same time, the number of studies of single or individual structures is decidedly limited. Perhaps it is not surprising that folklorists and architectural historians have carried out most of these investigations. Among the most useful of these types of studies by folklorists are those by Warren Roberts, Henry Glassie, John Vlach, Howard Marshall, and Simon Bronner, although this list is by no means exhaustive.[2] Representative of the research of architectural historians are works by Russell Keune and James Replogle, Richard Perrin, and Donald Millar, although, again, this is not a complete list.[3]

The thrust of research by folklorists generally involves an attempt to discover the rationale of the structure, particularly how the building reflects the ethos of its builders. Architectural historians, on the other hand, are more concerned with the specific details of construction and the impetus for any observable variations in technique. For the most part, however, these historians have avoided vernacular architecture in favor of academic architecture. Examples of studies of individual structures by scholars in other disciplines would

Fig. 8–1 Model of Cultural Landscape Studies

Mode of study → Level of investigation ↓	Structure	Space	Culture
Individual	A. Individual building or landscape element	B. Individual farmstead or single group of elements	
Local	C. One building type or landscape element in a restricted locality	D. All types or elements in a restricted locality	E. All or several structures or elements of one ethnic group in a restricted locality
Regional		F. All or several types or elements in a large area or region	G. All or several structures or elements of one ethnic group in a large area or region
Comprehensive	H. One type or element everywhere it occurs	I. Comparative studies of one or several types or elements in two or more regions	J. Study of the landscape associated with one ethnic group everywhere it occurs

135

include those of Terry Jordan (cultural geographer), Paul Jenkins (historian), J. J. Brody and Anne Colberg (archaeologists). Even enthusiastic and talented amateurs can produce fine studies.[4]

No house, barn, or other farm structure exists in a void, but surprisingly few researchers have recognized the significance of the farmstead as an integral cultural unit. In the final analysis, these studies may prove of greater benefit than those of the single house or barn, since they usually attempt to place structures in relationship to one another within a single grouping of buildings. Some examples of these kinds of studies include those of Glassie, Philip Dole, and Thomas Carter.[5]

Research carried on at the level of the individual structure or grouping (see fig. 8–1) represents the best point at which to test the validity of hypotheses and observations made for larger areas. Therefore, such individual studies should be encouraged and opportunities for the publication of this most necessary and basic work should be made more widely available. Local historical societies and groups of local preservation organizations could well become the key agencies for providing the kind of documentation required at this level. Care must be taken, however, that the investigators be thoroughly trained and that the quality of the research be maintained at a consistently high level.

Research at a local scale

At the scale of local investigations, many more studies have been performed. Three types at this level can be distinguished (see fig. 8–1). First are the treatises covering a single building type or landscape element. Examples of such research might include the work of Susanne Ridlen, Thomas Hubka, Charles Calkins and William Laatsch, and Richard Hulan.[6]

A second kind of study done on a local scale includes works that treat all or several building types and/or elements within a restricted area. These studies generally attempt to explain the composition of the local landscape and to reconcile it with larger historical, economic, social and/or cultural phenomena. Examples would include those of David Sutherland, Brian Coffey, and Charles Martin. The U.S. Army Corps of Engineers has produced or sponsored a number of excellent works that also fit into this category.[7]

The final group of studies at this scale are different only in that they examine elements of an ethnic group in a local area, and they always give at least some emphasis to the ethnic connection that helps to make the local landscape distinctive. Authors who have contributed works with this orientation and scale include Ingolf Voegler, Hubert Wilhelm, Douglas Meyer, and, of course, many others.[8]

Regional scale investigation

The third scale of investigation is that of the region. It is here that the greatest difficulties are encountered in attempting

to classify research on material culture. One reason may be that although researchers often examine phenomena on the local scale, beyond that they seem to opt for a comprehensive study of the feature. Furthermore, at this scale of investigation much detail must be suppressed in favor of synthesis, but, of necessity, studies must be essentially incomplete. Perhaps this is not a very satisfactory scale at which to work for anyone except geographers, who are trained to look for various spatial patterns of expression.

Two rather different types of study exist at this scale. One looks at the buildings or elements within large regions to attempt to explain patterns of distribution.[9] The other analyzes the components of particular culture regions.[10]

Comprehensive studies of the settlement landscape

There is, ultimately, a scale of investigation in which an attempt is made to be comprehensive, at least as far as geographical coverage is concerned. At this level a distinction can be made among three types of approach. First are those works that are comprehensive because they examine a single building type or element throughout its entire range. Jordan's study of the American windmill, Vlach's articles on the shotgun house, and Wilbur Zelinsky's work on the New England connected barn fall into this category.[11]

A second group comprises those studies that attempt to be comprehensive by examining phenomena in two or more areas on a comparative basis. This is often done to try to identify the origins of elements, or to examine the modifications that have occurred due to the transfer of settlement.[12] These kinds of studies are not numerous because they require an intimate knowledge, best based upon fieldwork, of widely separated areas.

Finally, investigations can be designed that are comprehensive in that they examine all the landscape elements associated with a particular ethnic group wherever they occur. These studies attempt to be definitive. Stephen Jett and Virginia Spencer's recent book on Navajo architecture may be cited as one of the best examples.[13] All structures and major landscape features are examined in detail and carefully analyzed.

Fig. 8–2 The Dutch settlement area in western Michigan

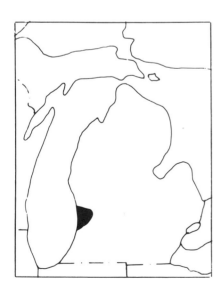

The settlement landscape

Obviously, much still remains to be accomplished before the entire range of cultural or regional settlement landscapes is identified and adequately studied. The balance of this chapter is devoted to a discussion of seven ethnic landscapes as examples of the uneven extent of materials that already exist, of the potential that is present for study, and of the directions that additional research may take. Three ethnic landscapes, the Dutch in southwestern Michigan, the Belgian in the Door peninsula of Wisconsin, and the Norwegian scattered over the upper Midwest, have received virtually no attention from scholars. More has been written about the material culture of the Ukrainians on the Canadian prairies and the Finns in the upper Great Lakes region, but no analysis of their entire cultural landscape exists at this time. The two remaining groups, the Amish and the Mormons, are unlike the previous five in that each has a landscape with a strong religious connection, which persists in the modern day. Additionally, both the Amish and the Mormons have been the subjects of considerable study, although the landscape settlement of the former has not received the attention paid to that of the latter.

A further reason to include discussion of the cultural landscapes of these seven groups is that each represents the most important concentration of its nationality or ethnic community, and its inclusion significantly broadens the range of this volume. One would hope that by including them, however briefly, other researchers may be encouraged to investigate these particular landscapes in the

detail and depth they deserve. Thereby, a valuable part of our North American heritage will have been preserved.

The Dutch landscape of southwestern Michigan

It seems strange that virtually nothing has been written about the settlement landscape of the Dutch in Ottawa and Allegan counties, Michigan (fig. 8–2), since the colony is so well known. In the colorful and appropriate language of Marcus Whiffen, who was speaking of different structures, these Dutch buildings are "an architecture which awaits its literature." Much of the area's fame is derived from the annual festival and spring flower display in Holland, Michigan, a rather characteristic example of Dutch business acumen. The Dutch settlers also have been successful farmers, and the prosperity of the settlement ultimately rests upon its rural foundation.

For up to ten miles in all directions from the city of Holland, a unique Dutch cultural landscape is encountered. Beginning in 1847, the swampy forests of this part of southwestern Michigan have been systematically cleared and drained. Generally, the first indication that travelers have that they have entered the Dutch area is the occurrence of large, tripartite, transverse gable barns—the Michigan Dutch barn (fig. 8–3). As one might suspect, the plans of these barns are quite similar to those of the earlier Dutch barns of New York and New Jersey (see chap. 2).

Fig. 8–3 A Michigan Dutch barn, near Holland, Michigan. Unpainted and weathered to a dark gray, the barn has painted red doors. (1982)

However, the Michigan Dutch barns are decidedly rectangular rather than squarish, their roof pitch is much lower, their dimensions are much greater, they are unpainted except for red doors, and the timber framing is lighter and less elaborate than the earlier New York–New Jersey barn.[14]

At a quick glance, the Michigan Dutch barn might be mistaken for other transverse-frame structures, particularly the Midwest three-portal barn (see chap. 1). What distinguishes the Michigan Dutch barn is the tripartite interior plan. The interior is frequently divided by lightweight partitions to provide stabling as well as equipment rooms. Often the roof of the barn is extended on the north side so that it reaches within a few feet of the ground, producing an asymmetrical gable profile (fig. 8–4), although the angles of pitch of each roof slope are the same. The side shed thus added is used to house either cattle or horses.[15] In addition to the Michigan Dutch barn, a number of gambrel-roofed barns also are present.

Houses, too, are distinct. Almost from the beginning of the settlement, frame houses were erected. A few log dwellings may have been built as well. However, the most unusual houses, and those that help to give a unique character to this area, are the patterned brick dwellings. Among the Dutch, brick has a certain prestige as a building material. It is looked upon as much more acceptable than timber. Admittedly, frame houses have always been cheaper and, hence, they predominate in the Dutch settlement, but whenever finances permitted, brick houses were erected. Ad-

Fig. 8–4 Many Michigan Dutch barns have an asymmetrical roof, usually on the north or west sides. Note the diamond windows, a feature sometimes seen in earlier Dutch barns in New York (see fig. 2–13). (Ottawa County, Michigan, 1982)

ditional study is needed to determine if particular house types can be identified. One house, which is numerous, is a one-story, squarish structure, with a low, hipped roof (fig. 8–5). Another possible type is two stories high, with a lower wing (fig. 8–6), although this may simply be the Dutch version of the upright-and-wing house (see vol. 1, chap. 10).

In any event, the distinguishing feature of all these houses is the patterned brick work. Most of the bricks are a deep red, and the decorative details are provided by employing a few bricks of a contrasting tan or brownish-yellow color. The design is geometric, most often consisting of a frieze, high up under the eaves. Window frames also are often decorated.

Closer inspection of the Michigan Dutch farmsteads may well reveal other ethnic landscape features worthy of study and recording. This process has barely begun here, a beginning rather similar to that for the much less well-known settlement of the Belgians in northeastern Wisconsin.

Fig. 8–5 A Michigan Dutch cottage. Unfortunately, the front windows of the house have been "modernized." (Ottawa County, Michigan, 1982)

Fig. 8–6 A Michigan Dutch upright-and-wing house (Allegan County, Michigan, 1982)

The Belgian landscape of the Door peninsula, Wisconsin

The only feature of Belgian settlement that has yet been studied carefully is the outdoor oven (see chap. 6). Calkins and Laatsch documented fifteen such ovens that have survived into the 1970s in Door County.[16] The urgent need now is for careful measuring and recording of details of each of these remaining structures, some of which are liable to disappear rather soon. This inventory would represent the beginning of the documentation of Belgian material culture in Wisconsin.

The ovens are just one feature of the rural cultural landscape created by French-speaking Walloons who settled in Brown, Kewaunee, and Door counties between 1853 and 1857 (fig. 8–7). The gently dipping, back slope of the Niagara cuesta, the same ridge of resistant dolomite that forms Niagara Falls

far to the east, provided an environment of rich limestone soils. The dense forests and scattered swamps, which covered the entire surface, effectively isolated the Belgian colony from other settlements for years. This probably accounts for the fidelity with which the Belgian landscape features have been preserved here.

The early settlers apparently built all their domestic structures—houses, barns, and outbuildings—of logs. Unfortunately, the great Peshtigo fire of 1871, the greatest conflagration in American history, was so awesome that it leaped the five-to-ten-mile-wide waters of Green Bay and proceeded to

Fig. 8–7 Belgian settlement in Wisconsin

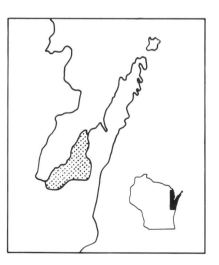

Fig. 8–8 A Belgian bakeoven built into the rear wall of a summer kitchen. The bakeoven platform and the summer kitchen are built of limestone, whereas the dome and the chimney are of brick. (Door County, Wisconsin, 1980)

ignite the Door peninsula, where it burned out a high percentage of these early Belgian log buildings.[17] When rebuilding began, the memories of the disaster were still fresh and the farmers turned to new fireproof materials, at least for some of their buildings. Clay pockets and small brickyards were widespread and they provided the red brick for houses.[18] Small quarries along the escarpment supplied the dolomitic limestone for house foundations and

corners, and for smaller structures such as summer kitchens and bakeovens (fig. 8–8). Roofs were often covered with metal as a further protection against fire.

A typical Belgian house is fairly large, reflecting the size of the families that live in them. Most houses are two or two-and-a-half stories and built entirely of brick or brick over hewn cedar or pine logs (fig. 8–9). Further study will be necessary to determine whether most of these houses adhered to a particular type or not. Only one floor plan of a Belgian house has ever been published (fig. 8–10), and because of the obviously larger than normal size of this house, it may not be representative.

Nevertheless, the Belgian house is not difficult to identify from its exterior characteristics (fig. 8–11). The foundation is Niagara dolomite and the walls are brick. In some instances, the wall

Fig. 8–9 A typical method of building in the Belgian Door peninsula settlement is to use bricks over a log base. (Door County, Wisconsin, 1980)

corners are quoined with blocks of dolomite. Door and window placement varies, but they are always elaborately treated, sometimes with fan-shaped brick segmental arches (fig. 8–12), at other times with decorated brick frames. The local bricks are of a deep red color, but light tan or cream-colored bricks, brought up Lake Michigan from the Milwaukee area, provided the decoration. Indeed, the farther east and closer to Lake Michigan one goes, the greater the amount of decorative trim.[19] The gable may incorporate tan bricks and usually has a fan-shaped window to provide light to the attic. The roof is of

Fig. 8–10 Plan of the Massart House, a Belgian brick house, town of Lincoln, Door County, Wisconsin (used with permission of William G. Laatsch)

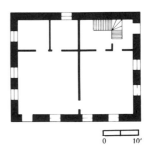

Fig. 8–11 The Wisconsin Belgian brick house

composition shingles or sheet metal.

The Belgians did not use brick for either barns or outbuildings. The barns, for the most part, are constructed of rough-hewn pine logs held in place with saddle, half, square, or full dovetail notching. Clay chinking keeps out the frigid winds that blow off Green Bay in the winter season. In plan, the Belgian barns are considerably elongated, roughly two or three times as wide as they are deep (fig. 8–13). Such a form,

Fig. 8–12 A two-room plan Belgian brick house. The back wall of the summer house is constructed of limestone to incorporate the bakeoven most safely. (Door Dounty, Wisconsin, 1980)

Fig. 8–13 A typical Door County Belgian barn. The logs are rough hewn with half notching. The gable is covered with vertical planks. (Door County, Wisconsin, 1980)

together with offset wagon doors and a series of smaller man-sized doors, is reminiscent of the Quebec long barn (chap. 2).

Among the most important of the outbuildings is the summer kitchen, usually constructed of stone (see fig. 8–8). Sometimes only the wall that incorporates the bakeoven is made of stone, with the other three walls of timber frame covered with clapboards (see fig. 8–12).

A third typical structure completes the ensemble. In the angle formed by the projecting bakeoven at the back of the summer kitchen, the frame privy is normally built (see fig. 6–21). Placed here, it can take advantage during the long winter of the warmth periodically generated by the bakeoven; it is also out of sight of the house.

The final Belgian component of these farmsteads is a tiny votive chapel (fig. 8–14), built of stone or lumber frame, with a gable roof. Sometimes its only opening will be a door on one gable wall. In other cases, the side walls will each have a single small window. Measuring only about six by four feet, these chapels can accommodate only two or three people at a time. The interior, which may even be carpeted, contains a small altar, a figure of the Virgin, perhaps a sacred picture or two, and a prayer rail. The motif of the cross is the most prominent exterior decoration (fig. 8–15). These chapels are a clear indication of the strong Roman Catholic orientation of the small and, until recently, isolated Belgian community.

Fig. 8–14 A Belgian votive chapel partially hidden by bushes. It is built of limestone blocks with a lumber frame roof. (Door County, Wisconsin, 1980)

The Norwegian landscape of the northern Midwest

The situation of the early Norwegian settlers was quite different from that of the Belgians.[20] They occupied a large number of widely scattered locations all across the northern Midwest (fig. 8–16). The land where the Norwegians established themselves was initially often in prairie openings in the forest. Later on, as additional Norwegian settlers filled up the land toward the West, all the territory which they occupied was treeless prairie. Thus they were spared part of the rigorous ordeal of clearing their land. They still built with logs, nevertheless, because their folk traditions encouraged it and timber was close by, plentiful, and cheap (see vol. 1, chap. 10). Surprisingly little has been written about Norwegian vernacular architecture. Perhaps because of the widely dispersed nature of Norwegian

Fig. 8–15 The cross motif on a Belgian votive chapel (Door County, Wisconsin, 1980)

settlement, few conscious attempts to preserve their folk architecture have been made. Furthermore, few Norwegian structures have been analyzed or even identified as yet.

One of the difficulties in locating examples of early Norwegian architecture is that Norwegians frequently settled on land of high quality that was easily accessible, so that in time they prospered and rebuilt more modern, less traditional buildings. Alternatively, they might sell their land to non-Norwegians if the price was right, and the Norwegian buildings would be replaced or altered in accordance with other traditions.

Although definitive evidence is not yet available, American Norwegian houses that have been described are all of one type, which may be called the Norwegian gallery or sval house. Its name is derived from the long, narrow, second-story gallery or *sval*, which runs along one side of the house (fig. 8–17). The sval is reached by an exterior, open flight of stairs at one end of the room. In

Fig. 8–16 Norwegian settlements in the northern Midwest

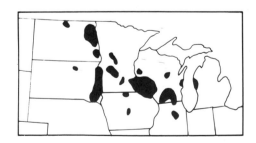

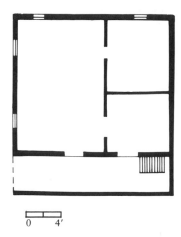

Fig. 8–17 Plan of a Norwegian gallery house

Fig. 8–18 A Norwegian gallery or sval house (Old World Wisconsin Outdoor Museum, 1979)

many instances, the space beneath the sval has been boarded in to create a room or hallway on the first floor to complement the two or three original rooms, which arc of unequal size. The ground-floor rooms are replicated by two or three unequal-sized rooms on the second floor. Sometimes the gable roof of the house is asymmetrical in order to incorporate the sval.[21]

The only specific discussion of a Norwegian gallery house in the American Midwest is the work of the Wisconsin architectural historian, Richard W. E. Perrin.[22] His description of the John Bergen House confirms that these structures are closely related to those reported in both Norway and Sweden.[23] Preserved in the Old World Wisconsin Outdoor Ethnic Museum is another Norwegian gallery dwelling (fig. 8–18). The plan of this house is not exactly that of a Scandinavian gallery house, but it is similar. The sval is incomplete, there is

no outside stairway, and the lower level of the sval is partially closed in. Other features of the structure are faithful to its Scandinavian predecessors; logs are tight-fitting, with little or no chinking, hewn in the Fenno-Scandinavian fashion (see vol. 1, chap. 10), and locked at the corners with full dovetail and tooth notching. A few other Norwegian gallery houses have been identified, mostly in Wisconsin,[24] but as yet they have not been carefully studied.

So little research has been attempted on American Norwegian buildings that virtually nothing can be said about the barns and outbuildings of the typical early Norwegian farmstead. They are, as would be expected, constructed of logs held in place by saddle notching or half-dovetail notching. In contrast, houses employ double notching, tooth, or full dovetail.[25]

One of the more unusual outbuildings of the Norwegian farm is the *stabbur* (fig. 8–19). In describing the stabbur on the farmstead of Mathias Lisbakken in Wisconsin, Alan Pape offers the following evaluation of the function of the building:

Two small outbuildings commonly associated with each other on Norwegian farms were the one-story *veslebur* and the two-story *stabbur*. These structures were often very ornate in appearance and were used for food, clothing and valuables storage, as well as unheated sleeping rooms. The Lisbakken stabbur is an American manifestation of this common Norwegian architectural farm-building style; in Norway its use is analogous to a larder and treasure-house, while in Wisconsin it functioned as a granary and storage chamber.[26]

Although it was essentially a store-house, the stabbur was much smaller than the gallery or sval house, and it was

143

Fig. 8–19 Sketch of a Norwegian stabbur with living quarters, c. 1852–1855 (by A. C. Pape; for source see n. 24)

often the first structure of the pioneering Norwegian settler. It normally measures only about eighteen to nineteen feet square, and could be designed to have one or two living rooms in addition to its storage loft, whereas the Norwegian gallery house might be twenty to twenty-four feet wide and thirty to forty feet deep, and normally had five or six rooms, hardly a likely structure for the frontier.

The Norwegian farmsteads, like those of the Dutch in southwestern Michigan and the Belgians in northeastern Wisconsin, have not been accorded the scholarly attention that they deserve, because these structures are so distinctive. Ukrainian and Finnish architecture is somewhat better known, but definitive studies are still lacking.

The Ukrainian landscape of Alberta

One of the last European groups to migrate in sizable numbers to North America was the Ukrainians, whose main movement to rural locations took place after 1890. By this late date, all the desirable land in eastern United States and Canada was already occupied, so that Ukrainian peasants had not very attractive alternatives open to them. They could become factory workers or miners, and many chose this. They could purchase barren and cutover land, and some fell into this trap. Most settlers who wanted to continue in farming could buy already developed farms with existing buildings, but in these cases they left a minimal cultural impact on the land. Additionally, in order to afford developed and proven agricultural land, these latecomers often had to spend a period of time working at urban occupations. Ukrai-nians who wished to go directly into farming were forced to homestead in the Dakotas, Montana, Wyoming, and the prairie provinces of Canada. In Wyoming, South Dakota, and most of Montana, Ukrainians settled among farmers of other nationalities and thus rarely formed a compact or cohesive community.[27] It is only in the northeastern corner of Montana, in the vicinity of Scobey, that a distinct Ukrainian settlement can be identified. The pattern of assimilation is also true of North Dakota, where Ukrainians are scattered in McHenry, McLeon, Billings, and Dunn counties in the western half of the state. In Canada, the most important Ukrainian settlements are in the aspen parkland belt of the prairie provinces, running in a broad arc from south of Winnipeg, Manitoba, through Saskatchewan into central Alberta, near Edmonton.

Fig. 8–20 Ukrainian settlements in Alberta (after Lehr).

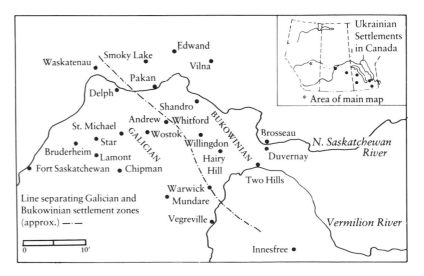

Fig. 8–21 The Ukrainian house, Galician subtype

The earliest Ukrainian settlers in Alberta arrived in 1892 from the province of Galicia. They were followed four years later by Ukrainians from Bukowina who settled to the north and east of the earlier group (fig. 8–20).[28] John Lehr has divided the Ukrainian folk houses in Alberta into two distinct variants of a basic type. One he calls the *Galician house* and the other, the *Bukowinian house,* based on the provincial origin of the Ukrainian settlers.

The Ukrainian house, Galician subtype. The typical Galician folk house (fig. 8–21) is a two-room, rectangular plan, log house.[29] The structure was always oriented to the south, in part to secure maximum sun exposure for doors and windows during the long prairie winters, and in part so that the holy wall of the larger of the two rooms would face east, the sacred direction. The interior surface of the holy wall was decorated with icons, religious calendars, and sacred paintings.

Although small, approximately eighteen feet deep by twenty-seven feet wide, the Galician house was quite sturdy. It rested on a foundation of large boulders, usually glacial erratics. In Saskatchewan the walls were sometimes of wattle and daub, but log wall construction was normal, especially in Alberta. Aspen generally was used because of its availability, but pine and spruce were preferred. The logs, which were rough hewn, were held in place by saddle notching and frequently by wooden dowels.

Over the log walls, thin, split, willow laths were nailed to provide a framework for the mud-plaster coating, which was the final element of the wall. This exterior covering is one of the most important diagnostic features of the Ukrainian cottage in Canada. The clay was mixed with water, straw, and animal dung, the latter to keep the mixture from cracking upon drying.

The viscous mixture was applied directly to the logs and smoothed over in a rough fashion. A secondary layer of clay and water, with a little sand added, was applied over the first to give a finely smoothed coating ready for liming. After drying, and the patching of any cracks, the plaster was limed with a mixture of active lime and water, often with skim milk or a little washing blue added to bring out the pure whiteness of the lime.

The exterior lime surface had to be renewed periodically if it were to perform its function of weather protection. Spring was the best time to do this, and the liming of house walls came to be part of the annual Easter celebration. On many houses, the white lime wall surface was highlighted by painting the window and door frames and other exposed wooden members with a bright blue trim.

The traditional roof covering was thatch, and this necessitated a high roof pitch. The use of thatch also apparently determined the roof style, with hipped and hipped-gable roofs very common. On the open prairies, sod roofs covered some of the earlier dwellings, with consequent lower roof pitch. Almost from the beginning of Ukrainian settlement, wood shingles also were employed as a normal roofing material.

Despite the frequently high roof pitch, the loft of Ukrainian houses functioned as an insulation space and not for storage or sleeping, in contrast to how this area was used in the small houses of many other ethnic groups. The base of this loft space was formed by a series of tie logs, running from front to back of the house and pegged to the top wall logs. "Poplar poles were then laid across these beams at intervals of two or three inches and the intervening gaps plugged with twists of mud, straw and cow dung. This constituted an effective roof insulation."[30]

The Ukrainian house, Bukowinian subtype. Although basically similar to the Galician house, the Bukowinian folk house (fig. 8–22) does display a range of different characteristics. One of the most important is the interior plan. Whereas the Galician house simply consists of two rooms of unequal size, the Bukowinian house has its two rooms separated by a large anteroom or hallway (fig. 8–23).

In both houses, a centrally located stove-furnace (*pich*) occupies a prominent position. In the Galician house, the stove is adjacent to the interior partition in the smaller room. The stove's location in the Bukowinian house is in the same relative position, but at the back of the center hallway. The size of this stove varies from house to house but is always quite large. In fact, one section of the top of the stove was commonly used as a sleeping shelf during the bitterly cold prairie winters. At a later period, cast-iron stoves were connected by horizontal stove pipes to the chimney of the original stove. The pipes, as well as the iron stoves themselves, help to heat the house's interior better.

The original chimney was often a haphazard affair, frequently going just above the ceiling into the loft. Smoke was left to find its way out through the thatch of the roof. In the Bukowinian house, eyebrow vents on the south slope of the roof were introduced to help dissipate the smoke. Even after installation of a chimney and the adoption of wooden shingle roofs, eyebrow vents were retained as relict features. The ex-

Fig. 8–22 A Ukrainian house, Bukowinian subtype, Smoky Lake County, Alberta (photo courtesy of John Lehr)

planation for the lack of a chimney that protruded beyond the roof line may be found in the ancient Rumanian practice of putting a tax on smoke (*fumarit*). For each unit of smoke, which was measured by recording smoke-producing chimneys, a fixed tax was levied. This was, of course, merely a household tax figured on the number of chimneys.[31]

The roof of the Bukowinian house typically is of a massive, hipped type with conspicuous overhanging eaves, sometimes extending over a front gallery. To support the heavy roof and especially the flaring eaves, the upper few wall logs on each side are progressively extended beyond the notch. This also contributes to the impression of a heavy roof line. Another distinguishing feature of the Bukowinian house is the use of green trim, rather than the blue of Galician houses.

Other Ukrainian buildings. The barns and outbuildings built by the Ukrainian settlers in Canada have not been fully analyzed. William Wonders and Mark Rasmussen have, however, provided a very brief description of Ukrainian barns in Alberta. The typical structure is an approximately twenty by thirty foot, "squared-beam, dovetail-cornered building . . . with a gambrel roof, covered in shakes. The extensive upper portion of the building was a one-room loft with small doors at each end. The ground floor also had two large doors opposing each other, usually on the narrow ends of the building, and centered. Sidewalls often had three small windows ($1' \times 2'$), evenly distributed on the wall."[32]

The known range of Ukrainian structures in Canada, in addition to houses and barns, includes wells with long sweeps, outdoor bakeovens, plaited willow fences, and small combination storage sheds and dovecotes.[33] A few photographs and drawings have been

Fig. 8–23 Floor plan of a Bukowinian house, showing the centrally positioned stove or pich

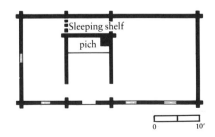

published, but no in-depth studies of these have yet appeared.

As the Ukrainian settlers in Alberta became established and prospered, they erected new houses that reflected their prosperity, but they also maintained some links with traditional building. Orientation and interior plan of the houses did not change, but form and some materials did. An upper half story was added, the roof pitch and eave line were changed, and a separately roofed front gallery was attached to the house. In some instances, timber or lumber frame was substituted for logs and, almost always, mud plaster gave way to weatherboard siding. These modifications produced a house that Lehr has described as "a Canadianization of the vernacular form."[34]

The Finnish landscape of the upper Great Lakes

Another ethnic group arriving in North America very late in the nineteenth and early in the twentieth century was the Finns. They settled in dispersed locations across the Canadian Shield, especially in the upper Great Lakes areas of Minnesota, Wisconsin, Michigan, and Ontario (fig. 8–24). The landscape here, although harsh and unattractive to other settlers, reminded the Finns of the rocky, wooded, and swampy land they had left behind. Furthermore, although the land was marginal in quality, they could acquire much more than they would have hoped to possess in Finland, because earlier immigrants had avoided settling there, for the most part.

Many observers have commented upon the large number of small structures, which appear to characterize the Finnish farmstead. Others suggest that the multiple roof line of Finnish buildings may give a false impression of a multiplicity of structures.[35] Although there is disagreement about the number, everyone agrees that the structures of the Finnish farmstead are small, a reflection of the paucity of resources in the upper Great Lakes, of the consequent poverty and lack of capital of the Finnish farmers, and of the slow expansion of farmsteads, which was done building by building.[36] Thus each separate structure is associated with a different farm function.

In most instances, the house was the first building erected on the farm. The early dwelling was apt to consist only of one room, plus a low loft (fig. 8–25 A, B). These log houses measured twelve to sixteen feet by sixteen to twenty feet.[37] The logs were carefully hewn and fitted, using wooden pins[38] and certain

Fig. 8–24 Finnish settlements in the upper Great Lakes

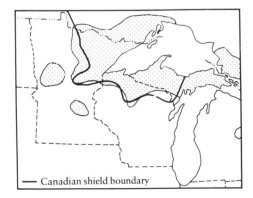

— Canadian shield boundary

notches, which produced a heat retentive structure. Gable ends were formed by gradually contracting the length of logs on the end walls. These upper logs were held in place by dowels and light pole purlins. The roof itself was of handsplit shingles. The combination of combustible roof materials, long cold winters that necessitated continual stove burning, the use of fire to clear out brush and stumps in expanding the farm, and the memory of disastrous forest fires kept the Finnish settlers acutely aware of potential fire danger. Few Finnish houses of any type were without a wooden ladder hung on an outside wall, leaning against the eaves or attached to the roof, which permitted quick access to the chimney area.[39]

A second but somewhat less common Finnish house is a two-room rectangular log dwelling with a large loft above (see fig. 8–25 C, D). The interior plan is easily revealed on the outside by the log partition, mortised into the longer exterior walls.[40] Finally, the Finns also employed the elongated Baltic three-room house (see fig. 8–25 E, F), described in chapter 10 of the first volume.

Despite the variance in number of rooms, certain features existed in common in all these Finnish houses. One was the carefully hewn, closely fitted, white pine log construction employing double, full dovetail, or tooth notching. Second, roofs were of the gable type and comprised of hand-split wooden shingles, usually of cedar.

Third, a small enclosed stoop provided

A

B

C

D

Fig. 8–25 The Finnish log house

E

F

a weather-insulated entrance to the house. In the one-room house, the entrance stoop was usually near one corner of the gable wall; in three-room houses it was typically in the center of one of the side walls; in two-room houses the stoop might be on either the gable or the side. Because of these entrance stoops, Finns normally entered the house and called out, rather than knocking on the door before entering.[41] Such a custom caused dismay among their non-Finnish neighbors because the Finns stepped unannounced directly into their houses which had no entrance stoops.

Finally, most houses were constructed without basements. The house sills were laid on glacial boulders, on wooden blocks, or on the ground itself. The lack of storage space created by this convention was made up for by a separate root cellar.[42]

By the 1920s, existing Finnish log houses were being sided over and new houses were being built of dimension lumber. Despite the status pressures that resulted from this shift to modern construction materials, the form of the structures persisted, continuing to be unmistakably Finnish. A generation later, at least half the buildings on Finnish farms had been sided over or were of frame construction.[43]

Finnish barns. A number of barns, each performing a specialized function, also characterized the Finnish farm. Close to the farmhouse was a cattle barn, sometimes almost as carefully constructed as the house itself (fig. 8–26). Although early barns were usually of hewn and fitted log construction, later cattle barns were tall, narrow, gambrel-roofed structures, timber framed with vertical planks (fig. 8–27).[44] The ground floor of both early and late barns was given over to housing cattle in winter, to equipment storage, and sometimes to grain storage; the loft held the hay.

In addition to the cattle barn, each Finnish farm had several *latos* or hay barns (fig. 8–28). These are loosely fitted log structures built to hold the winter hay supply for the cattle. The logs are left round, held by saddle notches, and separated from one another to encourage air circulation. The side walls are inclined slightly outward toward the eaves, so that the end profile of the latos vaguely resembles that of a corncrib. Such inward-toeing walls are designed

148

to offer additional weather protection to the hay. The floor of the lato consists of a series of large poles or logs raised up on the sills, a foot or two above the ground to further encourage air circulation.[45] Latos follow the rule of Finnish farm structures and are always small. One is normally built in the farmstead for use in mid-winter, and others are located in the hay fields themselves, so that the cattle can be driven to their vicinity in both early and late winter.

Several reasons can be offered for constructing multiple latos of small size, rather than one large hay barn. First, the hay fields were frequently widely separated and a small lato could conveniently be loaded from the yield of a single field, thus reducing labor. Second, few Finnish farmers could afford horses at first, and the dispersed lato pattern alleviated the necessity of hauling the hay some distance to a main barn. Third, the

danger of fire was greatly reduced. If a fire did occur, only a small part of the crop would likely be destroyed when the latos were scattered. Fire in a main barn might mean the loss of all the feed for the cattle for the entire season. Fourth, constructing smaller barns was easier than building large structures because the logs that had to be handled were smaller. The Finnish farmer rarely had much help, and even neighbors lived at some distance. Furthermore, the traditions of communal assistance, so strong among Germans, for example, seem not to have been a characteristic among the independent Finns. Fifth, the Finnish farm grew slowly as the farmer gradually cut down the forest, burned off the brush, and dynamited the

Fig. 8–27 The Finnish cattle barn

Fig. 8–26 A Finnish log cattle barn (Old World Wisconsin Outdoor Museum, 1980)

stumps and boulders. As the farm expanded, new hay storage capacity was needed, but it was always added in small increments.

In Finland, at least in the areas of South Ostrobothnia from which most North American Finnish migrants originated, nineteenth-century farmsteads tended to be arranged around two or three internal courtyards.[46] In the upper Great Lakes, such an arrangement was not continued, but the associated practice of constructing smaller barns and outbuildings in a line apart from one another and roofing over the intervening open space was continued, up to a point.[47] The most likely combination was that of a small lato and an animal shed, with an open driveway between. The resulting connected structures have

149

Fig. 8–28 The Finnish *lato* or hay barn

all the look of a double-pen crib barn (see chap. 1).

Another special purpose Finnish barn is the *riihi*, or grain processing barn, although it was never widely introduced into North America.[48] The distinctive feature of the riihi is a large, chimneyless, earthen and stone furnace occupying one corner (fig. 8–29). Its function is to provide the heat needed to dry harvested grain. Because the climate of the upper Great Lakes is considerably drier than that of western Finland, artificial drying of grain was not normally needed. Furthermore, the New World farms produced little grain, preferring to concentrate on hay for dairy cattle. The little grain that was grown could be dried in the sauna.[49]

The sauna. The Finnish farmstead always can be identified by the sauna. Although apparently of Scandinavian origin, the sauna is now recognized as distinctly Finnish. Normally located somewhat away from the other build-

ings of the farmstead, partly because of the potential danger of fire, and partly to be near a source of water for washing, the sauna was among the first buildings erected by a Finnish settler. The earliest saunas are termed *savusauna*, or *smoke sauna*, because these buildings are without window or chimney, and the smoke from the fire has to escape through the partially open sauna door or through a tiny smoke vent, a square hole cut high up in the opposite gable wall.[50] Typically, the interior of the sauvasauna is black from the smoke of years of use.[51]

These early saunas are small, one-room buildings about nine by twelve feet,[52] constructed of tightly fitted logs, which are locked together by full dovetail, double, or other notches. Such construction is designed to conserve heat, as are the general absence of windows, the small-sized doorway, and the low ceiling. The walls of the sauna are between six and eight inches wide, and

Fig. 8–29 Cross section of a Finnish riihi (from Matti Kaups, "A Finnish Riihi in Minnesota, *Journal of the Minnesota Academy of Science* 38, nos. 2–3 [1972], p. 67)

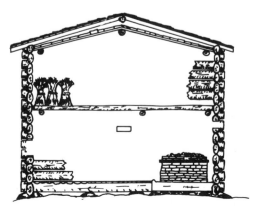

normally of pine logs "because their form is affected relatively little by temperature changes."[53] Seasoned timber is preferred, because green logs stay damp for up to a year and thus cannot absorb much moisture, which is critical in the sauna. Generally, the inside of the sauna is not painted, stained, or oiled because such treatment would reduce the capacity of the walls to absorb moisture.[54] The ceiling surface is comprised of split boards, covered by tar paper, overlaid with moss, sand, sod turned upside down, and straw.[55] A narrow open space separates the ceiling from the wooden shingle roof.

The smoke sauna was generally abandoned or modified in the late 1920s or the 1930s,[56] largely in response to the pressure of insurance companies who would not issue fire insurance on farmsteads with smoke saunas, and because of the introduction of the local safety laws forbidding the construction of such saunas.[57] The most common modifications were to install a chimney for the smoke and to enclose the open fire within a stove that became the dominant feature of the sauna. Comprised of large glacial boulders forming the side walls and smaller fieldstones making up the slightly domed top, the stove stood about four feet square and three feet high.[58] The object of the fire was not so much to heat the sauna directly as it was to heat the stones and boulders, which in turn provided a constant heat over a considerable time. The only other major interior feature of the savusauna was a wooden stepped platform, called the *lavo*, on which the bathers sat or reclined.

As Finnish farms became larger and more financially secure, the sauna frequently was built with an attached dressing room, or a frame dressing room was added to an earlier, modified sauvasauna (fig. 8–30). The addition of a dressing room also expanded the functions of the sauna, so that it could be used as a summer kitchen, laundry, smoke house, borning room, and as a craft room for weaving rugs, making birch-bark shoes, woodcarvings, and candles, and as a facility to dry grain, meat, flax, herbs, and berries, to germinate barley, and to prepare spruce and willow bark for tanning, and even as "sleeping quarters for the farm boys, who found some relief from plaguing mosquitos in its smoky-adorned atmo-

Fig. 8–30 A Finnish log and frame sauna (Old World Wisconsin Outdoor Museum, 1979)

sphere."[59] Clearly, the sauna lies close to the center of Finnish farm life. It, indeed, is the most persistent of Finnish farm structures. As time passes, all the other buildings are undergoing modification and the Finnish farmstead is becoming more American all the time. Such is not so clearly the case with Amish farms.

The Amish and Mennonite landscape

The Amish and Mennonites are often confused with one another. The two groups are related, both originating as Anabaptist followers of Menno Simons, a Dutch reformer priest of the sixteenth century. Frequently their farmsteads appear to be similar, and both groups have dress restrictions, although the Amish are more extreme in theirs.

North American Mennonites trace their origins back to two different groups in two parts of Europe. The first group to arrive in the New World, beginning with migrants to Pennsylvania in the eighteenth century, came mostly from southern Germany and northern Switzerland. They are sometimes called

Fig. 8–31 Location of major Amish-Mennonite settlements in northeastern United States

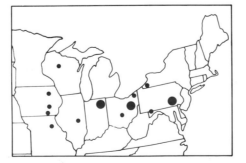

the Swiss Brethren. The Amish are a splinter group of the Swiss Brethren, founded by Jacob Amman in the late seventeenth century. Because they felt that the Mennonites and other Protestant reformers had not gone far enough in purifying the Christian Church, the Amish have been characterized as the "reformers of the Reformation."[60] Although some Amish came in the eighteenth century, most migrants to America arrived between 1815 and 1840.

Although the Amish avoided those areas where Mennonites had settled earlier, today the pattern of Amish and Mennonite settlements is similar (fig. 8–31), since many Amish have rebelled against rigid discipline and restrictions and have joined less severe Mennonite congregations, which thus have grown up in proximity to the Amish.[61] Consequently, it is difficult to separate the landscape of Amish and Mennonites, because neither group has formed a homogeneous settlement anywhere. Amish, Mennonites, and "English" farmers are always intermixed.

The Amish-Mennonite landscape is one in which religion accounts for a large number of the components, or at least the method in which the components are treated. Among the Amish, a strict regulation of the lives of the adherents requires conformity in the matter of house decoration, if not the form of the house. Certain features are acceptable and others are not. Among the Mennonites such proscription is less pervasive, but, nevertheless, the hand of tradition lies heavily upon the society.

151

An air of plainness and severity pervades both Amish and Mennonite homesteads, although more so in the former than in the latter. "The absence of all pictures or portraits of present or past generations, of all wall decorations, including wall paper, of rugs or carpets, of knickknacks or art objects, of fancy quilts, covers, or pillowcases heightens the impression of sobriety and austerity."[62]

Several characteristics have long been used by observers to locate and identify Amish-Mennonite farms, but such features are by no means infallible as indicators. Because electrical power is forbidden, the presence of a windmill is one such feature (fig. 8–32). However, in Mifflin County, Pennsylvania, one group popularly called the "White Buggy Amish" prohibits the use of windmills, which were considered too worldly when first introduced in the nineteenth century.[63]

Another feature often mentioned is that there are no lightning rods on either house or barn, since these are considered by the Amish to be against God's will. However, because many young Amish occupy tenant farms while saving to purchase their own farms, English owners frequently insist on the lightning rods being left in place to protect their investment. The same is true with electricity connections. While true Amish houses of most congregations will not have electric lines leading to the house or barn, properties occupied by Amish tenants may have them. It is also reported that the Amish, who purchase

Fig. 8–32 Windmill on an Amish farm. Note the buggies in front of barn. (Wayne County, Ohio, 1978)

houses having large, one-piece windows, replace the single glass with small panes.[64] Obviously, such modifications require capital and will not be made in tenant quarters.

Certain other features can be mentioned that provide clues in identifying Amish and Mennonite farmsteads. These would include distinctive aspects of the barn, the farmyard, and the house. For the most part, Amish and Mennonite barns are large versions of the Sweitzer German bank barn (see chap. 2). The barns are large, not just in anticipation of extensive farm operation but also, in some instances, to provide space for church services, which each farmer is expected to do periodi-

cally. If the house itself is large enough, the service will be held there, but, if not, the barn suffices. Indeed, many casual observers have suggested that the tall, narrow, slotted louver ventilators often found on these barns give them, together with the large proportions of the structures, a cathedrallike appearance. Some of these barns may be 50 feet wide and up to 120 feet long. Such large size does have a very practical aspect, however. Not only is grain and hay storage capacity increased, but the great superstructure of these two-and-a-half-story barns ensures that rapid temperature fluctuations in the basement stable and stall area will be kept to a minimum.[65] Another identifying characteristic of the

Amish-Mennonite barn is a series of geometric cut-outs high up on the gable wall (fig. 8–33). Such openings facilitate ventilation of the loft and may have been provided originally to attract barn swallows and other birds, considered to be beneficial and auspicious. A final aspect of the typical Amish barn is the presence of a large straw stack in the barnyard feeding lot (fig. 8–34).

Several features of the farmyard also mark the farm as Amish or Mennonite. Most farms have at least one kitchen garden, placed conspicuously so that it is in front or at the side of the house and easily seen from the road (fig. 8–35). The progress of the gardens and the diligence with which they are tended are carefully watched by neighbors and friends. A larger "truck patch" containing potatoes, sweet corn, and other vegetables also is cultivated, but its location is usually not so conspicuous.[66]

Fig. 8–34 Barnyard straw stack on a Mennonite farm. The German bank barn overhang has been boarded over. (Holmes County, Ohio, 1982)

Fig. 8–33 Gable cut-outs on a Mennonite barn (Ashland County, Ohio, 1977)

Fig. 8–35 A Mennonite farmstead in Wayne County, Ohio. The area in the foreground is the kitchen garden, plowed up and ready for planting. The garden fronts on a state highway which is just to the left of the photograph. (1982)

Fig. 8–36 A Mennonite farmstead in Berks County, Pennsylvania. Note the whitewashed board fence, the Sweitzer barn, and the four-over-four house. (1962)

Fig. 8–37 Bird houses on a Mennonite farmstead (Holmes County, Ohio, 1982)

The garden may be surrounded by a whitewashed board fence, another typical element. The barn feeding lot, and even the fields near the farmstead, also may be enclosed by such fences (fig. 8–36). Whitewashing appears to be equated among the Amish and Mennonites with cleanliness and order, so that not only are the board fences annually whitewashed, so also are stone walls, some of the smaller outbuildings, and even the farmstead tree trunks.[67] On the lawn of the farmstead, usually away from the garden but often close to the barn and/or animal pens, will be one or two multiple bird houses, painted white and perched high on slender poles (fig. 8–37).

The Amish or Mennonite house also offers some clues to the identity of its inhabitants. In the Kishocoquillas valley of Pennsylvania, where Amish have resided since the eighteenth century, Amish houses can be identified by the lack of projection of roofs beyond the gable line.[68] In all areas, one of the more reliable indicators of Amish and Mennonites is the presence of solid color, blue or green cloth curtains, drawn back to one side of the window frame during the day.

The houses of the Amish-Mennonites are large for several reasons. Families are large; seven or more children are not uncommon. Second, the family group is an extended family with three generations frequently housed in the dwelling. Third, many Amish build houses large enough to hold church services. Certain interior design features of Amish houses also are related to the holding of periodic church services. Doors between major first-floor rooms are especially wide, so that the congregation members seated in other rooms may see and hear those conducting the service (fig. 8–38). Some walls are made of removable panels for the same reason. Finally, hallways and closets are reduced or eliminated, so that only large rooms suitable for seating the congregation remain.[69]

Although usually greatly modified by additions, the most common house type encountered in Amish-Mennonite regions is the four-over-four house, previously discussed in chapter 5 of the first volume. In Ohio and Missouri, Amish-Mennonite houses also may be of the I-house type (see vol. 1, chap. 6), and in Indiana, Illinois, and Iowa, the Cornbelt cube house (see vol. 1, chap. 10) is fairly common. These latter houses were usually built by non-Amish settlers and acquired by the Amish when the farm was purchased. Because the Amish and Mennonites are expanding rural communities, many occupy nontraditional farmsteads and, when buildings need replacement, some use nontraditional materials and designs, further obscuring this community in the landscape.[70]

Finally, the institution of the grandfather (*gross-vater* or *gross-dawdy*) house is undeniably Amish or Mennonite. In many instances, grandparents simply live in an apartment or separate section within the Amish farmhouse, but usually an entirely separate structure is built. The grandfather house is a physical expression of the strength of the Amish or Mennonite family organization. Smaller than the main house, it may be built to the left and slightly in front of the older house, so that the corners of the two dwellings adjoin.[71] The proximity of the dwelling is symbolic of the closeness of the family. Even when the houses do not touch, a common porch frequently connects the two houses (fig. 8–39). The grandfather house accommodates the parents when they retire from active direction of the farm and turn over responsibility to the youngest son and his wife, following the rules of ultimogeniture which prevail among the Amish. In many instances, however, the house has already served a useful career as a residence for newly married, elder sons and their young, small families before they move to farms of their own.[72]

Fig. 8–38 Floor plan of an Amish house

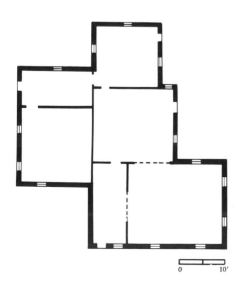

Fig. 8–39 An Amish I house to the left and the new grandfather house to the right (Wayne County, Ohio, 1978)

The Russian-Mennonite landscape of Manitoba

The second major group of Mennonite migrants to North America originated in Friesland, and later migrated to northern Germany and Russia. Beginning in 1874 many of the Mennonites residing in Russia fled to North America to escape military conscription. A few came to the United States, but most went to Canada, where the government was willing to reserve large tracts of land for communal settlement.[73] In southern Manitoba, the Russian group, unlike their Swiss counterparts, at first established agricultural villages from which the farmers tilled fields at some distance. The original villages assumed the form of *strassendorf,* a settlement of a single, exceptionally wide street upon which every residential property fronted. Individual lots were 200 feet wide and 500 or more feet deep.[74]

The earliest structures of the Manitoba Mennonites included dugouts, sod buildings, and log houses, all intended as temporary dwellings. The dugout (*sarai* or *semlin*) appears to have been the prototype for the later Mennonite structures. The typical dugout measured about twenty-six by twenty-six feet and had a thatch roof on a light, poplar frame, resting directly on the ground. The front of the structure sheltered farm animals, whereas the rear part was divided into two rooms for the family.[75] None of these has survived into the twentieth century.

When settlers became more affluent

and sought to replace the early temporary dwellings, they retained the basic form of connected house and barn. "The joining of the house and barn had the advantage of greater warmth, comfort and protection for humans and animals alike, especially in winter."[76] Chores could be done without going outside in inclement weather, especially during the great prairie blizzards. What would seem like an obvious problem of hygiene in a combined structure appears not to have been significant, because housebarns have continued to be built into the present century. Even fire danger failed to dissuade Mennonites from following the practice, perhaps because a fire wall was sometimes inserted between the house and barn portions of the building.[77]

In the Mennonite settlements southeast of Winnipeg, in the area called the East Reserve, structures were made of a variant of Red River frame construction, but those to the southwest, in the West Reserve, normally were built of horizontal, hewn logs locked together

by dovetail corners. However, by the turn of the century, dimensional lumber had largely supplanted both logs and Red River frame.[78] In many cases two by fours or two by sixes were laid one atop the other to form solid walls.

The house and barn were oriented so that roof ridges ran in the same direction in the earliest period (fig. 8–40). At first, a single gable roof covered both parts, but later, the roof of the house was separately framed and perhaps one to three feet lower than the barn roof, although at the same pitch. Initially, all roofs in both Mennonite areas were of light, poplar construction, clearly derived from the *sarai* and European antecedents. Early houses have massive sills and exposed beam ends.

The house part of the structure measures roughly twenty-four to twenty-five feet wide by about forty feet long. The gable faces the street, and thus the main door opens into the side yard in most instances, and in virtually all the earlier houses. After the turn of the twentieth century, houses were shifted

Fig. 8–40 Manitoba Mennonite housebarn

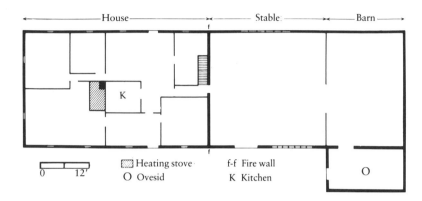

Fig. 8–41 Floor plan of a Manitoba Mennonite housebarn

House — Stable — Barn

0   12'
▨ Heating stove
O Ovesid
f-f Fire wall
K Kitchen
K
O

ninety degrees, and connected to the barns only by a lower profile, intermediate, hall-like structure. In these houses the front door faces the street.

The most unusual features of the Manitoba Mennonite house, aside from the large rooms, are the central location of the kitchen (fig. 8–41) and the brick stove-furnace, which not only provided an ample cooking place but was a source of space heating as well. This interior oven frequently stood six feet high and covered about twelve square feet of floor space. It was built in such a fashion that although it served the kitchen, its walls formed parts of other rooms so as to aid in their heating. In this respect, the interior stove represents a joining of a Slavic feature to a North German house.[79] Similar stove-furnace ovens are encountered in Ukrainian houses and in German-Russian houses on the Great Plains (see above in this chapter and chapter 10 in the first

volume). The central location of the kitchen in Manitoba Mennonite houses clearly places them within the group of houses derived from the southern shore of the Baltic Sea.[80]

Little detailed information can be provided on the barn portion of the Manitoba Mennonite housebarn because no detailed studies apparently have been made. Generally speaking, the barns, which approximate a size of twenty-five by forty-five feet, are divided into two unequal sections.[81] The larger, front part functions as a stable, housing both cattle and horses. The smaller rear area is used for grain, straw, and equipment storage. Projecting sideways from the end of the barn, and thus helping to enclose the farmyard, is a small addition called the *ovesid*. Sometimes this is used for tool and gear storage and at other times it may function as a milk house. The ovesid is covered by an extension of the main barn roof, creating an off-

center, unbalanced roofline. Although many of these barns remain unpainted, barn doors, by way of contrast, are almost always painted white. The final distinctive feature is a row of small, closely set windows along the side walls of the stable. No description of the framing of these barns has yet appeared. The same is true for the various outbuildings, although E. K. Francis has mentioned the common occurrence of summer kitchens, icehouses, smokehouses, implement sheds, chicken houses, and granaries.[82]

The Mormon landscape

As did the Manitoba Mennonites, the Mormons created an agricultural village landscape. In both cases, the impetus for this seems to have been the same, a need to conserve the religious structure and cohesion of the group. Two additional reasons contributed to the Mormon preference for village settlement over scattered individual farms. The danger of Indian attack in mid-nineteenth-century Utah was an important consideration, and the most effective agricultural production resulted from irrigation, which required a ready labor force to construct, maintain, protect, and operate the irrigation works. Farmers settled in villages were more suitable for this than those scattered across the countryside.

The Mormon settlement pattern and the form of the Mormon villages have received considerable study.[83] Unlike

157

the *strassendorf* of the Manitoba Mennonites, the Mormon villages utilized a grid plan, and the features of the grid are sufficiently distinctive to give a unique character to all Mormon towns. The streets are exceptionally wide, long, and straight, and oriented to the cardinal compass points. Town blocks may be as large as ten acres with individual lots up to two and a half acres in size. The large size of the lots permits the erection of barns and farm outbuildings, so that towns have a distinctive, cluttered, but rural appearance.

Such a mixed rural-town settlement also has certain important disadvantages.[84] Sanitation becomes a problem if livestock are kept in large numbers, and much time and effort is required each day to travel between home and the fields.

The form of the Mormon town plan owes much to the influence of the centralized Mormon faith.[85] Joseph Smith himself worked out and promulgated the plans for the "City of Zion" which became the model for all Mormon settlement in the West.[86] The encouragement of settlement in villages rather than in the open countryside, thus, became a central item of Mormon faith.[87] But as Richard Jackson notes, "the Mormon village is more important as the hearth from which the landscape was modified than as an example of the unique sacred city of Zion."[88]

Mormonism, which did not adhere to all the characteristics of nineteenth-century communal, utopian societies, nevertheless did attempt to influence its members to settle on small farms in order to accommodate a continuous influx of new converts. Such settlement also greatly reduced the cost of fencing and irrigation facilities for individual farmers.[89] Rick Francaviglia defines the unique Mormon landscape by identifying ten "visual clues" that reveal that landscape: wide streets; roadside irrigation ditches; barns and granaries in town; unpainted farm buildings; open field landscape around the town; hay derricks (see chap. 6); the "Mormon" fence (see chap. 7); a high proportion of I houses; the dominant use of brick; and Mormon ward chapels.[90]

Jackson has proposed a somewhat different set of elements that combine to create the Mormon landscape. He suggests: nucleated settlement with large-scale grid pattern morphology; the persistence of poplar trees as a relic feature; mini-farms accompanying each residence; impoverished appearance of farmsteads; brick homes "with their distinctive architectural style."[91]

Combining the lists of both Jackson and Francaviglia produces a surprisingly detailed description of the Mormon cultural landscape. Nevertheless, certain further statements or elaborations about Mormon buildings and other features should be made.

Building Mormon houses. Mormon converts were drawn from wide backgrounds and origins. Some built their new Utah houses and farm buildings following the folk traditions they had known in the old country. Danes, for example, built long, low-appearing houses with asymmetrically positioned doors and windows, thatched roofs, and chimneys placed near the center.[92] However, such structures were the exception rather than the rule. As Richard Poulsen has noted of the stone buildings erected in the town of Beaver, Utah, Mormon structures show a "blend of European folk architecture, eastern United States building tradition and Mormon utilitarianism."[93]

Part of the explanation for the successful suppression of foreign ethnic traits is undoubtedly related to the converts' commonly held idea that they were making a fresh start in a new land. As a consequence, old traditions could be abandoned with little hesitancy. Another factor in ensuring a uniform architecture in Mormon communities is probably the important cooperative village aid that was given to newly arrived Mormons, of both domestic and foreign origins, in constructing their new homes.[94] This assistance, provided by Mormons of diverse backgrounds, resulted in a blending of techniques, with a heavy emphasis on what was pragmatic and the most cost effective.

The initial period of Mormon settlement was one in which the immediate need for shelter was paramount. Families built their own houses with the aid and counsel of earlier settlers. The materials used were those readily available or most easily utilized. The need to obtain shelter almost instantaneously "required temporary reduction of known folk housing ideals; no family could immediately build the dream house it sought or attained in Nauvoo or Kirtland."[95]

Dugouts and log houses. Some early settlers constructed rough dugouts consisting of a "nearly square room measuring somewhere between 12 and 18 feet and dug to about 3 or 4 feet below the surface."[96] Sometimes the earth walls were lined with logs, and sometimes the upper walls were merely logs laid on top of the ground. The roof, composed of layers of light poles, willow branches, and dirt, was not unlike that used in the Southwest. Roofs were mostly gable form, but shed roofs have also been reported for early dugouts.[97] The entrance to the structure was in the gable wall. These dugouts had all the disadvantages common to sod dugouts (see vol. 1, chap. 8) and were usually abandoned within a year or two.

Because they could be built about as quickly and cheaply as dugouts, log or adobe houses were much preferred by early settlers. Of the two, log was less popular, since it was considered crude and unattrctive in comparison to stuccoed adobe.[98]

Several reasons explain the bias of Mormon settlers against log construction. Timber was in short supply in much of the mountain West and, hence, it was needed as fuel more than as building material. Second, many of the most influential early Mormons derived from a postfrontier New England heritage in which log construction was considered crude, rough, and socially inferior.[99] Finally, the Mormon leadership had publicly urged adoption of adobe, brick, or stone construction because of perceived fire hazards.[100]

Log houses were one or two room structures that were quite similar, both in form and notching, to those encountered in eastern North America. The major difference was the use of the "dirt" roof in many instances.[101] Various woods were employed for these houses depending upon their availability; the cottonwoods of the lowland river banks were used most commonly. Unfortunately, cottonwood has an uneven, spiral grain, so its use produced a shabby, uneven building. Quaking aspen is even less desirable, and it was used only for barns and outbuildings.[102] The long, easily hewed, straight-grained conifers of the mountains were the most valued construction woods.

Only in the northern reaches of Mormon settlement were log houses built in substantial numbers. In Idaho, where abundant conifer forests occur, log construction continued to be important almost until World War II.[103]

Mormon adobe houses. In most parts of Mormon territory the basic early building material was sun-dried adobe brick. A closely related, alternative method of construction, using mud concrete or poured adobe, was possible in areas having a high lime content in the clay.[104] However, the use of this technique was quite limited; it was adobe bricks that became the standard building material throughout most of the Mormon area until well into the twentieth century. As late as 1925, nearly a quarter of all the houses in Provo, Utah, for example, were of adobe.[105]

Several factors explain the adoption of adobe building methods by the Mormons, who lacked such a tradition before coming to the West. First, of course, was the dry climate and the consequent restriction of good timber supplies. This also meant that fuel was not available to produce kiln-fired bricks.

Only upon the completion of railroads to the Utah coal deposits in 1875 would the cheap fuel that was necessary for brick making become widely available.[106] Initial isolation of the settlements also meant that nails were in extremely short supply. Again, the coming of the railroad made nails available for lumber frame construction.[107] Finally, building with adobe was simple. Completely untrained individuals could successfully erect a building, and they could do it even faster than they could build a log or timber structure, because those materials usually had to be collected and hauled to the building site.

Still, the early Mormon builders did have problems with adobe. They were inexperienced in selecting and mixing the component soil materials. If they selected too much clay, the bricks shrank and cracked upon drying; if too much sand was used, they crumbled and failed to bond properly. Furthermore, in their haste to erect shelters, they often attempted to use the adobe bricks before they were thoroughly cured.[108]

Another important problem was that unless the annual precipitation was very low, adobe walls had to be protected by a mud plaster or stucco in order to keep them from weathering badly. Writing in 1945, Joseph Spencer observed that "relatively low annual rainfall, good workmanship, perfected techniques, and the exceedingly greasy, sticky clay from which the bricks were made have allowed retention of pioneer adobe houses in the south long after a more rigorous climate, poor materials, and

159

changing public fancy caused replacement in northern Utah."[109]

Mormon brick and frame houses. Many writers have commented on the widespread use of fired brick in Mormon house construction. But brickyards were not widely established until the 1860s, which was almost a generation after original settlement. Initially, bricks were used primarily as a veneer over adobe walls, but gradually, as fired bricks became more plentiful, they began to be employed in load-bearing walls and foundations.[110] Brick became so popular that by the 1880s it began to dominate wherever suitable clays occurred. Only in those communities where bricks could not be procured cheaply were stone, adobe, and lumber used.[111]

Lumber frame house are not very common in Mormon settlement areas. Virtually none were constructed until the completion of railroads in the 1880s, although sawmills were established in the early 1850s. Most of the lumber produced in these early mills went for rafters, doors, window frames, and furniture. After 1870 many of the early adobe houses were covered with clapboard or weatherboard siding. After the turn of the century, commercial lumberyards began to import quantities of precut lumber of superior quality from outside areas.[112]

Mormon stone houses. Much more extensively utilized than lumber framing is a wide variety of building stones. The type of underlying bedrock varies throughout Mormon territory so that stone houses demonstrate a considerable range of composition and color. Because of weight, building stone use is restricted to towns near quarries or bedrock deposits. Towns such as Beaver City, Spring City, Willard, Manti, and Farmington have high concentrations of stone dwellings, whereas other settlements may have very few. A second factor contributing to the uneven distribution of stone dwellings is the presence or absence of stonemasons. Most of the converts who built stone buildings in Mormon territory were Europeans.

The stone structures, even the small, one-story ones, give an impression of solidity, strength, and permanence. Walls are frequently between sixteen and twenty-two inches thick, window and door openings are small and rather few in number, and roof pitch is often somewhat low and combined with a heavy eave line.[113] Despite these particular characteristics, Mormon stone houses, together with other Mormon houses built in other materials, fit into a series of types that apparently depend upon the time of construction.

Mormon house types. Among the earliest structures is the single-room Mormon house (fig. 8–42A). Nearly square, its most typical dimensions are fourteen by sixteen or fifteen by seventeen feet. These measurements are evidence that this structure derives from the English traditions (see vol. 1, chap. 8). Other features of the one-room Mormon house type include an inside gable chimney, often a rear lean-to ad-

dition, either one offset door and one window or a centered door with small windows on either side, and one or one-and-a-half-story elevation.[114] Few of these one-room houses have survived. Much more common are dwellings with a two-room plan.

In both plan and elevation, the one-story Mormon house resembles double pen or saddlebag houses. However, because they are built mostly of adobe or brick, these terms, which were earlier associated with log construction in eastern North America, never have been applied to the Mormon structures. However, Mormon houses have been generally labeled "central hall" houses,[115] which is true, unfortunately, only for certain houses, usually those built after the Civil War. What *is* almost universally true is that Mormon houses have centered doors, whether or not the door opens into a central hallway. In some two-room plan houses, however, one finds two front doors instead of a centered door. This is further evidence to suggest a double pen house, but, emphatically, it has no connection with polygamy, a folk tale with considerable tenacity.

The Mormon two-room house, subtype 1 (see fig. 8–42B) has a one-story elevation, a rectangular plan of two equal or nearly equal rooms, interior gable chimneys, one or two front doors, windows in the front wall but not elsewhere, very little roof overhang, and a general absence of decoration.[116] Built of adobe or brick, these houses are concentrated in the central and southern parts of Mormon territory.

The Mormon two-room house, subtype 2 (fig. 8–42C) occurs primarily in the central and northern Mormon re-

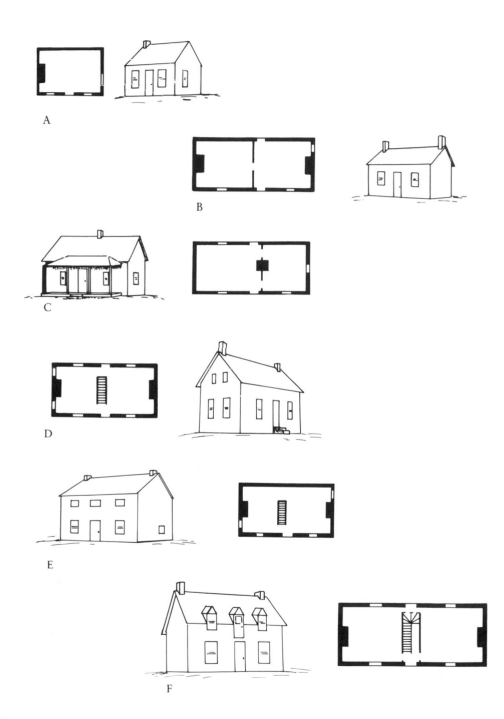

gions. It is characterized by rooms of unequal size, a centered doorway balanced by two windows, often additional small, offset windows in each gable wall rather than rear windows, a gable roof, and a centered chimney.[117] It may be built in stone, brick, or lumber frame. In the latter case, a porch often covers the facade of the dwelling (fig. 8–43).

The Mormon two-room house, subtype 3 (see fig. 8–42D) is distinguished from earlier subtypes by its one-and-a-half-story elevation. The facade is balanced with a central door and flanking windows, and the interior consists of equal-sized rooms separated by a straight flight of stairs that gives access to the upper level. This house is built usually in brick and its modest decoration consists of brick window arches and corbeled chimneys (fig. 8–44).

The Mormon two-room house, subtype 4 (see fig. 8–42E) is reminiscent of the one-and-a-half New England cottage (described in chapter 10 of the first volume) and may well be a derivative of this earlier structure. Such a circumstance is not unreasonable given the strong Mormon connection with the areas in which one-and-a-half New England cottages were built. Subtype 4 houses are limited to the northern areas of Mormon settlement. They are built either of lumber frame or of stone, and have chimneys at the gables. The facade is always balanced, whether or not a central hallway is present. The most easily recognized feature of this house is

Fig. 8–42 Early Mormon house types

Fig. 8–43 A Mormon two-room house, subtype 2, located near Logan, Utah. Greek Revival styling includes the gable pediment, the low porch roof, and the porch columns. (1977)

Fig. 8–44 A Mormon two-room house, subtype 3

the very small windows of the upper level. It is this feature that makes identification swift and certain.

The second-story windows of subtype 5 houses are treated quite differently (see fig. 8–42F). Instead of being reduced, they remain at full scale, but are positioned so that they interrupt the eave line. These very distinctive windows are called *Dixie dormers,* probably because they were first described in that part of southern Utah locally called *Dixie.* They occur throughout the state of Utah and perhaps beyond, however. Probably for the sake of balance, a full-sized door occupies the space midway between the Dixie dormers. Speculation

has long centered on the purpose of these doors "that lead to nowhere," an apparent contradiction in the otherwise pragmatic Mormon architecture. The explanation seems to be that the small balcony that accompanied these doors was constructed of wood (in contrast to the house, which was built of brick or stone). The thin pieces of unpainted wood, much more susceptible to weathering and decay than the sturdy brick or stone, rapidly deteriorated and ultimately disappeared—hence, the "doorway to nowhere."[118]

Considerable changes were introduced into Mormon architecture by about 1860 or slightly thereafter. Larger, two-story houses began to appear in numbers. Most were designed and constructed by professional builders, but they still retained a strong tradi-

tional aspect. Generally, they can be classified as either I houses (see vol. 1, chap. 6 for basic descriptions) or four-over-four houses (see vol. 1, chap. 5).

At the same time that houses were reaching a full two stories, building materials were changing. Brick and lumber frame began to predominate. The walls of many adobe or log houses were stuccoed or covered with wooden siding or brick. As houses continued to expand, rear wings were added to I houses, producing L-plan and T-plan houses.[119]

Most significant of all, Greek Revival stylistic elements came into vogue.[120] Greek Revival had been the dominant architectural style in New York, Ohio, and Illinois when the initial Mormon colonies were established in those areas.[121] In those earlier times, Greek Revival represented the most modern and up-to-date architecture in the areas the Mormons left, but it usually could not be used under the frontier conditions of Utah. Gradually, as these conditions ameliorated, the Greek Revival style began to take hold. And it persisted long after the style had died out elsewhere, because the self-imposed isolation of the Mormons prevented other styles from developing until late in the nineteenth century.[122]

Mormon barns and outbuildings. Except for hay derricks (see chap. 6), Mormon structures other than houses have not received much attention. Both transverse and side-entry barns occur. Some of these resemble the double-crib or English barns of eastern North America (fig. 8–45). Constructed of unhewn logs held in place by saddle notch-

Fig. 8–45 An English type barn, near Paragonah, Utah. The logs are unhewn and held in place by saddle notching. The gables and roof are covered with sawn planks. (1967)

ing, both the roof and the gables are covered by vertically laid planks. The major function of these barns, in addition to providing some stabling space on the ground floor, is to store the large amounts of hay needed for winter feeding of stock. Additionally, the barns often contained calving pens, grain bins, and harness and implement rooms.[123]

Very similar in plan (which may suggest a common origin) is a second type of hay barn that originally had gable doors.[124] The plan dimensions are on the order of 1:2 and the barn is almost as tall as it is long, giving the structure a distinctive form (fig. 8–46). Early versions had gable roofs, but later the gambrel roof was used. In both instances, however, vertical planks provided the roof covering. Another modification in the later barns was the addition of hay hoods, which permitted the elimination of the gable doors and increased interior

storage.[125] Animal shelter and storage functions were moved to flanking sheds, which became common features of most Mormon barns in the later nineteenth and early twentieth centuries.

Because the climate in the mountain West is quite dry, many farmers found that complete barns were not really necessary. Hay could be stored in the open (hence, the importance of hay derricks), or in hay shelters, which were nothing more than barns without sides (fig. 8–47). The dry climate also may have been a factor in the construction of what have been called "inside-out" granaries, in which the studs are not covered by exterior cladding.[126] Not all Mormon granaries are of this type, however. Some are built of stone or adobe, particularly in the southern sections of Mormonland.

Finally, a recent study has been made of thatched-, flat-, or shed-roofed cow shelters, and this work extends a bit fur-

Fig. 8–46 Sheds have been added to the basic Mormon barn, near Randolph, Utah. Siding has been left off at the eave line of the main structure to permit light to enter and for ventilation. (1977)

ther the range of identifiable Mormon features.[127] These structures consist of a post-and-beam framework of poles covered with a rough roof of loose straw.

Despite the many studies that have been made of Mormon houses and of Mormon village patterns, the definitive study of the pioneer Mormon landscape remains to be done. But here, as elsewhere with other cultural groups, time is short before some of the most important elements are irreparably lost.

Fig. 8–47 A hay shelter near Provo, Utah (1977)

9 Settlement Landscape Study: Agenda for the Future

The preceding nineteen chapters collectively represent the first comprehensive study of North American rural settlement forms. In addition to much new research, combined with various methods of interpretation, each chapter relies heavily on previously published studies, so that the present book can be said to be a summary of the current state of settlement landscape or folk building research in North America.

In the roughly two decades that have elapsed since Fred Kniffen, in a presidential address to the Association of American Geographers, called for a concerted research campaign to unlock the secrets of American folk building,[1] an increasing number of American and Canadian geographers have taken up the challenge. One can trace most of their work in the references listed for each of the preceding chapters. Within the same period, the most comprehensive volume on material culture has been produced, not by a geographer but by a folklorist, Henry Glassie.[2] His work has acted as a stimulus for a later generation of folklorists, whose research also has contributed to the present volume.

Both geographers and folklorists seem to be fully committed to landscape studies. Architects, landscape architects, historians, anthropologists, and scholars in other fields generally have been less active. Nonetheless, individuals in such disciplines frequently have written excellent works. Some of these are reviewed in chapter 8.

Despite the efforts already made, much still remains to be accomplished in order to reconstruct the settlement landscape of North America. Furthermore, as this research continues, intriguing questions arise pertaining to the relationships between apparently unconnected structures, various techniques, and research methods. The balance of this chapter raises a very large number of such problems, as well as identifying those areas that will require further investigation. It thus functions as a research agenda for future studies of the settlement landscape of North America. Of course, there will be research topics that cannot be foreseen at present that will have to be added as time passes.

Bibliographies and terminology

Because the study of the settlement landscape is such a relatively young field of inquiry, certain of the most basic concerns have yet to be resolved. For example, the widely dispersed publication outlets for this research require the preparation of both general and specialized bibliographies in order to facilitate additional study. Only by locating and consulting the widely scattered materials can the quality of new research be maintained. A few bibliographies already exist, but many more are needed.[3] The value of such bibliographies will increase as time passes.

A related problem is the lack of a totally accepted terminology. Furthermore, the nomenclature that is employed has not been standardized, so considerable confusion currently exists. The use of the term *bungalow* to describe one-story, gable-entry houses in Louisiana is a case in point. Perhaps such a term should properly be reserved for those houses that derive from the bungalow movement of the early twentieth century (see vol. 1, chap. 11). At a different scale, one might cite the term *eyebrow window*, which has been used to describe the small, upper level windows of both saltbox houses and one-and-a-half New England cottages (see vol. 1, figs. 3–14 and 10–5). Such windows really should be called *knee windows, lie-on-your-stomach windows,* or *half windows,* but emphatically *not* eyebrow windows, a term properly reserved for small, half-circular windows let into the roof (fig. 9–1).

In some instances, early workers have applied names that later proved not to be entirely appropriate. The Quaker-

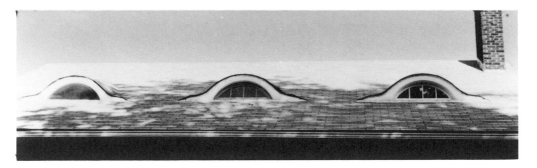

Fig. 9–1 Examples of eyebrow windows (Akron, Ohio, 1981)

plan house (vol. 1, chap. 5) and the Flemish cottage (vol. 1, chap. 4) are two of the most conspicuous examples. Although acceptance of an agreed-upon terminology is essential to the growth of this field of study, all researchers would do well to coin new terms only with the greatest reluctance.

Another aspect of the problem of terminology is the difficulty in securing clear identification of relationships (or perhaps lack of relationship) between similar appearing phenomena. By way of illustration, an investigation is needed into the possible connection between Red River frame construction used by the Ukrainian settlers of southern Manitoba and *pièce-sur-pièce* construction, which derives from French origins. Several questions need to be answered. First, in what particulars do the two methods differ? Second, did the Ukrainians borrow the technique from the French or was it independently derived from their own traditions? If borrowed, when and how did the process operate? And what could this tell us about possible links between other ethnic groups in other areas?

Classification and identification of types

For some structures not even the most basic classification system has been agreed upon. Barns are the most noticeable example. Although several scholars have produced works dealing wholly, or in part, with various kinds of barns, the present work is the first to attempt to relate all barns to one another. Additional attention certainly needs to be given to this subject. Hay hoods, the gable projection of many barns (chap. 1), also are in need of a clear classification system as well as further study.

The lack of adequate research on many aspects of settlement landscape prevents full development of the field. In some cases, this hiatus covers great spans. For example, no study exists of Russian structures in North America, beyond the reconstructions of Fort Ross, California. In the case of another quite different group, the buildings erected by the Scandinavian immigrants have received virtually no attention.[4]

165

Certain particular structures need more careful analysis. A study of the component elements, the geographical distribution, and the relationship to other houses of the one-and-a-half New England cottage is warranted. Similar studies of I houses, German-Russian houses, and Baltic three-room houses also are needed. Such research is especially critical because of the wide geographical extent of each of these structures.

Potential relationships between structures of similar morphology also require investigation. Among the more obvious is the possible connection between Italianate style houses and the Cornbelt cube house, or that between the double pen and the hall-and-parlor.

Comparative folk building studies

Many important questions remain about the possible connections between the structures of different ethnic groups. First, to what degree do particular environmental conditions evoke the same or similar cultural response in different peoples? For example, dwellings consisting of a single file of rooms, such as the Charleston single house and the shotgun house, seem to be concentrated in southern United States. How important has climatic influence been in molding the plans of these houses?

A second consideration is to track down whatever connection exists between the structures of quite different ethnic groups to determine, if possible, the effect of one structure upon another. In Canada, a question arises concerning the influence that the Ontario cottage may have had on the German-Russian house (vol. 1, chap. 10). In the American southwest, a rather different study needs to be undertaken to determine whether Spanish vertical *jacal* construction, which resembles French *poteaux-en-terre*, is in fact derived from it. Perhaps this might be undertaken as part of a larger study of jacal construction methods and techniques in the American southwest.

Finally, within a single nationality group, the links that may exist between structures in widely separated geographical locations or at different times frequently have received little scholarly attention. The most obvious case is that of French building in the St. Lawrence valley and, later, in the mid-Mississippi valley and in Louisiana. Why were certain forms and techniques transferred, but not others? Another important series of relationships are those that exist among the structures built by the various German communities in Pennsylvania, Wisconsin, Missouri, Texas, and elsewhere.

Unanswered questions

The longer one examines the subject of material-settlement landscape study, the greater the number of unanswered questions that comes to mind. Listed below, in no particular order of significance, are some of the more obvious and basic ones:

1. Why did the Dutch in the Hudson valley hearth leave virtually no distinguishing impact on land division, boundaries, and settlement pattern?

2. Why were roofing tiles more commonly employed around Charleston, South Carolina, than elsewhere in colonial America?

3. What is the origin (or ethnic connection) of the built-in or recessed porch on houses of southeastern and central United States?

4. Why didn't any early French houses built of stone survive in the St. Louis, Missouri, area?

5. What was the process by which shotgun houses migrated across the southeastern United States and the Mississippi valley areas?

6. Is upstate New York the origin of the raised or basement barn type?

7. Why does one find saddlebag houses in some areas, double pen houses in others, and dog-trot houses in still others? When single-room dwellings were expanded, what governed the choice of the particular mode of expansion?

8. Where did the four-crib barn originate and what relationship does it have to other crib barns?

9. If the transverse-frame barn evolved from the four-crib barn, why were the side openings closed in rather than the gable-end openings?

166

10. Robert Bastian has identified a porch barn apparently from Pomerania and occurring in central Wisconsin, and Charles Calkins and Martin Perkins have found a Pomeranian stable barn of different morphology in the same state. What is the relationship, if any, of these two kinds of structures.[5] Additionally, Robert Ensminger has raised important questions about Wisconsin porch barns and Pennsylvania forebay barns.[6] These questions need further discussion.

11. What outbuildings occur on farmsteads having New England connected barns? How do they differ from those of farmsteads having smaller barns, such as the English barn?

12. When, where, and why did the Erie Shore barn originate? The radical departure in both plan and form of this barn from virtually all other types requires investigation and explanation.

13. Why were round-roof barns adopted?

14. What is the origin of the pole barn? Where did it first appear?

15. Why is there a concentration of Wisconsin dairy barns in north central West Virginia?

16. Crib barns have been reported in the lower peninsula of Michigan and across Illinois. Is this information accurate and correct? How is this geographical distribution accounted for?

17. What is the date of erection of the first silos in West Virginia and Missouri?

18. To what extent was the Ukrainian Galician house influenced by Polish cultural elements, or the Ukrainian Bukowinian house by Rumanian elements?

19. The centrally positioned, interior stove is a characteristic of Ukrainian houses, German-Russian houses, and Manitoba Mennonite housebarns. What are the connections between these structures?

20. What was the impetus for the turning of the house part of the Manitoba Mennonite housebarn ninety degrees from the barn, around the turn of the twentieth century?

21. Why did Mormons shift to an end entry for dugouts and log cabins when they arrived in Utah, and then shift back to a side entry in later houses?

22. How does the form of shotgun houses vary from area to area?

23. What is the specific relationship between the Cornbelt cube house and the western bungalow?

Wilbur Zelinsky has raised additional questions about the use of stone in the material culture of North America, which still await investigation: "Why the contradiction in New England between the ubiquitous stone fence and the non-use of stone as a house-building material? Why was stone an important house material in some parts of southeastern Pennsylvania where it was distinctly subsidiary as a fencing material? And why was stone employed so widely for the underpinnings of houses and for chimneys in the southern Piedmont and Appalachians and almost never for any other purpose?"[7]

The whole question of the selective use of building material has thus far been studied on a quite limited basis for geographically restricted areas and in rather generalized terms. Much has been written on the techniques and methods of construction, especially for both log and timber frame structures, but few scholars have attempted to examine the rationale for the choice of particular materials. The best of such studies are those by Richard Pillsbury, Charles Gritzner, Richard Jackson, and John Hudson.[8]

These questions by no means exhaust the list of as-yet-unanswered questions facing researchers (see chap. 8, for example). Perhaps they don't even touch the most important aspects of material-settlement landscape study.

A research agenda for the future

A number of basic, and sometimes quite comprehensive, investigations remain to be launched. By identifying them, a research agenda can be formulated that offers numerous possibilities for scholars in a wide variety of disciplines. Indeed, the greater the number of viewpoints from which research is undertaken, the greater the possibility of cross-checking results, and consequently of avoiding error. Given herewith are the projects, tasks, or areas of study that at least one worker in the field feels ought to be undertaken in the future. The order of listing is not significant.

1. Existing works in French that cover the material-settlement landscape of the St. Lawrence valley should be translated into English.

2. Dutch houses, barns, and house-barns are the antecedent structures of those erected in the New York–New Jersey Dutch hearth and, subsequently, in southwestern Michigan. The relationships between buildings in the two areas requires detailed and careful investigation.

3. An attempt to generalize the regional distribution for the colonial period of brick, stone, timber frame, and log construction could provide a foundation for similar studies of structures from later periods.

4. An in-depth study, including origins, evolution, subtypes, and geographical distribution of the four-over-four house is needed.

5. A definitive study of structures, especially dwellings, of Indians of the eastern woodlands of North America will confirm that existing studies are tentative, fragmentary, or provincial.

6. A comprehensive examination of Huguenot-plan houses is long overdue.

7. In fact, the evolution of the entire range of structures in southeastern United States needs to be carefully traced.

8. Little has been written specifically about the Spanish-Mexican material-settlement landscape. The impact of this culture in the landscape of the Southwest needs to be assessed, along with the types of structures developed in the process.[9]

9. A study of the camelback house ought to be undertaken, especially a comparative study of the house in, say, Louisville, Kentucky, with that in Louisiana.

10. The southern pyramid-roof house extends over the entire southeastern quarter of the United States. It is the dominant folk type in many parts of this area, yet its origin, characteristics, and evolution never have been investigated in depth. Research on this house is long overdue.

11. No scholar has yet produced any study exclusively devoted to the upright-and-wing house, although this is one of the most important dwellings of the eastern Midwest. Its study should be quite rewarding.

12. Also lacking is a careful geographical survey of the distribution of log corner-notching types. What is needed is almost a census of notches, and, consequently, such a survey would probably have to be undertaken by a national organization like the Pioneer America Society. Techniques that could be employed have already been worked out for the state of Texas by geographer Terry Jordan.[10]

13. No study has yet been made of diamond notching, a type apparently limited to southern Virginia and northern North Carolina.

14. Despite its great importance, the Upland South folk culture has not been the subject of detailed analysis. Its existence has long been recognized by cultural geographers, folklorists, and others, but many of its salient characteristics have not been clearly identified and studied (see vol. 1, chap. 10).

15. Much has been written on log building techniques, but very little has been written of the form of log houses. The major exception is the works of Eugene Wilson.[11]

16. No study has yet been made of the western bungalow despite the fact that it may be a link between the German-Russian house, on the one hand, and the most typical plains house type, the Cornbelt cube, on the other.

17. The Cornbelt cube, despite its popularity in the Midwest and elsewhere, has never been the subject of specific and detailed study.

18. A series of regional studies of academic architectural style, similar to those produced by Zelinsky and Bastian, will considerably broaden our understanding of the geographical distribution and local impact of nineteenth-century architecture.[12]

19. A precise definition for terms such as *bungalow, bank barn, cottage,* and *cabin* must be sought.

20. The particular relationship of crib barns to German and English barns requires clarification.

21. It is to be hoped that someone will

undertake to trace the geographical distribution of the various types of hay hoods and hanging gables.

22. Particular barn types should be the subject of additional inquiry. For example, investigation of the Appalachian barn would be especially rewarding.

23. Despite their importance, virtually nothing beyond Glassie's basic studies, has been done to analyze crib barns and crib-derived barns.[13]

24. The entire subject of barn types in the Midwest has been largely ignored by scholars up to this point.

25. The Belgian barn of the Door peninsula, Wisconsin, does not appear to resemble barns in Belgium. How does one explain this discrepancy? Or do we not know enough about barns in Belgium?

26. Some quite distinctive small, log barns with gambrel roofs (fig. 9–2) occur in eastern Missouri. Some attention needs to be given to these barns, which are in an advanced state of decay.

27. The middle Mississippi valley has numerous French derived houses, but what about barns? Do any exist and how are they different from barns of other ethnic groups?

28. The excellent work of Jordan and Ensminger tracing the European antecedents of the German barn[14] should be expanded to investigate whether or not several types of German barns may have been introduced into the New World.

29. For a much larger group of structures, the potential European sources have to be identified and the connection established. Such studies would be the forerunners of comparative investigations.

30. Except for the Sweitzer subtype, German barns have not been studied

Fig. 9–2 A previously unidentified barn type from southeastern Missouri (Near Old Mines, Missouri, 1980)

carefully in North America, yet they have a very wide distribution and large numbers of early barns still survive.

31. Another barn type that warrants fuller attention is the gable-entry banked barn. We need to know where it originated and where it was built in this continent, as well as exactly what its morphology is and whether it differs in this respect from raised or basement barns.

32. A census of both active and relict flue-cured tobacco barns should be an interesting and rewarding research topic in North Carolina, because of the proliferation of various shed subtypes there.

33. There is an urgent need for studies of both the Ontario tobacco barn and the Connecticut valley tobacco barn before these structures entirely disappear. The latter is in a particularly critical position.

34. Up to the present time no one has undertaken a definitive study of any barn type over its entire range.

35. A study is needed of the distribution of various silo types. Research on the Harvestore silo could be particularly useful, especially because it might reveal something about the process of cultural diffusion (chap. 5).

36. The pattern of crib barns (chap. 4) suggests an origin for this type somewhere in the Chesapeake Bay area. This possibility needs further investigation.

37. Reports of transverse barns in the Driftless area of Wisconsin, in eastern Michigan, and in coastal Maine may provide starting points for several re-

search projects, or the reports may prove to be incorrect (chap. 4).

38. The occurrence of Midwest three-portal barns in eastern Ontario and southern New England seems to be illogical (chap. 4). All indications are that the three-portal barn diffused westward from an Appalachian source region. A careful analysis of barns in these two areas should determine whether or not these barns are of the Midwest three-portal type, or whether they are barns of an as-yet-identified and unstudied type.

39. An unnamed barn type occurs in southeastern Ohio and northern West Virginia (see fig. 4–12). Its form is quite distinct from those of other types. The questions of its origin, the limits of its range, the functions it performs, and other, similar ones, need to be answered.

40. Secondary or outbuildings have been largely ignored by scholars. Unfortunately, many of these structures have been altered, removed, or so neglected that they are in an advanced state of decay.

41. The rationale for the form of the squirrel-tail oven (chap. 6) has not yet been provided. Perhaps a comparative study of Pennsylvania German bakeovens and bakeovens in Germany could provide answers.

42. An in-depth study of summer kitchens is needed.

43. The hop house of central New York has never been carefully scrutinized and should be.

44. The hay barrack seems to have a strong Dutch connection, but the reported occurrence of hay barracks in North America suggests different origins. The subject requires additional study.

45. Maple sugar houses are fast disappearing as suburbanization encroaches upon the farms of northeastern North America. Research on this structure must be undertaken quickly.

It should be apparent by now that considerable basic work remains to be done by researchers in the field of material-settlement landscape study. Many of the topics and questions raised in this chapter do not resolve the complicated problems that have been, and will be, generated by research in this field. They deal merely with identification of structures, classification, and taxonomy. Some are designed to resolve the problems of developing terminology. But answering these questions and solving these problems is a necessary initial step.

Notes

1 The North American Farm Barn: Simple Cribs and Transverse Frame

1 Ray Y. Gildea, "The Legacy of Early American Barns," *Virginia Geographer* 9 (1974): 10–12.

2 Alvar W. Carlson, "Bibliography on Barns in the United States and Canada," *Pioneer America* 10, no. 1 [1978]: 65–71.

3 Charles F. Calkins, *The Barn as an Element in the Cultural Landscape of North America: A Bibliography* (Monticello, Ill.: Vance Bibliographies, 1979).

4 R. W. Brunskill, *Illustrated Handbook of Vernacular Architecture* (London: Faber and Faber, 1970), p. 132.

5 Fred B. Kniffen, "Folk Housing—Key to Diffusion," *Annals of the Association of American Geographers* 55, no. 4 (1965): 549–77.

6 Two early studies that attempted primarily to provide classifications of barn types were Richard Francaviglia, "Western American Barns: Architectural Form and Climatic Considerations," *Yearbook of the Association of Pacific Coast Geographers* 34 (1972): 153–60, and Peter M. Ennals, "Nineteenth-Century Barns in Southern Ontario," *Canadian Geographer* 16, no. 3 (1972): 256–70. The journal *Pioneer America* also contains important articles on the comparative study of barns and farm outbuildings.

7 The term *crib* can be confusing because it is applied in two ways. In its simplest application, it refers to a pen composed of logs of small diameter that is used for crop or equipment storage or animal shelter. A crib may also be a more specialized structure, often of frame construction, used essentially for the storage of corn left on the cobs. See chapter 6 for a discussion of these specialized corn cribs.

8 William Lynwood Montell and Michael Lynn Morse, *Kentucky Folk Architecture* (Lexington: University Press of Kentucky, 1976), p. 53.

9 Henry Glassie, "The Double Crib Barn in South Central Pennsylvania, Part Four," *Pioneer America* 2, no. 2 (1970): 28.

10 Henry Glassie, "The Pennsylvania Barn in the South, Part I," *Pennsylvania Folklife* 15, no. 2 (1965–66): 12–17 (citation from p. 13).

11 Glassie, "The Double Crib Barn, Part Four," p. 23.

12 Henry Glassie III, "The Double-Crib Barn in South Central Pennsylvania, Part One," *Pioneer America* 1, no. 1 (1969): 16.

13 H. Wayne Price, "The Double-Crib Log Barns of Calhoun County," *Journal of the Illinois State Historical Society* 73, no. 2 (1980): 140–60.

14 Howard Wight Marshall, *Folk Architecture in Little Dixie: A Regional Culture in Missouri* (Columbia: University of Missouri Press, 1981), pp. 78–80.

15 Price, "Double-Crib Log Barns," p. 144.

16 Henry Glassie III, "The Old Barns of Appalachia," *Mountain Life and Work* 45 (Summer 1965): 28.

17 Montell and Morse, *Kentucky Folk Architecture*, pp. 61, 62.

18 Glassie, "The Double-Crib Barn, Part One," p. 10, see fig. 2.

19 Marshall, *Folk Architecture*, p. 72.

20 Francaviglia, "Western American Barns," pp. 156–57.

21 Montell and Morse, *Kentucky Folk Architecture*, p. 56.

22 Glassie, "The Old Barns of Appalachia," p. 22.

23 Montell and Morse, *Kentucky Folk Architecture*, p. 68.

24 Kniffen, "Folk Housing—Key to Diffusion," p. 563.

25 Montell and Morse, *Kentucky Folk Architecture*, p. 68.

26 See, for example, Josef Schepers, *Westfalen-Lippe*, in *Haus und Hof deutscher Bauern*, ed. Gustav Wolf (Munster: Aschendorff, 1961), vol. 2.

27 Montell and Morse, *Kentucky Folk Architecture*, p. 53.

28 Karl B. Raitz, "The Barns of Barren

County," *Landscape* 22, no. 2 (1978): 19–25 (citation from p. 23).

29 Bruce Rueber, "Factors Influencing Barn Styles in Fayette County, Iowa" (Master's thesis, San Diego State University, 1974), p. 93.

2   The North American Farm Barn: Early Ethnic Origins

1   Ronald C. Carlisle, *An Architectural Study of Some Folk Structures in the Area of Paintsville Lake Dam, Johnson and Morgan Counties, Kentucky* (Pittsburgh: Department of Anthropology, University of Pittsburgh, 1982), p. 119.

2   Allen G. Noble and Albert J. Korsok, "Barn Variations in Columbiana County, Ohio," *East Lakes Geographer* 12 (1977): 98–111.

3   R. W. Brunskill, *Illustrated Handbook of Vernacular Architecture* (London: Faber and Faber, 1970), pp. 140–41.

4   Henry Glassie, "The Variation of Concepts within Tradition: Barn Building in Otsego County, New York," *Geoscience and Man* 5 (1974): p. 185 (special issue, *Man and Cultural Heritage*).

5   This term is also the origin of the English unit of measurement termed the *rod*.

6   Fred B. Kniffen, "Folk Housing—Key to Diffusion," *Annals of the Association of American Geographers* 55, no. 4 (1965): 558.

7   R. L. Séguin, *Les Granges du Québec*, Bulletin 192 (Ottawa: Musée National du Canada, 1963), p. 11.

8   Eric Arthur and Dudley Witney, *The Barn: A Vanishing Landmark in North America* (Greenwich, Conn.: New York Graphic Society, 1972), p. 120.

9   Victor A. Konrad and Michael Chaney, "Madawaska Twin Barn," *Journal of Cultural Geography* 3, no. 1 (1982): 64–75.

10   Theodore H. M. Prudon, "The Dutch Barn in America: Survival of a Medieval Structural Frame," *New York Folklife* 2 (Winter 1976): 125.

11   John Fitchen, *The New World Dutch Barn* (Syracuse: Syracuse University Press, 1968), p. 22.

12   Peter O. Wacker, "Folk Architecture as an Indicator of Culture Areas and Culture Diffusion: Dutch Barns and Barracks in New Jersey," *Pioneer America* 5, no. 2 (1973): 38.

13   Arthur and Witney, *The Barn*, p. 45.

14   Peter O. Wacker, *The Musconetcong Valley of New Jersey* (New Brunswick: Rutgers University Press, 1968), and "Folk Architecture as an Indicator of Culture Areas and Culture Diffusion," pp. 37–47; Fitchen, *The New World Dutch Barn;* and Prudon, "The Dutch Barn in America."

15   Fitchen, *The New World Dutch Barn*, p. 65.

16   The subject is well reviewed in Terry G. Jordan, "Alpine, Alemannic, and American Log Architecture," *Annals of the Association of American Geographers* 70, no. 2 (1980): 154–80.

17   Charles H. Dornbusch and J. K. Heyl, *Pennsylvania German Barns*, vol. 31 of the publications of Pennsylvania German Folklore Society (Allentown, Pa., 1965).

18   Henry Glassie, "The Double Crib Barn in South Central Pennsylvania, Part Four," *Pioneer America* 2, no. 2 (1970): 23.

19   Alan G. Keyser and William P. Stein, "The Pennsylvania German Tri-Level Ground Barn," *Der Reggeboge* 9, no. 3–4 (1975): 1–25; citation from p. 1.

20   Susanne S. Ridlen, "Bank Barns in Cass County, Indiana," *Pioneer America* 4, no. 2 (1972): 27.

21   Henry Glassie, "The Pennsylvania Barn in the South, Part II," *Pennsylvania Folklife* 15, no. 4 (1966): 14–16.

22   Ibid., pp. 16–17.

23   Joseph W. Glass, "The Pennsylvania Culture Region: A Geographical Interpretation of Barns and Farmhouses" (Ph.D. diss., Pennsylvania State University, 1971), p. 99.

24   J. William Stair, "Brick-end Decorations," in *The Pennsylvania Barn,* ed. Alfred L. Shoemaker (Lancaster: Pennsylvania Dutch Folklore Center, Franklin and Marshall College, 1955), pp. 70–86.

25   Robert W. Bastian, "Southeastern Pennsylvania and Central Wisconsin Barns: Examples of Independent Parallel Development?" *Professional Geographer* 27, no. 2 (1975): 200–204.

26   Robert F. Ensminger, "A Comparative Study of Pennsylvania and Wisconsin Forebay Barns," *Pennsylvania Folklife* 32, no. 3 (1983): 98–114.

27   Bernice M. Ball, *Barns of Chester County, Pennsylvania* (West Chester, Pa.: Chester Day Committee of the Women's Auxiliary, Chester County Hospital, 1974), p. 148.

28   Frederick Watts, "The Pennsylvania Barn," *Report of the Commissioner of Agriculture for the Year 1864* (Washington: Government Printing Office, 1865), p. 291.

29   Ibid., p. 289.

30   Keyser and Stein, "The Pennsylvania German Tri-Level Ground Barn."

31   Dornbusch and Heyl, *Pennsylvania German Barns.*

32   Glass, "The Pennsylvania Culture Region."

33   Bastian, "Southeastern Pennsylvania and Central Wisconsin Barns."

34   Glassie, "The Pennsylvania Barn in the South, Part II," p. 22, fig. 19.

35   Charles F. Calkins and Martin C. Perkins, "The Pomeranian Stable of Southeastern Wisconsin," *Concordia Historical Institute Quarterly* 53, no. 3 (1980): 121–25.

36   Ibid., p. 124.

37   Ensminger, "A Comparative Study of Pennsylvania and Wisconsin Forebay Barns," p. 99.

38   Hubert G. H. Wilhelm, "Amish-Mennonite Barns in Madison County, Ohio: The Persistence of Traditional Form Elements," *Ohio Geographers: Recent Research Themes* 4 (1976): 1–8.

39   Ensminger, "A Comparative Study of Pennsylvania and Wisconsin Forebay Barns," p. 112.

40   Charles van Ravenswaay, *The Arts and Architecture of German Settlements in Missouri* (Columbia: University of Missouri Press, 1977), pp. 263–94.

41   Glassie, "The Double Crib Barn in South Central Pennsylvania, Part Four."

42   Hubert G. H. Wilhelm, "The Pennsylvania-Dutch Barn in Southeastern Ohio," *Geoscience and Man* 5 (1974): 155–62 (special issue, *Man and Cultural Heritage*).

43 Ridlen, "Bank Barns in Cass County," pp. 25–43.

44 Glassie, "The Double Crib Barn in South Central Pennsylvania, Part Four."

45 Henry Glassie, "The Pennsylvania Barn in the South, Part I," *Pennsylvania Folklife* 15, no. 2 (1965–66): 8–19.

46 William I. Schreiber, "The Pennsylvania-Dutch Barn in Ohio," *Journal of the Ohio Folklore Society* 2, no. 1 (1967): 15–28.

47 Glass, "The Pennsylvania Culture Region."

48 Terry G. Jordan, "A Forebay Bank Barn in Texas," *Pennsylvania Folklife* 30, no. 2 (1980–81): 72 77.

49 M. D. Learned, "The German Barn in America," in *University of Pennsylvania Lectures* (Philadelphia: University of Pennsylvania, 1915), pp. 338–49.

50 Robert F. Ensminger, "A Search for the Origin of the Pennsylvania Barn," *Pennsylvania Folklife* 30, no. 2 (1980–81): 50–71; and Jordan, "Alpine, Alemannic, and American Log Architecture."

51 Amos Long, Jr., *The Pennsylvania German Family Farm* (Breinigsville, Pa.: Pennsylvania German Society, 1972).

52 Henry J. Kauffman, "Pennsylvania Barns," *Farm Quarterly* 9, no. 3 (1954): 58–61, and 80–81. The earlier article is "Pennsylvania Barns," *Pennsylvania Cultivator*, August 1848, pp. 14–15.

3 The North American Farm Barn: Changes in Time and Space

1 Thomas C. Hubka, "The Connected Farm Buildings of Southwestern Maine," *Pioneer America* 9, no. 2 (1977): 152.

2 Russell V. Keune and James Replogle, "Two Maine Farmhouses," *Journal of the Society of Architectural Historians* 20, no. 1 (1961): 38–39.

3 Hubka, "The Connected Farm Buildings of Southwestern Maine," pp. 171, 147.

4 Wilbur Zelinsky, "The New England Connecting Barn," *Geographical Review* 48, no. 3 (1958): 544.

5 Hubka, "The Connected Farm Buildings of Southwestern Maine," p. 155.

6 R. W. Brunskill, *Vernacular Architecture of the Lake Counties* (London: Faber and Faber, 1974), p. 82.

7 Peter M. Ennals, "Nineteenth-Century Barns in Southern Ontario," *Canadian Geographer* 16, no. 3 (1972): 256.

8 David K. Butterfield and Edward M. Ledohowski, *Architectural Heritage: The Brandon and Area Planning District* (Winnipeg: Manitoba Department of Cultural Affairs and Historical Resources, 1983), pp. 57–74.

9 Stewart McHenry, "Vermont Barns: A Cultural Landscape Analysis," *Vermont History* 46 (Summer 1978): 153–56.

10 Ennals, "Nineteenth-Century Barns," p. 256.

11 N. S. Fish, *Building the Dairy Barn*, University of Wisconsin, Agricultural Experiment Station, Bulletin 369 (Madison, 1924), p. 7.

12 Ennals, "Nineteenth-Century Barns," p. 263.

13 Ibid., passim.

14 Byron D. Halstead, *Barn Plans and Outbuildings* (New York: Orange Judd, 1881), p. 39.

15 Fish, *Building the Dairy Barn*, p. 256.

16 Ibid., p. 11.

17 Alvar W. Carlson, "Designating Historical Rural Areas: A Survey of Northwestern Ohio Barns," *Landscape* 22 (Summer 1978): 32.

18 Halstead, *Barn Plans and Outbuildings*, p. 55.

19 Carlson, "Designating Historical Rural Areas," pp. 32–33.

20 John Fraser Hart and Eugene Cotton Mather, "The Character of Tobacco Barns and Their Role in the Tobacco Economy of the United States," *Annals of the Association of American Geographers* 51, no. 3 (September 1961): 279.

21 Laura Scism, "Carolina Tobacco Barns: History and Function," in *Carolina Dwelling*, ed. Doug Swaim (Raleigh: North Carolina State University, School of Design, 1978), p. 119.

22 Maurice Corina, *Trust in Tobacco* (New York: St. Martin's Press, 1975), p. 291.

23 A fine photograph illustrating this may be found in Hart and Mather, "The Character of Tobacco Barns," p. 278.

24 The idea for this exercise is based upon material in Ligon Flynn and Roman Stankus, "Carolina Tobacco Barns: Form and Significance," in *Carolina Dwelling*, pp. 112–17; citation is from p. 114.

25 See Scism, "Carolina Tobacco Barns," p. 124, for a photograph.

26 Ibid., p. 127 n.8.

27 Amos Long, Jr., *The Pennsylvania German Family Farm* (Breinigsville, Pa.: Pennsylvania German Society, 1972), p. 495.

28 Robert A. Barakat, *Tobaccuary: A Study of Tobacco Curing Sheds in Southeastern Pennsylvania* (Ann Arbor: University Microfilms, 1972), p. 331.

29 Ibid., p. 247.

30 Ibid., p. 210.

31 William Lynwood Montell and Michael Lynn Morse, *Kentucky Folk Architecture* (Lexington: University Press of Kentucky, 1976), p. 79.

32 Arthur Greenburg, "The Bluegrass Tobacco Barn and the Physiographic Sub-divisions of the Kentucky Bluegrass: A Case Study in Areal Association" (M.A. thesis, University of Cincinnati, 1965), p. 13.

33 Hart and Mather, "The Character of Tobacco Barns."

34 Karl B. Raitz, "The Wisconsin Tobacco Shed: A Key to Ethnic Settlement and Diffusion," *Landscape* 20 (October 1975): 32–37; citation from p. 35.

4 Diffusion of the Farm Barn in Northeastern United States

1 Allen G. Noble and Gayle A. Seymour, "Distribution of Barn Types in Northeastern United States," *Geographical Review* 72, no. 2 (1982):

155–70. The methods used in collecting the information are given here.

2   Fred B. Kniffen, "Folk Housing—Key to Diffusion," *Annals of the Association of American Geographers* 55, no. 4 (1965): 559.

3   Robert F. Ensminger, "A Comparative Study of Pennsylvania and Wisconsin Forebay Barns," *Pennsylvania Folklife* 32, no. 3 (1983): 98.

4   Josef Schepers, *Westfalen-Lippe,* in *Haus und Hof Westfälischer Bauern,* ed. Gustav Wolf (Münster: Aschendorff, 1980), p. 129.

5   Howard Wight Marshall, *Folk Architecture in Little Dixie: A Regional Culture in Missouri* (Columbia: University of Missouri Press, 1981), pp. 72–76.

6   Henry Glassie III, "The Barns of Appalachia," *Mountain Life and Work* 40 (Summer 1965): 29.

7   Marshall, *Folk Architecture in Little Dixie,* pp. 72–76; Douglas K. Meyer, "Diffusion of Upland South Folk Housing to the Shawnee Hills of Southern Illinois," *Pioneer America* 7, no. 2 (1975): 61.

8   Wilbur Zelinsky, "The New England Connecting Barn," *Geographical Review* 48, no. 3 (1958): 540–53.

9   Stewart G. McHenry, "Vermont Barns: A Cultural Landscape Analysis," *Vermont History* 46 (Summer 1978): 153, 156.

10   Peter M. Ennals, "Nineteenth-Century Barns in Southern Ontario," *Canadian Geographer* 16, no. 3 (1972): 256–70.

11   Jerry Apps and Allen Strang, *Barns of Wisconsin* (Madison, Wisc.: Tamarack Press, 1977), pp. 25–26, 39, 131.

12   Alvar W. Carlson, "Designating Historic Rural Areas: A Survey of Northwestern Ohio Barns," *Landscape* 22 (Summer 1978): 29–33.

5   The Diffusion and Evolution of the Silo

1   Portions of this chapter are based upon material that appeared earlier in Allen G. Noble, "The

Evolution of American Farm Silos," *Journal of Cultural Geography* 1, no. 1 (1980): 138–48, and "Diffusion of Farm Silos," *Landscape* 25 (February 1981): 11–14.

2   Manly Miles, *Silos, Ensilage and Silage* (New York: Orange Judd Co., 1913), p. 31.

3   H. M. Jenkins, "Report of the Practice of Ensilage at Home and Abroad," *Journal of the Royal Agricultural Society of England* 20, no. 11 (1884): 135.

4   Ibid., p. 137.

5   F. W. Woll, *A Book on Silage* (Chicago: Rand McNally and Co., 1898), p. 8.

6   George Thurber, *Silos and Ensilage* (New York: Orange Judd Co., 1881), p. 8.

7   Miles, *Silos, Ensilage and Silage,* p. 37.

8   Thomas A. Williams, "Succulent Forage for the Farm and Dairy," *Yearbook of the United States Department of Agriculture* (Washington: Government Printing Office, 1899), p. 617.

9   Henry E. Alvord, "Is Ensilage a Success in New England?" *Thirty-fifth Annual Report of the Secretary of the Massachusetts Board of Agriculture* (Boston: Wright and Potter, 1888), p. 123.

10   National Silo Association, *The History of Concrete Tower Silos and the Silo Association* (Waterloo, Iowa, 1977), p. 7.

11   Ibid., p. 12.

12   U.S. Department of Agriculture, *Silos and Ensilage: A Record of Practical Tests in Several States and Canada,* Special Publication no. 48 (Washington: Government Printing Office, 1882).

13   John M. Bailey, *The Book of Ensilage or the New Dispensation for Farmers* (Billerica, Mass.: published by the author, 1880).

14   J. F. Hickman, "Has the Silo Come to Stay?" *Ohio Farmer,* March 29, 1890, p. 245.

15   H. P. Miller, "Silos and Silage," *Ohio Farmer,* July 2, 1910, p. 4.

16   Ulysses P. Hedrick, *A History of Agriculture in the State of New York* (1933; reprint, New York: Hill and Wang, 1966).

17   Woll, *A Book on Silage,* p. 10.

18   *Modern Silage Methods* (Salem, Ohio: Silver Manufacturing Company, 1903), p. 10.

19   Miller, "Silos and Silage," p. 4.

20   J. R. McCalmont, *Farm Silos,* Agricultural Research Service, Misc. Publication no. 810 (Washington: U.S. Department of Agriculture, 1960), p. 1.

21   "Ohio Fourth in Silos," *Ohio Farmer,* April 19, 1924, p. 28-574.

22   Allen G. Noble, "Barns and Square Silos in Northeastern Ohio," *Pioneer America* 6, no. 2 (1974): 17.

23   Ibid.

24   Woll, *A Book on Silage,* p. 77.

25   Eric Sloane, *An Age of Barns* (New York: Ballantine Books, 1967), p. 65.

26   Allen G. Noble, "The Silo in the Eastern Midwest: Patterns of Evolution and Distribution," *Ohio Geographers: Recent Research Themes* 4 (1976): 13.

27   Thurber, *Silos and Ensilage,* p. 17.

28   Robert Suter, *The Courage to Change* (Danville, Ill.: Interstate Printers and Publishers, 1964), pp. 52, 77.

29   David J. DeTemple, *A Space Preference Approach to the Diffusion of Innovations: The Spread of Harvestore Systems Through Northeast Iowa,* Geographic Monograph Series, vol. 3 (Bloomington: Department of Geography, Indiana University, 1971); Edward K. Scorgie, "The Diffusion of Harvestore Structures in Southwestern Ontario, 1962–1970" (M.A. thesis, London, Ontario: University of Western Ontario, 1973).

30   Suter, *The Courage to Change,* p. 35.

31   Ibid., p. 36.

32   Noble, "The Silo in the Eastern Midwest," p. 17.

33   McCalmont, *Farm Silos,* p. 22.

6   Secondary Farm Structures

1   Henry J. Kauffman, *The American Farmhouse* (New York: Hawthorn Books, 1975), p. 183.

2   Terry G. Jordan, "The Evolution of the American Windmill: A Study in Diffusion and Modification," *Pioneer America* 5, no. 2 (1973): 7.

3   Walter P. Webb, *The Great Plains* (New York: Grosset and Dunlap, 1931), p. 337.

4   Ibid.

5 Leon S. Pitman, "Domestic Tankhouses of Rural California," *Pioneer America* 8, no. 2 (1976): 84–97. Citation from p. 86.

6 Ibid., p. 87.

7 Ibid., pp. 96–97.

8 Lauren Post, *Cajun Sketches: From the Prairies of Southwest Louisiana* (Baton Rouge: Louisiana State University Press, 1962), p. 24.

9 Amos Long, Jr., *The Pennsylvania German Family Farm* (Breinigsville, Pa.: Pennsylvania German Society, 1972), pp. 206, 218, 229.

10 Ibid., p. 207.

11 Byron D. Halstead, *Barn Plans and Outbuildings* (New York: Orange Judd Co., 1881), p. 140.

12 Ibid., p. 143.

13 Long, *Pennsylvania German Family Farm*, p. 218.

14 Kauffman, *The American Farmhouse*, p. 231.

15 Long, *Pennsylvania German Family Farm*, p. 230.

16 J. H. Hammond, *The Farmers and Mechanics Practical Architect* (Boston: John P. Jewett, 1858), p. 150.

17 Long, *Pennsylvania German Family Farm*, p. 156.

18 Kauffman, *The American Farmhouse*, p. 213.

19 The material on dryhouses in this section was obtained from Long, *Pennsylvania German Family Farm*, pp. 197–205.

20 Halstead, *Barn Plans and Outbuildings*, p. 187.

21 Peter O. Wacker, "Cultural and Commercial Regional Associations of Traditional Smokehouses in New Jersey," *Pioneer America* 3, no. 2 (1971): 25.

22 Long, *Pennsylvania German Family Farm*, p. 190.

23 Halstead, *Barn Plans and Outbuildings*, p. 187.

24 Long, *Pennsylvania German Family Farm*, p. 187.

25 Halstead, *Barn Plans and Outbuildings*, p. 188.

26 Long, *Pennsylvania German Family Farm*, p. 189.

27 Ibid., p. 188.

28 Kauffman, *The American Farmhouse*, p. 222.

29 Ibid., p. 221.

30 Amos Long, Jr., "Smokehouses in the Lebanon Valley," *Pennsylvania Folklife* 13 (Fall 1962): 26–30.

31 Wacker, "Regional Associations of Traditional Smokehouses," pp. 33, 30.

32 Long, *Pennsylvania German Family Farm*, p. 179.

33 Henry Glassie, "The Smaller Outbuildings of the Southern Mountains," *Mountain Life and Work* 40, no. 1 (1964): 21–25.

34 Terry G. Jordan, *Texas Log Buildings: A Folk Architecture* (Austin: University of Texas Press, 1978), pp. 77, 177–179; John B. Rehder; John Morgan; Joy L. Medford, "The Decline of Smokehouses in Grainger County, Tennessee," *West Georgia College Studies in the Social Sciences* 18 (June 1979): 75–83.

35 Howard W. Marshall, *Folk Architecture in Little Dixie: A Regional Culture in Missouri* (Columbia: University of Missouri Press, 1981), p. 87.

36 Richard W. E. Perrin, "Wisconsin's Stovewood Architecture," *Wisconsin Academy Review* 20, no. 2 (1974): 5; William Tishler, "Stovewood Architecture," *Landscape* 23, no. 3 (1979): 29; William Tishler, "Stovewood Construction in the Upper Midwest and Canada: A Regional Vernacular Architectural Tradition," in *Perspectives in Vernacular Architecture*, ed. Camille Wells (Annapolis: Vernacular Architecture Forum, 1982), p. 126; Edward M. Ledohowski and David K. Butterfield, *Architectural Heritage: The Eastern Interlake Planning District* (Winnipeg: Manitoba Department of Cultural Affairs and Historical Resources, 1983), pp. 92–95.

37 Thomas Ritchie, *Canada Builds, 1867–1967* (Toronto: University of Toronto Press, 1967), pp. 158–59.

38 Tishler, "Stovewood Architecture," p. 29.

39 Ibid., p. 31.

40 Don Yoder, "Folk Cookery," in *Folklore and Folklife,* ed. Richard M. Dorson (Chicago: University of Chicago Press, 1972), p. 342.

41 Ibid., p. 343.

42 Amos Long, Jr., "Bakeovens in the Pennsylvania Folk-Culture," *Pennsylvania Folklife* 14, no. 2 (1964): 18.

43 Victor Mindeleff, *A Study of Pueblo Architecture: Tusayan and Cibola,* Eighth Annual Report of the Bureau of American Ethnology (Washington: Smithsonian Institution, 1891), p. 175.

44 E. Boyd, *Popular Arts of Spanish New Mexico* (Sante Fe: Museum of the New Mexico Press, 1974), p. 15.

45 Edith M. Thomas, "Old Dutch Bakeovens," *A Collection of Papers Read before the Bucks County Historical Society* 4 (1917): 576.

46 Fred B. Kniffen, "The Outdoor Oven in Louisiana," *Louisiana History* 1 (1960): 30.

47 Ibid., p. 32.

48 Excellent photographs and a discussion of such ovens may be found in Michel Lessard and Gilles Vilandre, *La Maison Traditionelle au Québec* (Montreal: Les Editions de l'Homme, 1974), pp. 255–64.

49 Michel Lessard and Huguette Marquis, *Encyclopédie de la Maison Québecoise* (Montreal: Les Editions de l'Homme, 1972), pp. 621, 624.

50 Lise Boily and Jean-François Blanchette, *The Bread Ovens of Quebec* (Ottawa: National Museums of Canada, 1979), p. 11.

51 Charles F. Calkins and William G. Laatsch, "The Belgian Outdoor Ovens of Northeastern Wisconsin," *PAST: Pioneer America Society Transactions* 2 (1979): 2, 9.

52 Ibid., pp. 2, 4.

53 Kauffman, *The American Farmhouse*, p. 206.

54 Thomas, "Old Dutch Bakeovens," p. 575.

55 Amos Long, Jr., "Outdoor Bakeovens in Berks," *Historical Review of Berks County* 28, no. 1 (1962–63): 11.

56 Thomas, "Old Dutch Bakeovens," p. 575.

57 Frederick B. Jaekel, "Squirrel-Tailed Bake-ovens in Bucks County," *A Collection of Papers Read before the Bucks County Historical Society* 4 (1917): 579.

58 Ibid., p. 581.

59 Long, "Outdoor Bakeovens in Berks," p. 11.

60 Long, "Bakeovens in the Pennsylvania Folk-Culture," pp. 18–19.

61 Long, "Outdoor Bakeovens in Berks," p. 32.

62 Kauffman, *The American Farm*, p. 191.

63 Amos Long, Jr., "Pennsylvania Summer Houses and Summer Kitchens," *Pennsylvania Folklife* 15 (1965): 10–19; Laszlo Kurti, "Hungarian Settlement and Building Practices in Pennsylvania and Hungary: A Brief Comparison," *Pioneer America* 12, no. 1 (1980): 34–53; Lessard and Vilandre, *La Maison Traditionelle*, p. 256; Lessard and Marquis, *Encyclopédie de la Maison Québecoise*, pp. 651–54; Calkins and Laatsch, "Belgian Outdoor Ovens," pp. 2–4; Hattie P. Williams, "A Social Study of the Russian German," *University Studies of the University of Nebraska* 16, no. 3 (1916): 127–227; and Thorpe M. Langley, "Geography of the Maple Area, Douglas County, Wisconsin" (M.A. thesis, University of Wisconsin-Madison, 1932), p. 30.

64 Long, "Pennsylvania Summer Houses and Summer Kitchens," p. 19.

65 Clarence R. Keathley, "Making Sorghum in Arcadia Valley," *Missouri Historical Review* 67, no. 2 (1973): 257.

66 W. T. Chamberlain, "Maple Sugar Making," *American Agriculturalist* 29 (February 1870): 58–60.

67 Darrell D. Henning, "Maple Sugaring: History of a Folk Technology," *Keystone Folklore Quarterly* 11, no. 4 (1966): 264, 265.

68 Lessard and Marquis, *Encyclopédie de la Maison Québecoise*, pp. 648–49, 651.

69 Putnam W. Robbins, *Production of Maple Sugar in Michigan*, Circular Bulletin no. 213 (East Lansing: Michigan Agricultural Experiment Station, 1949): 9.

70 Lessard and Marquis, *Encyclopédie de la Maison Québecoise*, p. 650.

71 Herbert B. Nelson, "The Vanishing Hop-Driers of the Willamette Valley," *Oregon Historical Quarterly* 64 (1963): 269.

72 Marion N. Rawson, *Of the Earth Earthy* (New York: E. P. Dutton, 1937), p. 132.

73 Charles F. Calkins and William G. Laatsch, "The Hop Houses of Waukesha County, Wisconsin," *Pioneer America* 9, no. 2 (1977): 191.

74 Charles Whitehead, "Fifty Years of Hop Farming," *Journal of the Royal Agricultural Society*, Ser. 3, 1 (1890): 347.

75 Charles Whitehead, "On Recent Improvements in the Cultivation and Management of Hops," *Journal of the Royal Agricultural Society*, Ser. 2, 6 (1870): 364–65.

76 W. A. Lawrence, "Hop Raising in New York State," in E. Meeker, *Hop Culture in the United States* (Puyallup, Wash.: E. Meeker, 1883), p. 94.

77 Herman C. Collins, "Culture, Drying and Baling of Hops," *American Agriculturalist* 24 (March 1865): 74.

78 D. B. Rudd and E. O. Rudd, *The Cultivation of Hops and Their Preparation for Market as Practiced in Sauk County, Wisconsin* (Reedsburg, Wisc.: Rudd and Rudd, 1868), p. 9.

79 Daniel Flint, *Hop Culture in California*, U.S. Department of Agriculture, Farmers Bulletin, no. 115 (Washington: Government Printing Office, 1900), p. 15.

80 G. R. Hoerner and Frank Rabak, *Production of Hops*, U.S. Department of Agriculture, Farmers Bulletin, no. 1842 (Washington: Government Printing Office, 1940), p. 22.

81 Gary S. Dunbar, "Hop Growing in Franklin County," *North Country Life* 8, no. 4 (1954): 23.

82 Halstead, *Barn Plans and Outbuildings*, p. 182.

83 Long, *Pennsylvania German Family Farm*, p. 341.

84 For floor plans and sketches of these buildings, see Halstead, *Barn Plans and Outbuildings*, pp. 183–84.

85 H. F. Raup, "The Pennsylvania-Dutch of Northampton County: Settlement Forms and Culture Pattern," *Bulletin of the Geographical Society of Philadelphia* 36 (Winter 1938–39): 6.

86 Henry Giese, "Trends in Farm Structures," in *A Century of Farming in Iowa, 1846–1946* (Ames: Iowa State College Press, 1946), p. 259.

87 Long, *Pennsylvania German Family Farm*, p. 452.

88 Nicholas P. Hardeman, *Shucks, Shocks, and Homing Blocks: Corn as a Way of Life* (Baton Rouge: Louisiana State University Press, 1981), p. 103.

89 Harold E. Gray, *Farm Service Buildings* (New York: McGraw Hill, 1955), p. 356.

90 C. K. Shedd, *Storage of Ear Corn on the Farm in the North Central States,* U.S. Department of Agriculture, Farmers Bulletin, no. 2076 (Washington: Government Printing Office, 1955), p. 6.

91 M. A. R. Kelley, *Corncribs for the Cornbelt*, U.S. Department of Agriculture, Farmers Bulletin, no. 1701 (Washington: Government Printing Office, 1933), p. 6.

92 Halstead, *Barn Plans and Outbuildings*, pp. 128–29.

93 Long, *Pennsylvania German Family Farm*, pp. 455, 458.

94 Amos Long, Jr., "Pennsylvania Corncribs," *Pennsylvania Folklife* 14, no. 1 (1964): 18.

95 Kelley, *Corncribs*, p. 2.

96 Henry Glassie, "Eighteenth-Century Cultural Process in Delaware Valley Folk Building," *Winterthur Portfolio* 7 (1972): 23.

97 Kelley, *Corncribs*, p. 16.

98 Giese, "Trends in Farm Structures," p. 259.

99 Shedd, *Storage of Ear Corn*, p. 11.

100 Marion D. Learned, "The German Barn in America," *University of Pennsylvania, University Lectures* (Philadelphia: University of Pennsylvania, 1915), p. 346.

101 Don McTernan, "The Barrack, A Relict Feature on the North American Cultural Landscape," *PAST: Pioneer America Society Transactions* 1 (1978): 57.

102 Peter O. Wacker, "Folk Architecture as an Indicator of Cultural Diffusion: Dutch Barns and Barracks in New Jersey," *Pioneer America* 5, no. 2 (1973): 38.

103 Alfred L. Shoemaker, "Barracks," *Pennsylvania Folklife* 9 (Spring 1958): 4.

104 Ledohowski and Butterfield, *Architectural Heritage,* pp. 77, 81.

105 Alan G. Keyser and William P. Stein, "The Pennsylvania German Tri-Level Ground Barn," *Der Reggeboge* 9, no. 3–4 (1975): 10–11.

106 Robert C. Bucher and Alan G. Keyser, "Thatching in Pennsylvania," *Der Reggeboge* 16 (1982): 1.

107 Z. Kuzela, "Folk Architecture," in *Ukraine: A Concise Encyclopedia,* ed. Volodymyr Kubijovyc (Toronto: University of Toronto Press, 1963), 1: 294.

108 For Massachusetts, Virginia, and Rhode Island, see Wacker, "Folk Architecture as Indicator," pp. 42, 44, 46 n. 26. For Maryland and Ohio, see William A. Craigie and James Hulbert, eds., *A Dictionary of American English on Historical Principles* (Chicago: University of Chicago Press, 1938), 1: 679. For Linn County, Iowa, see *The Portrait and Biographical Album of Linn County, Iowa* (Chicago: Chapman Brothers, 1887), p. 386. For Muscatine and Scott counties, see A. T. Andreas, *Illustrated Historical Atlas of the State of Iowa* (1875; reprint ed., State Historical Society of Iowa, 1970), pp. 72, 354, 361. For Illinois, see Russell G. Swenson, "Illustrations of Material Culture in Nineteenth-Century County and State Atlases," *PAST: Pioneer America Society Transactions* 5 (1982): 63–70 (see esp. the illustration on p. 69). For western New York, see Shoemaker, "Barracks," p. 5. For Prince Edward Island, see Eric Arthur and Dudley Witney, *The Barn: A Vanishing Landmark in North America* (New York: New York Graphic Society, 1972), p. 208. For Manitoba, see Ledohowski and Butterfield, *Architectural Heritage,* pp. 77, 81. And for Newfoundland, see John J. Mannion, *Irish Settlements in Eastern Canada* (Toronto: University of Toronto Press, 1974), pp. 129–31.

109 The idea was suggested by a paper presented at the 1982 Pioneer America meetings. See Swenson, "Illustrations of Material Culture."

110 Giese, "Trends in Farm Structures," p. 252.

111 Rick Francaviglia, "Western Hay Derricks: Cultural Geography and Folklore as Revealed by Vanishing Agricultural Technology," *Journal of Popular Culture* 11, no. 4 (1978): 926.

112 Austin E. Fife and James M. Fife, "Hay Derricks of the Great Basin and Upper Snake River Valley," *Western Folklore Quarterly* 7 (July 1948): 228.

113 Ibid., pp. 225–26.

114 The classification used herein is a combination and modification of those offered by Fife and Fife, ibid., and Francaviglia, "Western Hay Derricks."

115 Francaviglia, "Western Hay Derricks," p. 924.

116 John A. Alwin, "Montana's Beaverslide Hay Stacker," *Journal of Cultural Geography* 3, no. 1 (1982): 42–50.

117 Ibid.

118 L. A. Reynoldson, *Hay Stackers and Their Use,* U.S. Department of Agriculture, Farmers Bulletin, no. 1615 (Washington: Government Printing Office, 1929), p. 5.

119 Ibid.

120 James A. Young, "Hay Making: The Mechanical Revolution on the Western Range," *Western Historical Quarterly* 14, no. 3 (1983): 319.

121 Reynoldson, *Hay Stackers and Their Use,* p. 9.

122 The material in this section is based upon Roger L. Welsch, "Sandhill Baled-Hay Construction," *Keystone Folklore Quarterly* 15 (Spring 1970): 16–34.

123 Long, *Pennsylvania German Family Farm,* p. 493.

124 Karl J. Ekblaw, *Farm Structures* (New York: Macmillan, 1914), p. 189.

125 Amos Long, Jr., "Chickens and Chicken Houses in Rural Pennsylvania," *Pennsylvania Folklife* 18, no. 3 (1969): 36.

126 Long, *Pennsylvania German Family Farm,* p. 393.

127 Halstead, *Barn Plans and Outbuildings,* p. 74.

128 Long, *Pennsylvania German Family Farm,* p. 442.

7 Fences, Walls, and Hedges

1 John Fraser Hart and Eugene Cotton Mather, "The American Fence," *Landscape* 6 (1957): 4.

2 Gerald L. Pocius, "Walls and Fences in Susquehanna County, Pennsylvania, *Pennsylvania Folklife* 26 (Spring 1977): 9.

3 H. F. Raup, "The Fence in the Cultural Landscape," *Western Folklore* 6 (1947): 7.

4 Hart and Mather, "American Fence," p. 7.

5 Douglas Leechman, "Good Fences Make Good Neighbors," *Canadian Geographical Journal* 47, no. 6 (1953): 221.

6 Ibid.

7 Raup, "The Fence in the Cultural Landscape," p. 1.

8 Eugene Cotton Mather and John Fraser Hart, "Fences and Farms," *Geographical Review* 44, no. 2 (1954): 215.

9 Pocius, "Walls and Fences," p. 15.

10 Ibid., p. 12.

11 Esther L. Larsen, "Pehr Kalm's Observations on the Fences of North America," *Agricultural History* 21 (1947): 77.

12 Donovan Clemson, *Living With Logs: Log Buildings and Rail Fences* (Saanichton, B.C.: Hancock House, 1974), p. 54.

13 Larsen, "Pehr Kalm's Observations."

14 Pocius, "Walls and Fences," p. 11.

15 Hart and Mather, "The American Fence," p. 6.

16 Amos Long, Jr., "Fences in Rural Pennsylvania," *Pennsylvania Folklife* 12, no. 2 (1961): 33.

17 Raup, "The Fence in the Cultural Landscape," p. 3.

18 Vera V. Via, "The Old Rail Fence," *Virginia Cavalcade* 12, no. 1 (1962): 33.

19 "Statistics of Fences in the United States," *Report of the Commissioner of Agriculture for the Year 1871* (Washington: Government Printing Office, 1872), pp. 502, 506.

20   Mather and Hart, "Fences and Farms," p. 214.

21   Long, "Fences in Rural Pennsylvania," p. 33.

22   Leslie Hewes and Christian L. Jung, "Early Fencing on the Middle Western Prairie," *Annals of the Association of American Geographers* 71, no. 2 (1981): 196; Leslie Hewes, "Early Fencing on the Western Margin of the Prairie," *Annals of the Association of American Geographers* 71, no. 4 (1981): 507.

23   Wilbur Zelinsky, "Walls and Fences," *Landscape* 8, no. 3 (1959): 18.

24   "New England Fences," *Scribner's Monthly* 19 (February 1880): 509; Harry Symons, *Fences* (Toronto: McGraw-Hill Ryerson, 1958), pp. 24–25.

25   "Statistics of Fences in the United States" (1872).

26   Zelinsky, "Walls and Fences," p. 18.

27   Long, "Fences in Rural Pennsylvania."

28   H. N. Humphrey, *Cost of Fencing Farms in the North Central States*, Bulletin no. 321 (Washington: U.S. Department of Agriculture, 1916), p. 21.

29   M. A. R. Kelley, *Farm Fences*, Farmers Bulletin, no. 1832 (Washington: U.S. Department of Agriculture, 1940), p. 21.

30   Henry Gross, "Old Fences in Bucks County," *Bucks County Historical Society Journal* 5 (1926): 430.

31   Raup, "The Fence in the Cultural Landscape," p. 4.

32   Leechman, "Good Fences," pp. 225–26.

33   "New England Fences," p. 510.

34   Milton D. Rafferty, "The Limestone Fenceposts of the Smokey Hill Region of Kansas," *Pioneer America* 6, no. 1 (1974): 41.

35   Kelley, "Farm Fences," p. 5.

36   Hart and Mather, "The American Fence," p. 7.

37   Raup, "The Fence in the Cultural Landscape," p. 2.

38   Leechman, "Good Fences," p. 230.

39   Mary Louise Rice, "The Role of the Osage Orange Hedge in the Occupation of the Great Plains" (M.A. thesis, University of Illinois, 1937), p. 3.

40   Ibid., p. 4.

41   Hewes, "Early Fencing on the Western Margin," p. 514.

42   Earl W. Hayter, "Barbed Wire Fencing—A Prairie Invention," *Agricultural History* 13 (1939): 194, 189.

43   Earl W. Hayter, "The Fencing of Western Railways," *Agricultural History* 19 (1945): 163, 164.

44   H. L. Dunlap, "On Fencing," *Illinois State Agricultural Society Transactions* (1859–60): 686.

45   Hayter, "The Fencing of Western Railways," p. 165.

46   Hewes, "Early Fencing on the Western Margin," p. 522.

47   John Winberry, "The Osage Orange: A Botanical Artifact," *Pioneer America* 11, no. 3 (1979): 135.

48   "Osage Hedges," *Report of the U.S. Commissioner of Agriculture* (Washington: U.S. Department of Agriculture, 1868), p. 245.

49   Hewes, "Early Fencing on the Western Margin," p. 506.

50   "Statistics of Fences in the United States," p. 505.

51   Hewes and Jung, "Early Fencing on the Middle Western Prairie," p. 196, fig. 10.

52   Rice, "Role of the Osage Orange Hedge," p. 46.

53   John A. Warder, *Hedges and Evergreens* (New York: A. O. Moore, 1858), pp. 25–40.

54   Ibid., pp. 23, 17–22.

55   "Osage Hedges," p. 250.

56   Winberry, "The Osage Orange," p. 138.

57   Rice, "Role of the Osage Orange Hedge," p. 39.

58   Horace Capron, "Wire Fences," *Illinois State Agricultural Society Transactions* (1856–57): 426–27.

59   Hayter, "Barbed Wire Fencing," pp. 189–90.

60   Walter Prescott Webb, "From Split Rails to Barbed Wire," *True West*, July–August 1960, pp. 28, 38.

61   R. D. Holt, "Barbed Wire," *Texas Monthly* 4 (September 1929): 175.

62   Hayter, "Barbed Wire Fencing," p. 194.

63   Hewes, "Early Fencing on the Western Margin," p. 513.

64   Leechman, "Good Fences," p. 233.

65   Holt, "Barbed Wire," p. 179.

66   Joe M. Carmichael, "Thorny Fence," *Cattleman*, January 1949, p. 24.

67   Holt, "Barbed Wire," p. 176.

68   Hayter, "Barbed Wire Fencing," pp. 197, 200.

69   J. Evetts Haley, "And Then Came Barbed Wire to Change History's Course," *Cattleman*, March 1927, p. 81.

70   R. D. Holt, "Barbed Wire Drift Fences," *Cattleman*, March 1927, p. 81.

71   R. D. Holt, "The Introduction of Barbed Wire into Texas and the Fence Cutting War," *West Texas Historical Association Year Book* 6 (1930): 70–74.

72   Wayne Gard, "The Fence Cutters," *Southwestern Historical Quarterly* 51, no. 1 (1947): 3–4.

73   Holt, "Introduction of Barbed Wire."

74   Leechman, "Good Fences," p. 226.

75   Austin E. Fife, "Jack Fences of the Intermountain West," *Folklore International* (1967): 52, 53.

76   Rick Francaviglia, *The Mormon Landscape* (New York: AMS Press, 1978), p. 67.

77   Ibid., p. 29.

78   Kelley, *Farm Fences*, p. 8.

79   Ray Holt, "Net-Wire Fences Changed Sheep Raising," *Sheep and Goat Raisers*, March 1951, p. 24.

80   Ibid., p. 46.

81 Raup, "The Fence in the Cultural Landscape," p. 6.

82 Holt, "Net-Wire Fences," pp. 46, 26.

83 Humphrey, *Cost of Fencing Farms*, pp. 5–6.

84 Hayter, "The Fencing of Western Railways," p. 167.

85 Kelley, *Farm Fences*, p. 44.

86 Symons, *Fences*, p. xlii.

87 Leechman, "Good Fences," p. 234.

88 Kelley, *Farm Fences*, p. 19.

8   The Settlement Landscape

1 Donald W. Meinig, "The Mormon Culture Region: Strategies and Patterns in the Geography of the American West, 1847–1964," *Annals of the Association of American Geographers* 55, no. 2 (1965): 191–220; Richard V. Francaviglia, *The Mormon Landscape* (New York: AMS Press, 1978); Lowry Nelson, *The Mormon Village* (Salt Lake City: University of Utah Press, 1952); Richard H. Jackson, "Religion and Landscape in the Mormon Cultural Region," in *Dimensions of Human Geography*, ed. Karl W. Butzer, Research Paper, no. 186 (Chicago: University of Chicago Department of Geography, 1978), pp. 100–27.

2 Warren E. Roberts, "The Whitaker-Waggoner Log House from Morgan County, Indiana," in *American Folklife*, ed. Don Yoder (Austin: University of Texas Press, 1976), pp. 185–207; Henry Glassie, "A Central Chimney Continental Log House," *Pennsylvania Folklife* 18, no. 2 (1968–69): 33–39; John M. Vlach, "The Canada Homestead: A Saddlebag Log House in Monroe County, Indiana," *Pioneer America* 4, no. 2 (1972): 8–17; Howard Wight Marshall, "The 'Thousand Acres' Log House, Monroe County, Indiana," *Pioneer America* 3, no. 1 (1971): 48–56; Simon Bronner, "The Harris House," *Pioneer America* 12, no. 1 (1980): 8–30. For additional studies, consult the lists of references at the end of each of the preceding chapters.

3 Russell V. Keune and James Replogle, "Two Maine Farm Houses," *Journal of the Society of Architectural Historians* 20, no. 1 (1961): 38–39; Richard W. E. Perrin, "John Bergen's Log House," *Wisconsin Magazine of History* 44, no. 1 (1960): 12–14; Donald Millar, "An Eighteenth-Century German House in Pennsylvania," *Architectural Record* 63, no. 2 (1928): 161–68.

4 Terry G. Jordan, "A Forebay Bank Barn in Texas," *Pennsylvania Folklife* 30, no. 2 (1980–81): 72–77; Paul B. Jenkins, "A 'Stove-Wood' House," *Wisconsin Magazine of History* 7 (1923): 189–92; J. J. Brody and Anne Colberg, "A Spanish Homestead near Placitas, New Mexico," *El Palacio* 73, no. 2 (1966): 11–20; and Bryan J. Stevens, "The Swiss Bank House Revisited: The Messerschmidt-Dietz Cabin," *Pennsylvania Folklife* 30, no. 2 (1980–81): 78–86.

5 Henry Glassie, "The Wedderspoon Farm," *New York Folklife Quarterly* 22 (1966): 165–87; Philip Dole, "The Calef Farm: Region and Style in Oregon," *Journal of the Society of Architectural Historians* 23, no. 4 (1964): 200–209; and Thomas Carter, "The Joel Cock House: 1885 Meadows of Dan, Patrick County, Virginia," *Southern Folklore Quarterly* 39 (1975): 329–40.

6 Susanne S. Ridlen, "Bank Barns in Cass County, Indiana," *Pioneer America* 4, no. 2 (1972): 25–43; Thomas C. Hubka, "The Connected Farm Buildings of Southwest Maine," *Pioneer America* 9, no. 2 (1977): 143–78; Charles F. Calkins and William G. Laatsch, "The Hop Houses of Waukesha County, Wisconsin," *Pioneer America* 9, no. 2 (1977): 180–92; Richard H. Hulan, "Middle Tennessee and the Dogtrot House," *Pioneer America* 7, no. 2 (1975): 37–46.

7 David Sutherland, "Folk Housing in the Woodburn Quadrangle," *Pioneer America* 4, no. 2 (1972): 18–24; Brian Coffey, "Nineteenth-Century Barns of Geauga County, Ohio," *Pioneer America* 10, no. 2 (1978): 53–63; and Charles E. Martin, "Head of Hollybush: Reconstructing Material Culture Through Oral History," *Pioneer America* 13, no. 1 (1981): 3–16. Two examples of works published by the Corps of Engineers are Ronald L. Michael and Ronald C. Carlisle, *Historical and Architectural Study of Buildings and Artifacts Associated with the Bulltown Historic Area, Burnsville Lake Project, Braxton County, West Virginia* (Huntington, W.V., 1979) and Ronald C. Carlisle and Andrea Ferenci, *An Architectural Study of Some Log Structures in the Area of the Yatesville Lake Dam, Lawrence County, Kentucky* (Huntington, W.V., 1978).

8 Ingolf Vogeler, "The Roman Catholic Culture Region of Central Minnesota," *Pioneer America* 8, no. 2 (1976): 71–83; Hubert G. H. Wilhelm, "German Settlement and Folk Building Practices in the Hill Country of Texas," *Pioneer America* 3, no. 2 (1971): 15–24; Douglas K. Meyer, "Diffusion of Upland South Folk Housing to the Shawnee Hills of Southern Illinois," *Pioneer America* 7, no. 2 (1975): 56–66.

9 Allen G. Noble and Gayle A. Seymour, "The Distribution of Barn Types in Northeastern United States, *Geographical Review* 72, no. 2 (1982): 155–70.

10 Richard Pillsbury, "Patterns in the Folk and Vernacular House Forms of the Pennsylvania Culture Region," *Pioneer America* 9, no. 1 (1977): 12–31.

11 Terry G. Jordan, "Evolution of the American Windmill: A Study in Diffusion and Modification," *Pioneer America* 5, no. 2 (1973): 3–12; John M. Vlach, "The Shotgun House: An African Architectural Legacy, Parts 1 and 2," *Pioneer America* 8, no. 1 (1976): 47–56, and no. 2 (1976): 57–70; and Wilbur Zelinsky, "The New England Connecting Barn," *Geographical Review* 48, no. 3 (1958): 540–53.

12 Robert W. Bastian, "Southeastern Pennsylvania and Central Wisconsin Barns: Examples of Independent Parallel Development?" *Professional Geographer* 27, no. 2 (1975): 200–204; Robert F. Ensminger, "A Search for the Origin of the Pennsylvania Barn," *Pennsylvania Folklife* 30, no. 2 (1980–81): 50–70; Terry G. Jordan, "Alpine, Alemannic, and American Log Architecture," *Annals of the Association of American Geographers* 70, no. 2 (1980): 154–80; and Arnold R. Alanen and William H. Tishler, "Finnish Farmstead Organization in Old and New World Settings," *Journal of Cultural Geography* 1, no. 1 (1980): 66–81.

13 Stephen C. Jett and Virginia E. Spencer, *Navajo Architecture* (Tucson: University of Arizona Press, 1981).

14 Loyal Durand, Jr., "The Lower Peninsula of Michigan and the Western Michigan Dairy Region: A Segment of the American Dairy Region," *Economic Geography* 27 (1951): 181.

15 Ibid. Durand is incorrect in his observation that the roof slopes are at different angles.

16 Charles F. Calkins and William G. Laatsch, "The Belgian Outdoor Oven of Northeastern Wisconsin," *PAST: Pioneer America Society Transactions* 2 (1979): 1–12.

17 William G. Laatsch, "A Plan to Restore the Massart Farm," Green Bay, Wisconsin: Heritage Hill State Park [1980], p. 3.

18 Math S. Tlachac, *The History of the Belgian Settlements in Door, Kewaunee and Brown Counties* (Algoma, Wisc.: Belgian-American Club, 1974), p. 33.

19 William G. Laatsch, personal communication, June 2, 1982.

20 This section is taken from Allen G. Noble, "Rural Ethnic Islands," in *Ethnic Minorities in the United States,* ed. Jesse McKee (Dubuque: Kendall Hunt Publishing Co., forthcoming).

21 Richard W. E. Perrin, "Log Houses in Wisconsin," *Antiques* 89, no. 6 (1966): 870.

22 Perrin, "John Bergen's Log House," pp. 12–14.

23 John Lloyd, "The Norwegian Laftehus," in *Shelter and Society,* ed. Paul Oliver (New York: Frederick A. Praeger, 1969), pp. 38–48; and Thomas Paulsson, *Scandinavian Architecture* (Newton, Mass.: Charles T. Branford, 1959).

24 Alan C. Pape, "Kvaale House: Architectural Analysis Report" (Unpublished internal report, Eagle, Wisc.: Old World Wisconsin Outdoor Ethnic Museum, n.d.), p. 2 and passim.

25 Lawrence R. Brandt and Ned E. Braatz, "Log Buildings in Portage County, Wisconsin: Some Cultural Implications," *Pioneer America* 4, no. 1 (1972): 37.

26 Alan C. Pape, "Lisbakken Stabbur: Architectural Analysis Report" (Unpublished internal report, Eagle, Wisc.: Old World Wisconsin Outdoor Ethnic Museum, 1980), p. 3.

27 Wasyl Halich, *Ukrainians in the United States* (Chicago: University of Chicago Press, 1937), pp. 47, 55.

28 John C. Lehr, "Ukrainian Houses in Alberta," *Alberta Historical Review* 21, no. 4 (1973): 14.

29 The material of this and the following section is drawn principally from John Lehr, *Ukrainian Vernacular Architecture in Alberta,* Historical Sites Service, Occasional Paper, no. 1 (Edmonton: Alberta Culture, Historical Resources Division, 1976), citation is from p. 19; and from John C. Lehr, "Colour Preferences and Building Decoration among Ukrainians in Western Canada," *Prairie Forum* 6, no. 2 (1981): 204.

30 Lehr, *Ukrainian Vernacular Architecture,* p. 12.

31 Paul Henri Stahl, "The Rumanian Household from the Eighteenth to the Early Twentieth Century," in *Europe as a Cultural Area,* ed. Jean Cuisenier (The Hague: Mouton, 1979), p. 217.

32 William C. Wonders and Mark A. Rasmussen, "Log Buildings of West Central Alberta," *Prairie Forum* 5, no. 2 (1980): 212.

33 Gilbert Parfitt, "Ukrainian Cottages," *Architecture Canada* 18 (August 1941): 132–33.

34 Lehr, *Ukrainian Vernacular Architecture,* p. 34.

35 Cotton Mather and Matti Kaups, "The Finnish Sauna: A Cultural Index to Settlement," *Annals of the Association of American Geographers* 53, no. 4 (1963): 501.

36 Henry S. Heimonen, "Finnish Rural Culture in South Ostrobothnia (Finland) and the Lake Superior Region (U.S.)—A Comparative Study," (Ph.D. diss., University of Wisconsin, 1941), pp. 380–81.

37 Thorpe M. Langley, "Geography of the Maple Area, Douglas County, Wisconsin" (M.A. thesis, University of Wisconsin-Madison, 1932), p. 24.

38 Michael Karni and Robert Levin, "Northwoods Vernacular Architecture: Finnish Log Building in Minnesota," *Northwest Architect* 36 (May–June 1972): 95.

39 Darrell H. Davis, "The Finland Community, Minnesota," *Geographical Review* 25, no. 3 (1935): 385.

40 Langley, "Geography of the Maple Area," p. 25.

41 Gladys Pierson, "Acculturation of the Finns in Milltown, Montana" (M.A. thesis, Montana State University, 1941), pp. 88–89.

42 Davis, "Finland Community," p. 390.

43 Karni and Levin, "Northwoods Vernacular Architecture," p. 98.

44 Richard W. E. Perrin, "Log Sauna and the Finnish Farmstead: Transplanted Architectural Idioms in Northern Wisconsin," *Wisconsin Magazine of History* 44, no. 4 (1961): 286.

45 Eugene Van Cleef, "The Finns in America," *Geographical Review* 6, no. 3 (1918): 192.

46 Heimonen, "Finnish Rural Culture," p. 146.

47 Alanen and Tishler, "Finnish Farmstead Organization," p. 76.

48 Matti Kaups, "A Finnish Riihi in Minnesota," *Journal of the Minnesota Academy of Science* 38, nos. 2 and 3 (1973): 66.

49 Matti Kaups, "A Finnish Savusauna in Minnesota," *Minnesota History* 45 (1976): 19.

50 Ibid., p. 15.

51 Yvonne R. Lockwood, "The Sauna: An Expression of Finnish-American Identity," *Western Folklore* 36, no. 1 (1977): 72.

52 Perrin, "Log Sauna," p. 284.

53 Kaups, "A Finnish Savusauna," pp. 14, 13, 12.

54 H. J. Vikerjuuri, *Sauna: The Finnish Bath* (Brattleboro, Vt.: Stephen Greene Press, 1965), pp. 28, 24.

55 Kaups, "A Finnish Savusauna," p. 14.

56 Ibid., p. 12.

57 Vikerjuuri, *Sauna,* p. 56.

58 Perrin, "Log Sauna," p. 284.

59 For the various uses made of the sauna, see Kaups, "A Finnish Savusauna," pp. 19, 17; Ranulph Glanville, "Finnish Vernacular Farmhouses," *Architectural Association Quarterly* 9 (1977): 38; Pierson, "Acculturation of the Finns," p. 24; Aili K. Johnson, "Lore of the Finnish-American Sauna," *Midwest Folklore* 1 (1959): 35; and Perrin, "Log Houses of Wiscon-

sin," p. 870, and "Log Sauna," p. 284. Citation is from Kaups, p. 17.

60   Maurice A. Mook and John A. Hostetler, "The Amish and Their Land," *Landscape* 6 (1957): 21.

61   James Landing, "Amish Settlements in North America: A Geographical Brief," *Illinois Geographical Society Bulletin* 12 (1970): 67.

62   William I. Schreiber, *Our Amish Neighbors* (Chicago: University of Chicago Press, 1962), p. 45.

63   John M. Zielinski, *The Amish: A Pioneer Heritage* (Des Moines: Wallace-Homestead, 1975), p. 122.

64   Schreiber, *Our Amish Neighbors*, p. 44.

65   Ibid., p. 48.

66   John A. Hostetler, *Amish Society*, 2d ed. (Baltimore: Johns Hopkins University Press, 1968), p. 98.

67   Mook and Hostetler, "The Amish and Their Land," p. 28.

68   Ibid., p. 26; Zielinski, *The Amish*, p. 122.

69   Mook and Hostetler, "The Amish and Their Land," p. 28.

70   Zielinski, *The Amish*, p. 71.

71   Arthur V. Houghton, "Community Organization in a Rural Amish Community at Arthur, Illinois" (M.A. thesis, University of Illinois, 1937), p. 27.

72   Mook and Hostetler, "The Amish and Their Land," p. 27.

73   Calvin Redekop, *The Old Colony Mennonites* (Baltimore: Johns Hopkins University Press, 1969), p. 5.

74   John Warkentin, "Mennonite Agricultural Settlements of Southern Manitoba," *Geographical Review* 49, no. 3 (1959): 348.

75   E. K. Francis, "The Mennonite Farmhouse in Manitoba," *Mennonite Quarterly Review* 28 (January 1954): 56.

76   Frank Epp, *Mennonites in Canada, 1786–1920* (Toronto: Macmillan of Canada, 1974), p. 219.

77   Francis, "Mennonite Farmhouse," p. 57.

78   Ibid.; Warkentin, "Mennonite Agricultural Settlements," pp. 351–52.

79   Francis, "Mennonite Farmhouse," p. 57.

80   Gustav Rank, *Die Bauernhausformen im Baltischen Raum* (Wurzburg: Holzner-Verlag, 1962).

81   Warkentin, "Mennonite Agricultural Settlements," p. 352.

82   Francis, "Mennonite Farmhouse," pp. 57, 58.

83   Francaviglia, *The Mormon Landscape*; Nelson, *Mormon Village*; Richard H. Jackson, "The Use of Adobe in the Mormon Culture Region," *Journal of Cultural Geography* 1, no. 1 (1980): 82–95; Kate B. Carter, "The Mormon Village," *Treasures of Pioneer History* 4 (1955): 133–88; Richard H. Jackson and Robert L. Layton, "The Mormon Village: Analysis of a Settlement Type," *Professional Geographer* 28, no. 2 (1976): 136–41.

84   Nelson, *Mormon Village*, p. 275.

85   Peter L. Goss, "The Architectural History of Utah," *Utah Historical Quarterly* 43, no. 3 (1975): 209.

86   Francaviglia, *Mormon Landscape*, p. 81.

87   Dean L. May, "The Making of Saints: The Mormon Town as a Setting for the Study of Cultural Change," *Utah Historical Quarterly* 45, no. 1 (1977): 77.

88   Richard H. Jackson, "Religion and Landscape in the Mormon Cultural Region," p. 118.

89   Wayne Wahlquist, "A Review of Mormon Settlement Literature," *Utah Historical Quarterly* 45, no. 1 (1977): 20.

90   Richard V. Francaviglia, "The Mormon Landscape: Definition of an Image in the American West," *Proceedings of the Association of American Geographers* 2 (1970): 59–61.

91   Jackson, "The Use of Adobe," p. 82.

92   Cindy Rice, "Spring City: A Look at a Nineteenth-Century Mormon Village," *Utah Historical Quarterly* 43, no. 3 (1975): 269.

93   Richard C. Poulsen, "Stone Buildings of Beaver City," *Utah Historical Quarterly* 43, no. 3 (1975): 281.

94   Joseph E. Spencer, "House Types of Southern Utah," *Geographical Review* 35, no. 3 (1945): 449.

95   Leon S. Pitman, *A Survey of Nineteenth-*

Century Folk Housing in the Mormon Culture Region (Ann Arbor: University Microfilms, 1973), p. 110.

96   Ibid., p. 112.

97   Nelson, *Mormon Village*, p. 182.

98   Goss, "Architectural History of Utah," p. 221.

99   Pitman, *Folk Housing in the Mormon Culture Region*, p. 59.

100   Jackson, "The Use of Adobe," p. 85.

101   Spencer, "House Types of Southern Utah," p. 447.

102   Pitman, *Folk Housing in the Mormon Culture Region*, p. 61.

103   Ibid., p. 65.

104   Goss, "Architectural History of Utah," p. 211.

105   Jackson, "The Use of Adobe," p. 91.

106   Ibid., p. 85.

107   Paul Goeldner, *Utah Catalog, Historic American Buildings Survey* (Salt Lake City: Utah Heritage Foundation, 1969), p. 10.

108   Pitman, *Folk Housing in the Mormon Culture Region*, p. 26.

109   Spencer, "House Types of Southern Utah," p. 449.

110   Teddy Griffith, "A Heritage of Stone in Willard," *Utah Historical Quarterly* 43, no. 3 (1975): 289.

111   Thomas Carter, "Cultural Veneer: Decorative Plastering in Utah's Sanpete Valley," *Utah Historical Quarterly* 49, no. 1 (1981): 70.

112   Pitman, *Folk Housing in the Mormon Culture Region*, p. 81.

113   Austin E. Fife, "Stone Houses of Northern Utah," *Utah Historical Quarterly* 40, no. 1 (1972): 15.

114   Pitman, *Folk Housing in the Mormon Culture Region*, pp. 138–43.

115   Richard V. Francaviglia, "Mormon Central-Hall Houses in the American West," *Annals*

of the Association of American Geographers 61, no. 1 (1971): 65–71.

116 Spencer, "House Types of Southern Utah," pp. 448–49; Pitman, *Folk Housing in the Mormon Culture Region*, pp. 146–49; Jackson, "Religion and Landscape," pp. 113–14.

117 Fife, "Stone Houses," p. 9.

118 Poulsen, "Stone Buildings of Beaver City," p. 283.

119 Goss, "Architectural History of Utah," p. 215.

120 Jackson, "Religion and Landscape," p. 114.

121 Robert M. Lillibridge, "Architectural Currents on the Mississippi River Frontier: Nauvoo, Illinois," *Society of Architectural Historians Journal* 19 (1960): 109–14.

122 Jackson, "Religion and Landscape," p. 114; Allen D. Roberts, "The Greek Revival Style in Utah," *Utah State Historical Society Newsletter* 26, no. 5 (1976): 1–4.

123 Pitman, *Folk Housing in the Mormon Culture Region*, p. 213.

124 This is the structure that is called the "intermontane barn" by Richard V. Francaviglia, "Western American Barns: Architectural Form and Climatic Considerations," *Yearbook of the Association of Pacific Coast Geographers* 34 (1972): 154.

125 Pitman, *Folk Housing in the Mormon Culture Region*, p. 213.

126 Richard V. Francaviglia, *The Mormon Landscape*, p. 24.

127 David R. Lee and Hector H. Lee, "Thatched Cowsheds of the Mormon Country," *Western Folklore* 40, no. 2 (1981): 171–87.

9 Settlement Landscape Study: Agenda for the Future

1 Fred B. Kniffen, "Folk Housing—Key to Diffusion," *Annals of the Association of American Geographers* 55, no. 4 (1965): 549–77.

2 Henry Glassie, *Pattern in the Material Folk Culture of the Eastern United States* (Philadelphia: University of Pennsylvania Press, 1968).

3 See volume 1, chapter 1, note 12.

4 The recently published Edward M. Ledohowski and David K. Butterfield, *Architectural Heritage: The Eastern Interlake Planning District* (Winnipeg: Manitoba Department of Cultural Affairs and Historical Resources, 1983) contains the first discussion of North American Icelandic buildings.

5 Robert W. Bastian, "Southeastern Pennsylvania and Central Wisconsin Barns: Examples of Independent Parallel Development?" *Professional Geographer* 27, no. 2 (1975): 200–204; Charles F. Calkins and Martin C. Perkins, "The Pomeranian Stable of Southeastern Wisconsin," *Concordia Historical Institute Quarterly* 53, no. 3 (1980): 121–25.

6 Robert F. Ensminger, "A Comparative Study of Pennsylvania and Wisconsin Forebay Barns," *Pennsylvania Folklife* 32, no. 3 (1983): 98–114.

7 Wilbur Zelinsky, "Walls and Fences," *Landscape* 8, no. 3 (1959): 20.

8 Richard Pillsbury, "The Construction Materials of the Rural Folk Housing of the Pennsylvania Culture Region," *Pioneer America* 8, no. 2 (1976): 98–106; Charles Gritzner, "Construction Materials in a Folk Housing Tradition: Considerations Governing Their Selection in New Mexico," *Pioneer America* 6, no. 1 (1974): 25–29; Richard H. Jackson, "The Use of Adobe in the Mormon Cultural Region," *Journal of Cultural Geography* 1, no. 1 (1980): 82–95; and John Hudson, "Frontier Housing in North Dakota," *North Dakota History* 42, no. 4 (1975): 4–16.

9 Two additional important works should be added to the list of references given in vol. 1, chap. 8: Robert C. West, "The Flat-roofed Folk Dwelling in Rural Mexico," *Geoscience and Man* 5 (1974): 111–32 (special issue, *Man and Cultural Heritage*); and John J. Winberry, "*Tejamanil*: The Origin of the Shake Roof in Mexico," *Proceedings of the Association of American Geographers* 7 (1975): 288–93.

10 Terry G. Jordan, *Texas Log Buildings: A Folk Architecture* (Austin: University of Texas Press, 1978).

11 Eugene M. Wilson, *Alabama Folk Houses* (Montgomery: Alabama Historical Commission, 1975); and "The Single Pen Log House in the South," *Pioneer America* 2, no. 1 (1970): 21–28; and "Form Changes in Folk Houses," *Geoscience and Man* 5 (1974): 65–71 (special issue, *Man and Cultural Heritage*).

12 Wilbur Zelinsky, "The Greek Revival House in Georgia," *Society of Architectural Historians Journal* 13, no. 2 (1954): 9–12; and Robert W. Bastian, "The Prairie Style House: Spatial Diffusion of a Minor Design," *Journal of Cultural Geography* 1, no. 1 (1980): 50–65.

13 See Henry Glassie III, "The Double-Crib Barn in South Central Pennsylvania," a four-part article in *Pioneer America* 1, no. 1 and no. 2 (1969): 9–16, 40–45, and 2, no. 1 and no. 2 (1970): 47–52, 23–34.

14 Terry G. Jordan, "Alpine, Alemannic, and American Log Architecture," *Annals of the Association of American Geographers* 70, no. 2 (1980): 154–80; Robert Ensminger, "A Search for the Origin of the Pennsylvania Barn," *Pennsylvania Folklife* 30, no. 2 (1980–81): 50–71.

Index